MID✳MOD

MAYOR

How Raymond Tucker
Shaped St. Louis

Andrew J. Theising

BARTHOLOMEW/CHAMBERS MEDIA
Bartholomew, Chambers, and Co. LLC
Saint Louis, Missouri

Dedicated to all the people who have worked to make St. Louis a wonderful place to call home, then and now.

Thank you.

THE THREE LIVING ST. LOUIS MAYORS in 1955. From left: Aloys P. Kaufmann, then president of the Chamber of Commerce (mayor from 1943-1949); Mayor Raymond Tucker (1953-1965); and Bernard F. Dickmann, then St. Louis Postmaster (mayor from 1933-1941). On the table is the model for the elegant Mid-Century Modern terminal at Lambert Field (1956), designed by Minoru Yamasaki. Note that the terminal only had three arched segments initially. City of St. Louis Photo, courtesy of the Tucker Family

Table of Contents

THE CITY'S HIGHEST HONOR, 1956.
Theising Image, courtesy of the Tucker Family

Prologue

What is Mid-Mod?

Design journalist Cara Greenberg popularized the term "Mid-Century Modern" with the publication of her 1984 book on furniture from the 1950s. She described the furniture as appealing to young families. It was simple, comfortable, childproof, and scaled to fit smaller postwar houses.[1] Old houses may have been large, but those homes could be dark and gloomy. This generation wanted to be ensconced "behind plate-glass picture windows" to escape "the stuffy old-fashioned" spaces of their youth. In a word, they wanted to be "modern."[2]

How did Mid-Mod take off? Top designers created it, new technology manufactured it, eager media promoted it, and the newly affluent bought it up![3] Greenberg writes of the "new mentality" that accompanied Mid-Century Modern (MCM). The departure from the stodgy past gave "a sense of relief and bright hopes for the future, mingled with money to be spent." Quite simply, "there was a market for good design" as well as new construction and a break from the past.[4]

This new mentality applied to cities as much as furniture after the war. Cities are products of design. They are organic and they grow in ways that are intentional and accidental.

Consider the dichotomy of American society in the 1950s and 1960s. We had great confidence (at home); at the same time we had great fear (abroad—the Cold War). We had great wealth (in metro areas); at the same time we recognized our great poverty (the rural south—the War on Poverty). We had great vision (the moon); at the same time we could not see that we were destroying irreplaceable space (urban renewal). We had great intelligence (modern science), at the same time we never thought of consequences (toxic waste).

And amid all this brilliance, there were times when society just didn't get it. Society's majority was racist. Society tolerated it. And maybe it wanted better, but society didn't do the work. The suffering of African Americans in America's cities is unforgivable. Walter Johnson looks at this violence in his outstanding book that focuses on St. Louis, *The Broken Heart of America*.

Affluence and Audacity at Mid-Century

The single greatest societal change of this era was disposable income. When Greenberg spoke of the "newly affluent," she was referring to the first generation to have a meaningful amount of disposable income thanks to union wages and affordable higher education. Add to this a postwar baby boom, a newfound desire for comfort, and keeping up with the neighbors, and the suburbanization of the United States resulted.

St. Louis was as caught up in this movement as any city, and boasted an incredible mix of vision, talent, and resources. The comprehensive city plan drawn up by St. Louis officials in 1947 stated that the city should be prepared for a population of 900,000 by 1970.[5] That number did not materialize, but it showed the big and bold thinking in which leaders engaged. St. Louis in the 1940s, 50s, and 60s pushed grand proposals—in the same spirit as President Kennedy calling for the moonshot in this era.

St. Louis had dreams! The city made a formal pitch to host the United Nations headquarters that ultimately went to New York, the Air Force Academy that went to Colorado Springs, the NASA Space Flight Training Center that went to Huntsville, and even the Walt Disney theme park that wound up in Orlando. Any one of those could have transformed St. Louis into a long-term global leader that easily met the population projections of that 1947 city plan. Greenberg called it MCM's "new mentality," and St. Louis had it.

St. Louis had commerce! It boomed during these decades. All the major automakers had plants there, so the city made more automobiles than anyplace outside of Detroit (including the classic Chevy Corvette). Its breweries rivaled Milwaukee's for top beer production in the country. St. Louis had two baseball teams—though the Browns left town after the 1953 season to become the Baltimore Orioles. The Hawks moved to St. Louis in 1955, bringing pro-basketball there. The NFL football Cardinals came to St. Louis in 1960. (Blues hockey would not arrive until 1967.)

The St. Louis Zoo didn't hire just any director, it had Marlin Perkins—one of the best-known zoologists in the country, who from St. Louis would entertain the nation on *Mutual of Omaha's Wild Kingdom*. The interstate highway system didn't just cut through St. Louis—it started there, with the first ground being broken on the Mark Twain Expressway in St. Charles County, August 13, 1956.[6] The city didn't just pursue urban renewal—its Mill Creek Valley project was the largest land clearance in the country to that time. The city developed public housing, and the infamous Pruitt-Igoe was one of the largest developments ever constructed.

One of the very first public television stations in the country, KETC, was begun there—and Oscar-winning filmmaker Charles Guggenheim was brought to St. Louis to run it.[7] World-class designers like Minoru Yamasaki (World Trade Center towers) and Buckminster Fuller (the geodesic dome) were working in the region. A dozen Nobel Prize scholars had done their work there. The hometown Pulitzer family ran one of the three daily papers. Everything of this era screamed new, modern, different, and sometimes biggest, best, or first.

The MCM era was a powerful time, yet the city was on a precipice. Its growth was uneven. Its power was unequal. It clung to old ways. It tolerated injustice. These dynamics had been around for a long time, and they came together after World War II and had to be addressed. In this era, Raymond Tucker was one of the leaders chosen to herd and harness this wild energy. He faced a significant challenge, but he had the vision, the ability, and the smarts to do the job—if only the voters who put him there would go along.

The Mid-Mod Mayor

Raymond Tucker certainly embraced the new mentality of MCM, but he was also bound by his own personality. There were four themes to his life that seem to inform all that he did.

1.) <u>Professionalism</u>: Tucker believed in professionalism (in contrast to partisanship). He recognized that in all city government decisions, there was the professional path and the political path. Sometimes they agreed, and sometimes they didn't. He always chose the professional path and he recognized the necessity of the partisan political path (though he did not always like it). He sought compromise and would rather have a compromised path forward than wait it out for some ideal path forward. He realized both sides had to "win."

2.) <u>Pragmatism</u>: He liked to get things done. He was not satisfied with just ideas, but he wanted to transform those ideas into real work visible at street level. He could have led the life of an academic—postulating theories and enlightening a new generation to his discipline's knowledge. Instead, he was drawn to public service and the idea of making his life's work meaningful for average citizens who would never study the details of mechanical engineering. For him, academic work should have a practical outcome.

3.) <u>His moral compass</u>: Shaped largely by his Catholicism (a progressive version thereof), he had a strong sense of right and wrong (ethics), good and evil (morality).   He embraced the morality of the Catholic Church and let professional ethics guide his decisions.

4.) <u>Institutionalism</u>: Tucker was absolutely an institu-tionalist. He believed in the division of work appropriately among specialists, and he valued these formal structures that could deliver a specific body of work in a meaningful and efficient way (e.g., a school district for education, a Congress or legislature to make laws for society, a church to advance acts of faith). He believed in the goodness of institutions (universities, cities, churches) and lived by the motto that we should obey the institutional rules or change the rules. He worked to change many of the rules of existing insti-tutions and cooperated with like-minded institutionalists.

And so this creates for us a solid foundation upon which we can analyze the administration of one of St. Louis's—nay, America's—greatest mayors.

ENDNOTES

[1] Greenberg 8

[2] ibid.

[3] ibid. 9

[4] ibid. 28

[5] Bartholomew et al 1947, 10

[6] Weingroff, Richard F, "Three States Claim First Interstate Highway. *Public Roads Magazine.* New Jersey: U.S. Department of Transportation. 60:1. Summer 1996. https://highways.dot.gov/public-roads/summer-1996/three-states-claim-first-interstate-highway. Posted: 1996. Accessed: 14 Jan 2024.

[7] "Timeline: Early History," The History of NinePBS. https://www.ninepbs.org/about/history/. Posted: n.d. Accessed: 14 Jan 2024.

Municipal bond discussion on KETC, the public television station. The program was "Your Money at Work," October 16, 1957. From left: William P. Sharpe (Mercantile Trust Co. VP), attorney Richmond Coburn, Sidney Maestre (Chairman, Mercantile Trust), Mrs. John H. Crago, Mayor Tucker, and Dr. Merle T. Welshaus (moderator). Ferman photo. Courtesy of the Tucker Family.

Introduction

The View from Art Hill

Atop the highest point in the city's Forest Park since the 1910s is a statue of Louis IX depicted in glorious fashion—his *apotheosis*. It is the high point of the man Saint Louis on a high point in the city of Saint Louis. The statue faces the northeast and looks over so much of the city's story. Immediately in front of it is the grand basin of Forest Park, and the cascading hillside was once the centerpiece of the city's greatest moment, hosting the 1904 World's Fair and Olympic Games. From that place, the view goes to the Dwight Davis Tennis Courts, named for the Olympic athlete, statesman, and benefactor of the tennis sport's highest trophy. Davis once lived nearby.

At the park's edge is the elite end of Lindell Boulevard, six or seven blocks of tree-lined street, broad sidewalks, and opulent mansions. Beyond that are the grand private neighborhoods that have been home to the wealthiest and most powerful families in the city.

Going another mile to the northeast is St. Louis's north side, a historic center of African American neighborhoods. It was a center of political power, industrial power, and more than a few opulent mansions of its own. It has fallen on hard times in recent generations.

The Apotheosis of Saint Louis atop Art Hill in Forest Park. Henry Bregstone photo, 1913, Theising image

Finally, the view (imaginary at this point) leaves the city, crosses the great Mississippi River, and into the Illinois suburbs. These places, at least the ones closest to the river, were industrial suburbs. It was here, downwind and sometimes downstream, where St. Louis placed most of its heavy industry, its smokestacks and slaughterhouses, and the people who worked in them.

The view from Art Hill is the view of a city's story: wealth and poverty, residents and industry, white and Black, city and suburb, Missouri and Illinois, memories and reality. St. Louis is a dichotomy. Charles Dickens told us this in his own tale of cities—being best of time and worst of time, at the same time.

More than that, St. Louis is a juxtaposition. It's not only that these dichotomies exist at the same time, but they are also juxtaposed in the same space. St. Louis at mid-century was a dynamic, flourishing, powerful city, and it was dying. As my student Sara Washington wrote in an essay years ago, St. Louis needed a "knight on a horse" to show up (picture the *apotheosis*) and that man—imperfect as he may have been—was Mayor Raymond R. Tucker.

The Tucker Brothers: Raymond Roche Tucker, 1896-1970; Robert Clarence Tucker, 1893-1948; William Joseph Tucker Jr., 1891-1979. Portrait c. 1910; Tucker Family

Coming up in St. Louis

The young boy named Raymond Roche Tucker never knew the opulent streets of power, except as he passed them outside the gates. He was of modest means, growing up in the old Carondelet neighborhood on the far south side of St. Louis. His father was an Irish immigrant, a devout Catholic, and held a government job in the city. That income provided for a very modest house at 7019 Minnesota Ave., not far from the Mississippi River, south of Loughborough

2

and west of Broadway—major streets of South St. Louis.

In 1907, when young Raymond was 11 years old, the family moved to a larger and nicer home at 6451 Vermont Ave. (probably enabled by an inheritance from his maternal grandmother). After his father died of cancer at age 58, and his mother died of pneumonia at 65, Raymond Tucker and his wife moved into the old family home. He lived the rest of his life in the place where he had grown up.

He attended Saint Louis University High School, the Jesuit preparatory school in town. He went on to Saint Louis University itself to receive a Bachelor of Arts in 1917.[1] He might have received his BA on an accelerated path of three years instead of four, as his brother William Jr. did in 1910, which would account for what would seem to be an early graduation.[2] He received his Bachelor of Science in Mechanical Engineering from Washington University in St. Louis in 1920, and was added immediately to the School of Engineering faculty in 1921 as an instructor. It must have been a part-time position, because he also worked as a safety engineer at ALCOA's Aluminum Ore Company in East St. Louis for a time before securing a full-time teaching position.[3]

His first full-time teaching assignment came in 1924, when he was promoted to Assistant Professor of Mining in 1924.[4] He became an Assistant Professor of Mechanical Engineering in 1927, which would be the department where he spent the bulk of his academic career.[5] He married Mary Edythe Leiber in 1928 and they had two children.[6] They rented a modest apartment close to the university at 5899 Nina Place for $65 a month before living in the old family home.[7]

He doesn't seem to have had an early interest in politics, but his own father may have shown him a prophetic path. His dad, William J. Tucker Sr., was active in his local Democratic ward committee in the 1880s and 1890s. When Progressive Mayor Rolla Wells took office in 1901, the mayor installed a new smoke inspector and five deputies—and one of those deputies was William J. Tucker at a salary of $1,200 per year (about $35,000 in today's dollars). His father held that job for eight years and that probably was the only job young Raymond Tucker knew his father to have. These inspectors played an important role. They visited places that were generating an offensive amount of pollution, and helped bring them into compliance. They helped ensure a measure of quality-of-life for residents in a crowded city. When Republican Fred Kreismann took office in 1909, the Democrat appointees were thrown out and the Republican appointees came in. A 13-year-old Raymond Tucker saw his father lose his job instantly simply because of partisan politics.[8] It made an impression on the boy in multiple ways, undoubtedly giving him a bad taste for politics—and perhaps appreciating the use of government power to abate nuisances in society.

Smoke, Politics, and Politicians

Smoke pollution from household chimneys and industrial smokestacks was a big problem in the late 19th century. Everything required coal. Steam engines needed coal heat to operate steam-driven mechanical equipment. Trains needed coal to fire the pistons required to move freight and passengers. Office buildings needed steam systems to power water and heating elements. Household furnaces needed the high heat of coal to keep homes warm. Smokestacks and chimneys were everywhere—and so was the soot and smoke. The city first adopted a smoke regulation ordinance in 1892.[9] It was focused on nuisance behavior rather than overall pollution levels, and the various inspectors had broad powers to enter private properties and firms to correct and/or abate the offending source—often a boiler or furnace.

Smoke remained a problem for decades. Things didn't get moving until the creation of the Citizens' Smoke Abatement League on April 21, 1926.[10] The effort stemmed from the Women's Smoke Abatement Committee that had existed a few years prior. A *St. Louis Star* commentary noted that the League would fight the city's smoke pall with "smoke inspectors free of any influence" to identify offending chimneys and report them to "a competent combustion engineer who can personally instruct their owners not only how to prevent the sable plumes, but how to save money on their annual fuel bills by so doing."[11] Wherever would they ever find "a competent combustion engineer" for such a task? Why, at Washington University of course.

The local smoke abatement league decided to create a new division to investigate smoke's detrimental effects, and the director of Washington University's new Industrial Research Department, A. S. Langsdorf, was the division's chair, and Arthur Kendall of the Washington University Medical School was the vice chair.[12] To be certain, Tucker must have been aware of this group, if not a resource for them. When Mayor Bernard Dickmann established a smoke abatement committee to develop the rules and legislation to create change in 1934, he named Raymond Tucker as its chair.[13]

Dickmann was in the real estate business and had an intimate knowledge of St. Louis at street level. He was a bachelor who was jovial and was skilled at closing a deal—be it political or business.

The year 1933 was pivotal in St. Louis. As Democrat Franklin Roosevelt ended a long reign of Republican control nationally and embarked on a bold new policy agenda, Democrat Bernard Dickmann became the first of his party to win the mayoralty since the turn the 20th century. He also had a bold new vision for the city.

Just as a real estate man can see the potential in a property before it materializes, the new mayor could see the potential to enact substantive change in his city. This New Deal Democrat knew that he owed his

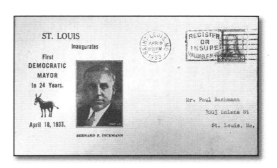

Inauguration postal cover acknowledging the Democrats' victory in the 1933 election. Theising image. Author's collection.

victory to sufficient support from African American voters, a voting bloc that was feeling alienated by broken promises from Republican mayors around the construction of a long-promised hospital for African Americans. Black voters turned out to support a major bond issue to build public infrastructure in 1923—with a new hospital in the budget. Ten years later, the bond money proved inadequate, and the hospital was not built.

Dickmann had a very impressive policy agenda. Some of his ideas, such as environmental initiatives, were ahead of their time.[14] He sought (with varying degrees of success) pollution control, riverfront park development, federal investment in local jobs programs, and personnel reforms. On a political level, though, he used old-fashioned political opportunity to his advantage and was guilty of political overreach.[15]

To Dickmann's credit, he surrounded himself with strong administrative people. Dickmann had the civic vision for the city but not necessarily the skillset to implement it. He surrounded himself with "doers" who could execute his plans. He knew what would have political payoff. He was willing to entertain lofty goals, but always had them connected to a strong dose of pragmatism. His team, over time, included Raymond Tucker as "secretary" (functionally chief of staff), Joseph Darst as the Director of Public Welfare (a job responsible for the city's public hospital system), and—after Tucker's attention shifted toward smoke abatement—John B. Sullivan as his replacement. These three men would play significant roles in St. Louis's development for the next quarter century.

Tucker and Darst became fast friends. Though eight years apart in age, both were lifelong city residents and had attended Saint Louis University High School. They socialized together, hosted card parties at their respective homes, and supported each other's professional careers. They were both excited by the prospect for change that the Dickmann Administration held, and both approached their work with alacrity.

Becoming Raymond Tucker

Raymond Tucker liked his first job at public affairs, but he had no taste for politics. Like his father, he was active in his neighborhood Democratic committee for a time but little beyond that. He enjoyed working for the public good. Like Dickmann, he could see a path forward for a better city—but it was one of policy, process, and practice. He believed in the power and potential of well-run institutions. He was a methodical professor. He embodied neutral competence when it comes to his work—always professional and eschewing partisan politics.

In his life, he also had a sense of duty and obligation, a sense of right and wrong. His work was never for personal power or material gain. His ego was in check by his moral compass.

He understood cause and effect. He was a systems thinker who could see how one side affected the other, and he understood how to take lofty vision and implement it at street level. He had a degree of utilitarianism, appreciating pragmatism and the common good. He always was focused on implementation and the practical application of policy.

He was remarkably consistent in his thoughts and actions, despite the tumult that sometimes engulfed the city. This was both a strength and a weakness.

ENDNOTES

[1] *Annual Commencement of the St. Louis University...Nineteen Hundred and Seventeen.* p. 3

[2] See "Junior Class, St. Louis University, Sets Record with 2 Years in One," *St. Louis Star*, 26 Jun 1910, p. 3.

[3] For his Wash U degree: see "Education Board Gives $470,000...," *St. Louis Post-Dispatch.* 10 Jun 1920. p. 23. and *The Hatchet*, 1921, p. 54 found at *WUSTL Digital Commons*, https://digitalcommons.wustl.edu/cgi/viewcontent.cgi?article= 1017&context=hatchet and for his faculty appointment see *The Hatchet* 1922, p. 28, also found at *WUSTL Digital Commons,* https://digitalcommons.wustl.edu/cgi/ viewcontent.cgi?article=1018&context=hatchet ; and for the Aluminum Ore reference, see "Ex-Mayor Tucker Dies...," *St. Louis Post-Dispatch.* 24 Nov 1970, p. 1A.

[4] "Nine Promotions in Washington U Faculty Announced," *St. Louis Post-Dispatch.* 09 Jun 1924, p. 3.

[5] "Two New Deans at Washington U.," *St. Louis Post-Dispatch.* 10 Sep 1927, p. 2.

[6] Marriage license issued 29 Nov 1928.

[7] *Fifteenth Census of the United States, 1930*, Ward 28, Block 5318, 19 Apr 1930. Lines 60-62.

[8] "Smoke I. and Aids to Go," *St. Louis Globe-Democrat.* 28 Jul 1909, p. 3.

[9] See "Burning Dollars: The Smoke Law Shows Manufacturers How to Stop It," *St. Louis Post-Dispatch.* 11 Dec 1892, p. 11.

[10] "The Smoke Abatement League," *St. Louis Post-Dispatch.* 24 Apr 1926, p. 12.

[11] "Preparing to Fight Smoke," *St. Louis Star.* 14 Jun 1926, p. 14.

[12] "Smoke Commission Will Meet Tuesday," *St. Louis Globe Democrat.* 17 Oct 1926, p. 7B.

[13] "Smoke Abatement League Seeks Membership of 10,000," *St. Louis Post-Dispatch.* 21 Mar 1934, p. 14C.

[14] Stein, Lana. *St. Louis Politics: The Triumph of Tradition.* St. Louis: Missouri Historical Society Press, 2002. p. 33.

[15] see Stein, pp. 41-43

An unfamiliar view of a familiar photo. Former Mayor Dickmann poses with his friend, Harry S. Truman. Dickmann usually was cropped out of the famous photo. It probably was Dickmann's biggest brush with fame. November 4, 1948 at St. Louis Union Station. Courtesy of Harry S. Truman Library, National Archives. Accession #64-861.

IN APPRECIATION OF

WHAT THE DEMOCRATIC ADMINISTRATION

. . . UNDER . . .

MAYOR BERNARD F. DICKMANN

HAS DONE FOR

100,000 NEGRO ST. LOUISANS

Vote Democratic April 6!

—— PREPARED AND ISSUED BY ——
NEGRO DIVISION
DEMOCRATIC CAMPAIGN HEADQUARTERS

Mayor Dickmann relied heavily on the African American vote in 1933, and wanted to keep that vote in 1937, as indicated from this brochure. Theising image, Author's Collection.

Chapter 1

The Start of a Career:

Tucker's Path to City Hall

Tucker's Pre-Mayoral Timeline

Tucker's Role		Mayor
On faculty at Washington University since 1921	1930	Bernard Dickmann [D] elected mayor, 1933
Tucker joins Dickmann Admin., 1934		
Tucker becomes Smoke Commissioner, 1937	1935	Bernard Dickmann [D] re-elected mayor, 1937
Tucker prepares the Griffenhagen Report, 1939-1941; writes civil service amendment, 1941	1940	Wm. D. Becker [R] elected Mayor, 1941
		Becker dies; Aloys Kaufmann [R] assumes mayoralty 1943
Tucker resumes faculty position at Washington University, 1941-1949	1945	Aloys Kaufmann [R] elected for full term, 1945
Tucker chairs Charter Reform, 1949		Joseph Darst [D] elected Mayor, 1949
Tucker writes STL Civil Defense Plan, 1951	1950	Raymond Tucker (D) elected Mayor 1953+
	1955	

THE ATTITUDE THAT DROVE the Mid-Century Modern movement did not just appear one day. It evolved over time, beginning with new thinking in the post-World War I years. Just as the Great War brought an end to many of Europe's old nineteenth-century monarchies, it opened a new chapter in the United States in term of technology, fashion, communication, and expectation. A popular song from 1919 captured it precisely: "how are you gonna keep 'em down on the farm after they've seen Paree?" The returning veterans of World War I helped push the rise of urban society, and the 1920 Census proved it—when, for the first time, more than half the country's population was living in cities instead of on farms.

In the years before he was mayor of St. Louis in the 1950s, Raymond Tucker showed his embrace of Mid-Century Modern attitudes in his many public projects of the 1930s and 40s. Each of these elements represents a unique preparation for being mayor of a large city. Taken together, these elements show how Tucker was willing to embrace change, let go of the past, and put forth bold new ideas—even as various constituencies pushed back.

Katherine Darst, columnist for the *Globe-Democrat* and sister-in-law of Tucker's friend Joseph Darst, ran a creatively favorable column on Tucker in 1939. She remarked that all St. Louisans should be thankful for Tucker, because otherwise "they would not have anyone to get mad at," embracing his techie (almost nerdy) approach.

> "To begin with, he's an engineer. As such, he has no flair for publicity. He looks simply awful in print, like Hoover. He uses big words we can't understand like 'the sulphurous acid content of our atmospheric air.' We don't know what atmospheric air is. We can only guess.

> "...Mr. Tucker is no editorial page duelist. Every time a writer slaps the Smoke Commissioner in the face with his glove, [the writer is] challenging him to fight without giving the Smoke Commissioner a choice of weapons. [The writer] fights professionals with their rapiers, and when the masters of words rip him to shreds, he looks like a gallant fellow beaten by a bully. Then we can't be mad at him anymore, only furious at his scheming opponents."[1]

CLEANING THE AIR

Most people of the Silent Generation remembered Raymond Tucker as the man who cleaned the air. Dirty air was just a fact of life in St. Louis at the turn of the last century. The buildings were dirty. Clothes were dirty. The air was dirty. When people opened windows for some kind of relief from the torturing summer heat, houses and rooms became dirty. It was just a fact of life.

St. Louis just learned to live with it. Coal was a part of our daily lives, and the factories that paid workers' wages depended on it. The trains that transported us depended on it. Most every family depended on it to heat homes during the bitter temperatures of a St. Louis winter. Rather than envisioning a world without coal, St. Louisans just learned to cope. Admire the architecture without noticing the grime on the surface. Cover your face while crossing a smoky street. Wear black! ...and clean your house with little pink balls of magic.

The Little Pink Balls of Magic

The year was 1891, the place was St. Louis, and a local businessman named H. R. Henderson invent- ed a new product he

Absorene was a common item in urban households across the industrial Midwest, as indicated by this 1919 advertisement in the Chicago Tribune. Newspapers.com

called "Absorene." The family still makes it in St. Louis today, and still sells it across the country. It is a pink rubbery product that homeowners would roll in ball across wallpaper or lampshades or tapestries to collect the coal dust that accumulated from open windows and leaky chimneys. It was not unusual that such a product would be invented in St. Louis, or that it would appear in 1891—because St. Louis had a smoke problem so severe that people pushed the city to act. In 1892, the city passed its first smoke regulation ordinance.

The smoke in St. Louis affected the quality of life. The sources were factories, railroad engines, commercial furnaces, and kitchen stoves. Stories of the smoke regularly appeared in the newspapers. In 1907, one article noted how the smoke blanketed the city worse on a Monday, since all the factories and heating plants began to "smoke up in unison to start the week's work."[2] With a light wind of 4 miles per hour, the smoke pall slowly pushed through the city. It was "dark as night" from Sarah Street to Taylor Avenue, a five-block swath of the Central West End neighborhood.[3]

In 1911, the Women's Organization for Smoke Abatement started working through other women's clubs to draw people to the cause. The smoke damaged books, paintings, and metal work, they noted, as well as killed lawns and trees. "Every woman knows that the smoke, even from her neighbor's chimney, ruins the tapestries, linen and laces in her home."[4] The group won the attention of some corporate sponsors and institutional directors, and was able to keep the issue before the citizens—though the problem did not seem to go away.

One of the most interesting newspaper features appeared on the *St. Louis Post-Dispatch* front page in February 1902. It was a narrative "pen picture" by a reporter who had ridden a streetcar through the smoke pall. He boarded the Olive Street line in the 4500 block, at Taylor Ave. As the car approached Vandeventer Ave. (3900 block), passengers began commenting that it was getting darker. By the time the streetcar crossed Grand Avenue (3600 block), "the car plunged into unmistakable night—it was as dark there as it will be at 10 o'clock tonight."[5]

"Women in the car grew timidly fearsome," the reporter noted, until the conductor turned on the electric lights. The driver had to clang the bell "almost incessantly" since visibility was only a few feet. [6] When an unknowing passenger commented to another how thick the fog was, the other retorted, "It's no fog—it's smoke!" There was a brief reprieve from the smoke at Compton Avenue (3200 block), but the darkness reappeared approaching 21st Street (2200 block). The reporter noted the source was the power plant on Locust Street and the neighboring factories with "huge columns of black smoke belching from [the] chimney stacks...."[7] In darkness all the way to Broadway (300 block), one passenger joked before reaching the terminus that maybe corrupt politicians brought the darkness "to cover a multitude of their sins and foil the grand jury!"[8]

Regulating Smoke for Real

Raymond Tucker was a mechanical engineer by training, but his specialty was combustion. He understood how things burned, and this is the real reason he was brought to Mayor Dickmann's staff in 1934. Though he was good at many things, Professor Tucker knew about smoke most of all. Therefore, he was put in charge of Dickmann's new citizens' smoke regulation committee.

The cause of St. Louis's smoke problem was rather simple—cheap high-sulfur bituminous coal from across the river in Illinois was being burned inefficiently, which caused it to smoke and generate a lot of particulate matter. Tucker identified two basic responses to the coal problem in a 1935 report.

1. Burn bituminous (soft) coal but invest in the equipment to do it right. High-sulfur coal could be burned cleanly, but it required sufficient oxygen and careful stoking. Large commercial or industrial furnaces sometimes had mechanical stoking devices that allowed for a very efficient burning of high-sulfur coal. The equipment was expensive to install and had to be maintained to ward off nasty smoke. One fix to the problem would be to inspect and supervise the installation of these stoking devices. Small residential units could not be expected to have these sophisticated devices.

2. Keep the existing equipment but burn anthracite (hard) coal instead. Anthracite burned cleanly without the expensive equipment, but it came from farther away and carried a higher price tag.

An intermediate strategy that could help in the short term was to remove the particulate waste matter that was attached to the pieces of coal. If pieces of coal were broken into smaller chunks and then washed, quite a bit of non-combustible pollutants could be removed. Tucker proposed this as a temporary approach to give some relief to the situation. Of course, this too would come at a higher price.

So, the city had an intractable problem that could only be fixed by having every household and business spend more money in one way or another. This was just not appealing to any constituent group or the politicians that represented them, especially during the Great Depression.

The First Public Hearing

Tucker's committee (well, Tucker) drafted a new smoke ordinance for the city. The first public hearing before the Board of Aldermen's Public Safety Committee was held on March 22, 1934—shortly after Tucker joined the mayor's staff. It did not go well.[9]

Seventy-five people showed up. The Operating Engineers Union sent its business agent to oppose the bill. "The trouble [with the present smoke laws] is that the [city smoke inspectors] are nothing but barbers and bartenders and don't know the first thing about engineering."[10] When one of the inspectors had shown up to the business agent's facility, the agent handed him a shovel and asked how to fire a boiler—and the inspector didn't know how to do it. Tucker responded that the new legislation only hired trained inspectors. It didn't help.

Opponents criticized the fees that were to be paid, asked for better enforcement of existing laws, and even cast blame on the industrial suburb of East St. Louis across the river as being the true source of downtown's smoke.[11] Tucker refuted it all. The Real Estate Exchange stated that it needed more time to study the issue, and the committee agreed. The bill was deferred to a later date, effectively letting the bill die in committee. The bill was re-introduced in the summer session, and again was left to die in committee.[12]

The third time proved to be the charm for the aldermanic committee. In January 1935, the committee finally released the bill, but the full board never picked it up. In May 1935, the

Citizens' Smoke Abatement League dissolved and turned the effort over to Mayor Dickmann and his administration. The presence of Raymond Tucker must have been encouraging to them, but once again Tucker saw political forces and uninformed constituents carry the day.[13]

Passing a Tougher Law

The Dickmann Administration prepared yet another bill for the Board of Aldermen early in 1936.[14] By the month of December, it had worked its way through the legislative process and hearings began. One of the provisions of this bill was the washing of coal—an idea that had been on the table for years.[15] It was a long and thorough bill (filled with years of lessons from Professor Tucker). Most significantly, it created a Smoke Commissioner to oversee the law's enforcement.

Once again, opposition poured from all directions. Southern Illinois coal producers called the mayor, others planned a protest march, and still others likened it to "the mistake of prohibition."[16] Something was different this time, though. Instead of coal companies opposing the matter, they decided to negotiate the regulation rather than contest it. They sat down with Tucker and the city counselor to work out definitions and standards.[17]

This provision proved controversial, and Tucker knew it. He believed that if this regulation could withstand legal challenge, it would open the door to tougher regulation in the future. Tucker got his wish. In May 1937, a Southern Illinois coal mine filed suit in federal court seeking an injunction. After a June hearing, Federal District Judge George H. Moore ruled that Tucker's ordinance was a proper regulatory measure enacted under the city's police power for public health and welfare.[18]

The new smoke ordinance passed unanimously and took effect on July 12, 1937. Now, the mayor needed to find someone to take on the role of Smoke Commissioner. Tucker was the logical choice, but his integrity prevented him from pursuing the job. He could not accept appointment to a position that he himself had designed.

Becoming Commissioner

The position was vacant for a few weeks as people turned down the highly technical job. However, after the Joint Engineering Council endorsed him for the position, he relented on the second ask.[19] Tucker accepted the position of Smoke Commissioner at a salary of $6,000.[20] He was sworn into office in October 1937. He was both praised and vilified.

- The *St. Louis Post-Dispatch* (the liberal paper) took a more pessimistic view of the appointment in an editorial titled "Brave Mr. Tucker." "Several engineers had coyly backed away from the job," and Tucker "offered himself as the sacrificial lamb...." The editorial continued, "Instead of waiting to watch Mr. Tucker grapple vainly with the problem, how about improving the shining hours by looking for a real solution?"[21]
- The *St. Louis Globe-Democrat* (the conservative paper) praised the choice: "In selecting Raymond R. Tucker to head the new Smoke Regulation section of the City Government, Mayor Dickmann has drafted technical knowledge, determination, and courage to meet one of the most harassing problems that face St. Louis."[22]

Tucker's time as city smoke commissioner showed his pragmatic side, where applied results mattered. It foreshadowed how he would behave as mayor. He was consistent in his behavior. He believed in rigid enforcement.[23] He was methodical in his enforcement.[24] He sought personal and professional integrity of his workers.[25] When one of his inspectors was implicated as being corrupt by a firm that was found in violation, Tucker made a public call for the evidence against his worker if true—or demanded an apology for the false accusation. He got the apology the next day![26]

Even personal friends were not exempt. When a family friend complained of being threatened for noncompliance, Tucker himself admonished the woman for wanting to be above the law.[27]

Tucker refused to use the police to enforce the law. He felt that their training could be called into question in a court action.[28] Therefore, he had a small team of smoke inspectors trained in the principles of engineering. He secured a $35,000 WPA grant (over $500,000 in today's dollars) to study where the smoke was most problematic in the city.[29]

The Impact on the Poor

Tucker was sensitive to the needs of the poor, but he did not make that point clear to all who watched him. The high-sulfur soft coal brought in from Southern Illinois was the cheapest form of fuel for many poor households. He knew from the WPA study that much of the residential pollution was coming from the districts east of Grand Avenue, including areas such as the Mill Creek Valley. This issue would dog him in later years.

When smokeless fuels were being considered, Tucker insisted that supplies be trucked to the poorer and smokier areas of town for cash-and-carry sales.[30] When an idea a smokeless coal product called Carbonite was raised, Tucker directed that it be given to poor households for its test run—diverting 200 tons of fuel to neighborhoods in need.[31]

One of the concerns Tucker had on behalf of the poor was the wastefulness of the coal they purchased. For every five tons of cheap coal they purchased, he noted, there were 500 pounds of slate—a completely inert material that only added to the weight.[32] Tucker explained to the Smoke Elimination Committee that smokeless coal could produce 14,000 BTUs of heating energy per ton, and that ton cost $9.75. Presently, he remarked, the poor were buying cheap Southern Illinois soft coal that produced 10,500 BTUs and cost $5 per ton. Over the heating season, the poor purchased $70 worth of dirty coal, versus $87 for the clean coal. The $17 additional annual expense would be recovered for residential, commercial, and industrial users, he said, by having less repair work, cleaning bills, and depreciation of property value.[33] Such logic, while true, was not consoling to persons for whom $17 was a great sum.

Winning the Newspaper War

The *Post-Dispatch* continued to be hard on Tucker. "[A]s a matter of principle, he would not allow a challenge to his method or his integrity to pass."[34] Editorials criticizing his smoke regulation work received stinging replies from him, replete with logic and technical details. The *Post-Dispatch* referred to him as a "brilliant epistolarian" who was part of a team that would not or could not fix the smoke problem.[35] Tucker fired back, citing the improvements already seen because of the program.[36]

When Tucker was taken to task in the newspaper by the Board Chair of St. Louis Children's Hospital, who said there were no efforts being made to clean the air, Tucker responded promptly. He retorted that her statement "must have been based on misinformation," and that a lasting solution required the proper "attitude on the part of individual citizens...."[37] Tucker had accomplished much.

November 1939 was a bad month for the Smoke Commissioner. Thanks to a natural thermal inversion over the city, the smoke palls were the worst ever recalled. Smoke mixed with fog in the center of a slow-moving high-pressure system. November 28 was called "Black Tuesday," and at noon the visibility was scant one block.[38] The *Post-Dispatch* already was lashing out at Tucker, stating that if the "brilliant epistolarian" would not do anything about the smoke, then the city should get someone who would—"something would be done if we had leadership with brains and courage."[39] The insulting editorial stirred Tucker to action.

Using his best epistolarian skills, he fired back at the editors with the successes of the program: less sulfuric acid in the air, reduction of fly ash, the oversight and proper maintenance of thousands of furnaces in St. Louis—all within two years.[40] He agreed with the paper that this was not enough, but the real solution was to stop burning Illinois coal. If that is what the editors were suggesting, he wrote, "let them so state in their editorials."[41] Tucker continued railing on the editors. The paper suggested using cheap processed fuels that were clean burning. Tucker retorted that such material does not exist, and that a scientist cannot simply create it on a whim. "Such an attitude," Tucker wrote, "is characteristic of the uninformed layman who is blissfully unaware of the difficulties that beset the scientist's path."[42]

Tucker's retort worked. Clearly, the editorial board had a meeting and took Tucker's response to heart. It changed their position. The *Post-Dispatch* had been critical of Tucker since his appointment, but thereafter took a new tone in dealing with him and his efforts. Within a week, the *Post* asked the question, "Has the community the brains, the courage, the initiative, and the leadership to tackle [the smoke problem]? We believe the answer to that is an emphatic 'yes.'"[43]

After Black Tuesday, the city shifted its attention from smoke *regulation* to smoke *elimination*. Once again, a blue-ribbon committee was assembled, and Raymond Tucker was their go-to staffer. Outside of Tucker, no one on the Smoke Elimination Committee knew anything about the subject. [44] Tucker presented important information to the committee but spent most of his time answering their questions. The professor in him relished the opportunity to educate a powerful circle of civic elite on his chosen field, but it showed that the committee itself was more symbolism than substance.

Drastic, Pragmatic Change

Tucker knew there was only one solution to ending St. Louis's smoke problem—quit burning Southern Illinois coal. This was unpalatable politically and economically to many. The Southern Illinois coal industry balked, as did railroads, manufacturers, landlords, and the coal distribution network. Committee members questioned the legality of such a ban.

Alternatives were put forward, but none were realistic. One group favored converting Southern Illinois coal into coke, in a city facility that would subsidize the cost. Tucker explained that it would not make sense to do that work in St. Louis; rather, it made the most sense to do it at the mine itself. Different mines require different coking processes. Another group favored using natural gas, but the Laclede Gas Light Company was not able to take advantage of the opportunity to switch the city from coal to gas. Due to antiquated supplier agreements and a general lack of distribution infrastructure in the city, Laclede was not an alternative energy source on the timeline that the committee needed.[45] Tucker was not afraid to disagree with his committee.

There was no one there who could out-maneuver him. The solution to the problem in 1939 was the same as it was in his first report on the subject in 1935. Now, it would finally be implemented. When the smoke elimination committee that Tucker coordinated won the "First Citizen" cash award of $1,000, the committee promptly gave the money to buy clean coal for the poor.[46]

The holiday season of 1940—for the first time that any could recall—was a largely smokeless winter. In the spring of 1941, a cherry tree planted by city hall in 1935 bloomed for the first time. The sulfuric acid from smoke had always killed the blossoms. [47] The city forester said it was the first time he had seen a tree in bloom since coming to St. Louis in 1904. Tucker had won.

THE PUSH FOR GOOD GOVERNMENT

Tucker's victory over smoke for Mayor Dickmann was major and lasting, yet he could not rest on his laurels. There was now an opportunity to do for city services what he had done for polluted air. A study was to be commissioned looking at the efficiency of government services. It would examine city services from top to bottom and side to side. Key leaders were involved, people who really could make a difference. The group would gather an overwhelming amount of data. No stone would be unturned. There was an opportunity for lasting change. It required a person who was detail-oriented, who understood big data, and knew how to transform data into conclusions, and conclusions into pragmatic steps for change. Mayor Dickmann knew the right man for the job and appointed Raymond Tucker. He also hired a nationally-prominent consultant, and man so well known for this kind of work that his name alone brought substance and credibility—Griffenhagen.

The Efficient Mr. Griffenhagen

Edwin Oscar Griffenhagen may not be a familiar name anymore, but there was a time when he had the attention of St. Louis' circles of power. One of his daughters married a prominent military surgeon whose life-saving feats were the stuff of front-page news. His other daughter married the great Columbia University political scientist David B. Truman. Griffenhagen was a scholar, an engineer, and a devotee of Progressive Era good-government systems—and he was well known by Raymond Tucker.

Griffenhagen was one of the practitioners who helped transform the country's Progressive Era thinking of the 1890s to the Cooperative Federalism of the 1930s. For the government, this was a new era of alphabet-soup bureaucracy—WPA, CCC, NRA, PWA, FERA, TVA, FDIC, etc. For people like Griffenhagen, it was an opportunity to practice the logic of efficiency.

There is a wonderful line in political scientist Mordecai Lee's *Bureaus of Efficiency* that is telling of today's world as much as a century ago: for some reformers, government was a solution; for others, government was the problem.[48] There is a considerable amount of wisdom in that idea. First, it implies that government is a dichotomy—a theme of this work. Second, so are reformers. Urbanist Lana Stein goes a step further: reform is only as good as the reformers. Dr. Lee, in a sense, builds on this, noting that a definition of efficiency could vary reformer to reformer and therefore so could the impact of the reformer's work.[49] Edwin Griffenhagen was a reformer. So was Raymond Tucker—and he saw government (as it was) as the problem, with government (as it could be) as the solution.

The notion of efficiency itself had broad importance because it bridged the public and private sectors. Lee acknowledges historian Samuel Haber's typology that defined efficiency in four terms: mechanical, commercial, personal, and social.[50] Efficiency could apply to individual and institution, to public and private, and even to the middle ground of nonprofits. Efficiency was universal, as were concepts of the common good and right/wrong.

Frederick Winslow Taylor is to blame. He went to deliver a paper on management systems to an engineering conference in 1895 and came out a pillar of Progressive Era thought! Obviously, it wasn't that simple but Taylor took his early notions of efficiency in private sector production and developed it over the next decade.[51] Taylor's quest to find the one-best-way to do anything morphed into "scientific management" and highlights the Progressive Era thinking in the private sector.[52]

Griffenhagen was a disciple of Frederick Winslow Taylor. As an efficiency expert, Griffenhagen's job was to find the "one best way" to do the work of city governments.

Departing from the Departure

Just as mid-century modern was a departure from the Progressive Era, the Progressive Era (an age of service to others) was, itself, a departure. To set the stage for this analysis, let us consider some political realities that rose in the old Gilded Age (an age of profit for self or firm) that sound eerily familiar to us today. There was a rise of commercial power and the generation of great wealth. It was not just great wealth, but a concentration of wealth at the top of society and a widening gap between the "haves" and the "have-nots." There were deep divisions within society, with streaks of racism and xenophobia in the public debate. There was uncertainty about who wielded power in the electorate and who wielded power in institutions.

There certainly were reformers that pushed for structural change, above and/or beyond process change. One of the classic ideals that came out of the Progressive Era was using science to improve existing conditions. Sometimes, state and municipal governments simply did not have the capacity for such endeavors. Implementing a scientific approach required data, methods, and scientists. Governments across the United States at all levels became swept up with the science and began creating research bureaus to develop measures, capture data, and identify pinch-points that held back progress. Some governments went further by creating specific bureaus designed to study work and suggest changes that would help maximize service delivery and make the best use of scarce resources.

St. Louis created one of these efficiency bureaus in 1914 (and it also created the "Citizens Bureau of Municipal Research" in 1922—these functions often went hand-in-hand).[53] Though these bureaus of efficiency were true structural change, they took on different forms in different cities—some as government agencies and some as publicly affiliated nonprofits. Cities creating these structures chose one or the other, or in the case of Chicago, Milwaukee, and St. Louis—both!

It makes sense logically that efficiency would be a Progressive Era concern. If Progressive Era reformers were to add structure and process to already-complex social systems in the name of making them better, then there should be some expectation that these changes would be beneficial. The bureaus of efficiency were kin to the bureaus of research that set out on a similar (yet distinct) path.[54] However, the term efficiency became so elastic that the name was applied confusingly across purposes.[55]

Griffenhagen carried efficiency ideas into the 1930s and 40s, and people like Raymond Tucker implemented them in new ways, using new methods—even to this day. Though bureaus of efficiency are long gone, the "cult of efficiency" is still quite strong.[56] Beginning in the 1980s, and ever more so since then, private sector measures have been used to examine the public sector. Lee notes that modern desires to "privatize" services really raise the old point of efficiency.[57] In this sense, Lee finds comfort that the work of those old bureaus did not end with the Progressive Era as the structures tended to do.

The business community will always pressure the government to behave in certain ways and it is not shy in asserting its wants. At the end of the day, though, government's purpose is to protect rights and provide what the marketplace will not—and the reason is because certain functions are simply too inefficient or inappropriate to be profitable for the private sector. Tucker understood this. While there may be one-best-way to accomplish anything, it also may be foolish to try to measure a public-sector product with a private-sector yardstick.

Making Government Better

Consider what leaders back in the Great Depression must have been thinking in the day. Here was the economy—this invisible external force—that completely upset the status quo. This upset was not a passing phase; it was a long-term problem that required a complete re-thinking of government services.

The national government was unleashing a myriad of new programs. In fact, the administration of Franklin D. Roosevelt was having difficulty managing all the new programs it had unleashed and invited University of Chicago political scientist Louis Brownlow to lead a commission studying the administration's efficiency. The resulting Reorganization Act of

1939 led to the creation of the Executive Office of the President, which today is a vital organ of the executive branch.

Mayor Dickmann, in his second term, conceived of doing a similar study at the local level in the summer of 1938. The local administration worked with the St. Louis Government Research Institute on laying the groundwork for the study. Edwin Griffenhagen, of Chicago, was the leading authority on the subject and was engaged to lead the effort as the primary consultant. It was Griffenhagen who would go into the weeds, where Raymond Tucker liked to be. He went down musty hallways, into basements as well as boardrooms. He would pore over the contents of filing cabinets and interview everyone from the director to the custodian.

His price tag was $30,000 (over $500,000 in today's dollars).[58] The Board of Aldermen funded the study in the spring of 1939 and a two-year effort was launched to examine all the workings of city government—and then recommend changes. Mayor Dickmann put his trusted assistant on the job. Raymond R. Tucker was named the group's secretary and documentarian. Tucker was at the table with an extensive list of St. Louis's elite—moneyed names like Bixby and Shapleigh, corporate scions like Maestre and Bakewell, as well as other civic elite. They all got to see the meticulous professor at work, down in the weeds, making sense of the morass that can be bureaucracy.

A Bad Report Card

There were three themes that emerged in the study that clearly stayed with Tucker over the years. First was disorganization. "No consistent principle seems to have been followed in the matter of the grouping of functions," noted the report. Like operations were spread among agencies, and unlike functions were combined.[59]

Second was disjointed executive authority. The weak-mayor, plural-executive model from 1914 was not serving St. Louis well. The matter confused even voters. "Voters in St. Louis are called upon to elect 98 officers of local government, in addition to the state and national elective officers.... It has been estimated that the average voter can at any one time express at the polls no more than five choices, based on conscious weighing of the merits of the candidates. Larger numbers result in more or less arbitrary selections as by the voting for whole slates without regard to the individual merits of the candidates."[60]

In what must be a section written by Tucker, the report stated, "It is a peculiar thing that, in the mind of the average American, the essence of democracy is bound up in the exercise of the elective franchise. The idea seems to be that the more officers there are to be elected, the more democratic is the form of government. Little thought seems to be given to the effects or results of the exercise of the elective franchise...."[61] The "*substance*" [emphasis Tucker's] of representation in policy determination is more important than the "*mere symbol*" [emphasis Tucker's] of popular choice.

The report opined that voters yield to emotional appeals, slogans, party loyalty, and racial or religious prejudices. [62] "Election is about the poorest possible method of choosing persons qualified to administer the various technical activities of any city government."[63] It continued, where "such routine, ministerial posts as those of the Recorder of Deeds and the clerks of courts...are filled by election, whereas such responsible places as those of the City Counselor and the President of the Board of Public Service are filled by appointment, no room is left for...claim of any logic or consistency."[64]

The third theme was the interference of partisan politics in administrative affairs. This was a point that must have struck home for Tucker, remembering his father's dismissal by a newly elected mayor. "There is no Democratic, as opposed to Republican, method of registering deeds, conducting autopsies, or collecting and accounting for money...."[65] The report favored the reduction of appointments without merit: "...there seems to be a very distinct impression prevailing among the...departments that [job hires] are chosen largely on the basis of political considerations."[66] It wasn't supposed to be this way necessarily. There was an "efficiency board" that was supposed to manage the process, but nothing really stopped favoritism from happening.

Therefore, the study prescribed some basic principles: centralizing executive structure and authority, preventing "legislative meddling" in the administration of approved services, and keeping administrative activities out of partisan politics.[67] Tucker held all these principles dear.

By the way, the Division of Smoke Regulation, established in 1937 under Tucker's guidance, passed muster with the committee with the recommendation that it continue "on its present basis"—no surprises there.[68]

To show the minutiae covered in the report, consider this excerpt from the section on the Street Department:

> "Of the eleven 2½ ton trucks operated by the section, six were purchased in 1928, one in 1931, two in 1934, one in 1937, and one in 1938. The cost of operation ranges from 2.9 cents for the 1937 and 1938 trucks to 12.4 cents per mile for one of the 1928 trucks. Indications are that repair costs are too high on the older trucks."[69]

Other mundane facts reviewed in the report are that the Chain of Rocks water plant has an operating cost of $0.0278 per hour during fiscal year 1938-39;[70] that judging from the amount of idle time of employees in the Treasurer's Office, it is somewhat overstaffed;[71] the cost per "inmate day" at the Bellefontaine juvenile delinquent farm for boys was $1.30—which was 2 cents higher than the facility for girls;[72] and the recommendation that the "head laundress" and "head seamstress" at City Hospital be assigned to the head employee of the laundry rather than the superintendent directly.[73]

The report mentioned multiple times utilizing the model charter offered by the National Municipal Association. The report provided a St. Louis-specific list of modifications to such a charter in the appendix. It prepared Tucker well when it came time to revise the city charter later in the decade.

In all, almost one thousand changes were suggested in the report that was released on February 20, 1941.[74] Mayor Dickmann, who was facing his toughest election battle just a few weeks away in April, pushed for a big change from the start—getting rid of the patronage jobs that were the lifeblood of the city's mayors and aldermen for decades.

It was that last point that stuck in Dickmann's craw (Tucker's too). The party bosses of St. Louis government won their roles by giving away jobs to key constituencies. It was a process that did not always put the best person for the job in the position, but it made the partisans happy—and expanded their power! They were the "patrons" and the jobs they gave away were the "patronage."

Patronage Jobs vs. Merit Employment

St. Louis had in the 1940s, and still has today, a mixture of professional and partisan hires to deliver city services. The professionals are hired under the merit system, also called civil service, while the political appointees are hired under patronage rules, historically called the spoils system (where they serve at the pleasure of the official that appointed them).

In the 19th century, St. Louis—like many other local governments at the time—employed people based on a patronage system, where hiring, firing, and promotion were done at the will of the boss or "patron." This system was common at the national level during the administration of Andrew Jackson. Jackson, at the time, raised the employment of political cronies to an art form. He relished both rewarding his allies with "spoils" while punishing political enemies where he could.[75] The national government abandoned this system in 1883 with the Pendleton Act, a response to the patronage-motivated assassination of President James Garfield in 1881. States and localities were slow to adopt the system—if ever. Missouri didn't seriously take up the discussion until its 1945 constitutional convention, and even then, it did not force much change. Today, only 39% of Missouri's bureaucracy is merit-based.[76]

Hiring people based on political affiliations rather than talent was antithetical to Raymond Tucker's sense of good governance. (This is not to say that people who serve in patronage positions today are not qualified for those jobs— merely to note that they were not hired first for their ability.) John Samuel Myers wrote in 1936 that building a merit-based system was a "campaign waged almost continuously" after the new charter and city-county split of 1876. (Corruption in county government was a motivator for the separation.)[77] A major attempt at merit reform was made in 1896, but it did not go very far. It did get the attention of the Civic League of St. Louis, which would prove influential in the next decade.[78]

Facilitating Change in St. Louis

The dismissal of Tucker's father in 1909 happened under the 1876 charter. The Civic League, whose blue-ribbon board of trustees was steeped in Progressive Era values, was a major proponent of the 1914 charter. In an open letter to "Mr. Citizen," the League asked if voters were tired of "the evils of mismanagement, inefficiency, and irresponsibility at the City Hall," noting that the new charter would fix it all.[79] However, as noted in the Griffenhagen Report, the protections put in place in 1914 were ineffective and/or unenforced, and the party bosses that benefitted from handing out jobs were reluctant to do anything differently. It was time for a change.

The Dickmann Administration took up the reform head-on. Civil service legislation had come out of the Griffenhagen Report and Raymond Tucker was its author. The bill went to the Board of Aldermen in January, was delayed with surveys and deal-making, but passed late in March and was signed by Mayor Dickmann on his way out of office in April 1941. It called for a special election in September. On election day, September 16, 1941, voters passed Tucker's charter amendment that put most (not all) of city hall's jobs under the Merit System.

The idea of patronage had not really been much of an issue in the minds of average St. Louisans before Dickmann since Republicans held city hall for decades and the perks of political employment had changed little from one Republican administration to another. However, the election of the New Deal Democrat in 1933 wreaked havoc on the political scene. Dickmann openly disregarded rules prohibiting politically motivated dismissals and announced that he intended to replace old Republican workers with Democrats "as rapidly as is consistent with efficient service." [80] The "upheaval" in employment shocked both residents and the editorial pages of the papers.

Mayor Bernard F. Dickmann casts his ballot, with fingers crossed, in the April 1941 election. He made some good decisions, and also some bad ones. He lost to Republican William Dee Becker after making high-profile state-level political blunders in 1940. See Stein's <u>St. Louis Politics</u>, pp. 41-45, for a deeper dive. AP Photo, 1941 (pub). Author's collection.

To be fair, Dickmann took advantage of lax enforcement of such laws just as his predecessors did. His actions had grave consequences, though. According to the influential *Post-Dispatch* newspaperman Carlos Hurd, twelve of those workers Dickmann ousted from city jobs at the height of the Great Depression committed suicide. [81]

Raymond Tucker's Speech

Tucker prepared a speech on October 12, 1942, where he laid out his views on public service. He took a swipe at patronage, partisan politics, and even uninformed citizens. (The audience is unidentified, but the timing would have been when he had returned to faculty at Washington University.) He felt that opinions from public officials did not carry the weight they should because people did not hold political leaders in positions of respect. He felt the public's attitude was that political jobs were highly paid and that all politicians were dishonest. [82] Tucker condemned "the attitude of the citizen who expected his representative to do dishonest favors for him, while criticizing the representative if he did the same thing for someone else."[83]

He pointed to the long history of patronage in the city. He criticized "the selection of public servants solely for partisan reasons rather than on merit or on the basis of a job well done."[84] Those days were ending, though, and the city was getting on a different path. He said that citizens were "too quick to criticize without being in full possession of the facts."[85] He pleaded for his fellow citizens to have tolerance and consideration for public officials, and "to offer constructive criticism not necessarily in public, but quietly, so that motives would not be misunderstood."[86]

People had a role in creating the government they wanted. "[G]ood government, honest and clean government, would not be obtained until citizens themselves respected their government and the officials who administered the laws of the community."[87] Furthermore, "Men of integrity and experience would not run for public office unless it carried with it the opportunity to perform a public service and not provide an opportunity only 'to be crucified for sound judgment and sincere enforcement of the laws of the community.'"[88]

Tucker had won another battle when it came to patronage, but it was a small victory when the city had much larger issues facing it (as the Griffenhagen report noted in detail). Though patronage was wounded, it was not dead. Too many citizens were content with a system driven by partisan politics more than professionalism. This indignity against true good government would come at the expense of public service. "Men of integrity…would not run," he said. When Raymond Tucker was asked to run for mayor in 1945, he turned it down.[89]

A CHANCE TO FIX IT ALL: A NEW CHARTER

The 1914 St. Louis City Charter was showing its age by the time Tucker came along. Recall that the Griffenhagen Report recommended that the city consider adopting a new charter back in 1941, based on the model provided by the American Municipal Association (today called the National League of Cities). This was a subject close to Raymond Tucker's heart. He saw charter reform as a powerful, yet difficult, way to build fairness and professionalism into the delivery of city services. The stronger the charter could be, the less chance that partisan hack could mess it up in the future. Charter reform would be an elusive goal of Tucker's for the rest of his life.

There are two basic models for building the executive branch of government. There is the strong-executive model where a single leader appoints the various heads of bureaucracy, like the President of the United States does with cabinet secretaries. Then, there is the plural executive model, where voters elect the leaders of executive divisions. This is found in many states, where voters select a governor, a secretary of state, an attorney general, etc. St. Louis, with its sordid past, functionally stripped its mayor of any real power and allowed voters to elect a variety of offices that, in other jurisdictions, would be political appointments.

St. Louis's 1914 charter, which remains in effect today, had become a mess by midcentury. However, it was less of a mess than what it replaced. At the time of the 1904 World's Fair, the city government had a gigantic legislature called the "Municipal

Assembly" with two chambers like the Congress. There was a "City Council" having 13 at-large members and a "House of Delegates" having one member from each of 28 wards. [90] Corruption was rampant, and an oft-told joke was that the House of Delegates could be nearly emptied by yelling, "Hey Mister! Your saloon's on fire!"[91]

Lincoln Steffens wrote *Shame of the Cities* at the same time St. Louis was hosting the world at its exposition and Olympiad. St. Louis was so corrupt that it warranted two chapters in the book, where other cities only had one.[92] After being lambasted in front of the whole country, Progressive leaders in St. Louis pushed for charter change. The charter of 1914 was a model of Progressive-Era thinking. It took power away from the mayor and vested it in various boards and commissions. The budget was now controlled by a "Board of Estimate and Apportionment," a three-member panel of which the mayor had only one vote. Any fiscal authority the mayor had remaining was shifted to a directly elected comptroller. Separate offices collected fees for licenses, oversaw the treasury and investments, and determined assessed values. The new charter basically stripped the mayor's power over the city's money. No wonder it's called a "weak mayor" system.

For all its improvements to city government in the days before World War I, the 1914 charter was not suitable for the mid-century city after World War II. The city's population was growing, new generations were demanding new amenities, technology was advancing rapidly, and it was difficult for the city to keep up. Many saw the need for sweeping changes in city operations and the need for a strong executive to lead it.

"Fighting" for Change

In 1949, Tucker's dear friend Joseph Darst was elected mayor. After Dickmann's defeat in 1941, Darst tried for other elective offices, unsuccessfully. He was the Democratic nominee for President of the Board of Aldermen (a citywide elected position) in 1943. He lost that election to Republican Aloys Kaufmann.

Darst's victory in 1949 marked the end of Republican rule in St. Louis. The Republican incumbent did not seek re-election. Not only did Darst defeat his Republican challenger, but

Democrats also won a majority on the Board of Aldermen. The Republicans would not take the loss in stride. It was fought tooth and nail—literally!

Aldermanic President Charles Albanese, a Republican, questioned the credentials of two newly elected aldermen: Raymond Egan and A. J. Cervantes. (Refusing to seat the two new members would allow the Republicans to maintain their majority for the moment.) Even though an aldermanic committee already had declared the men eligible for office, Albanese wanted to read a letter he received questioning their ability to serve. [93] When Democratic aldermen objected, Albanese ignored them and instructed the clerk to read the letter anyway. A raucous back-and-forth erupted, and the furor continued until noon, the time when Darst was to be inaugurated. [94] Albanese declared a recess so the Board members could attend the inauguration ceremony. However, during the break, Egan and Cervantes were taken over to the City Register's office and sworn in.

Of course, when Republican board members learned of this, the chamber exploded with rage. The whole time, Mayor Darst was waiting to give his inaugural address to the newly elected Board of Aldermen. In fact, the delay was so long (five hours in total), Darst had time to run over to Sportsmen's Park to throw out the first pitch at the baseball game.[95] Both parties took a break to caucus but made no progress. By the end of the afternoon, President Albanese refused to swear in *any* of the new aldermen and moved to adjourn the meeting. The existing Republican majority voted to adjourn, and the Republicans— new and old—promptly left the chamber. The Democrats stayed and reconvened the meeting. At some point, the parliamentarian got involved; he had asserted that the oaths were invalid, and so was the continued meeting. This infuriated Sheriff (and political boss) Thomas Callanan. Callanan struck the parliamentarian in the jaw, knocking him off the dais, telling him he was fired.[96]

In the Democrats' session (convened by the new majority), they installed new leadership, promptly stripped President Albanese of all power save running meetings and maintaining decorum, and invited Mayor Darst to make his speech later in the week.[97] Mayor Darst's first day—and that of A. J. Cervantes too—was tumultuous, but it marked the passing of the old guard and the installation of the new.

Considering a New Charter

In Darst's speech, which already had been delivered to the press before the tumult, he criticized old laws and old ways of thinking, and noted how they held the city back.[98] He didn't mention the charter explicitly, but he clearly had changes in mind.

The idea of charter reform had been swirling for a while. Aloys Kaufmann, Darst's predecessor, had worked with the business community to advance the idea. Kaufmann did not seek re-election in April 1949, and soon after was chosen to lead the Chamber of Commerce. While in office, he did push through a ballot measure to create a Board of Freeholders to make a deep examination of the old 1914 charter.

In an editorial from early in 1949, the *Post-Dispatch* declared that the Board of Freeholders that would draft a charter needed to "study the city government in detail" and "draft the best organic law it can to control its organization and functions."[99] Raymond Tucker was one man who clearly fit that bill, and he filed for election to be one of the 13 freeholders.[100] So did 63 other people!

On the same ballot that elected Joseph Darst, Raymond Tucker was elected to the Board of Freeholders, getting the third highest vote count out of the 64 candidates. (It should be noted that two women were elected to the board, but it does not appear that any African Americans were. Creamus Evans, a professor at Stowe Teachers College, and Emmett Golden fell about 5,000 votes short of consideration.)[101]

The first meeting was held on April 21, about two weeks into Darst's term. The photograph of the meeting that appeared in the *Post-Dispatch* shows the members seated and standing in the mayor's conference room, with Darst at the head of the table and Tucker standing behind him with a hand on the back of the mayor's chair. Rumors were circulating that Tucker would be asked to join the mayor's cabinet, but Tucker quashed them saying he didn't want a city position.[102] Once again, the man of integrity didn't want a city hall job—he was focused on finishing the reform work he started years ago.

Darst addressed the group, saying they had an "exacting" task ahead of them, and that there was "a crying need" to change the 1914 charter that reflected old thinking from "an early day of political science."[103]

Former Mayor Kaufmann, who got the matter on the ballot, reminded the freeholders of the Griffenhagen Report. He called the current organization of functions in the city "illogical." The group also was reminded that the services of the Government Research Institute were "at the command of the freeholders."[104]

A week later, Raymond Tucker was chosen to be the board's chairman.[105] The choice made sense—he had been an astute observer of city hall for more than a decade and was liked by the community broadly. His organizational skills, his rational understanding of problems, and his sense of professionalism and public service would serve him well in this role. Tucker also liked to be in charge of change efforts.

The resulting document was unlike anything the city had seen before. The simplification was not done with a scalpel; rather, it was a chainsaw. The weak-mayor system was gone, and the mayor was given the power to appoint all department heads. The Board of Estimate and Apportionment was replaced with mayoral budgetary controls. A new city Department of Finance was called for, replacing several of the "county" offices where patronage lived—Revenue Collector, License Collector, and City Treasurer. Further, the city would enjoy greater home-rule power and bring all the remaining "county" functions under the control of the city charter and the city's budget. The number of appointed officers and boards was cut in half, and ex-officio roles for key officials were eliminated.[106]

The change didn't stop with the executive branch. There would be an auditor appointed by the Board of Aldermen to monitor the mayoral departments, and the auditor was empowered to initiate court action. The Board of Aldermen, which still had 28 members like the old House of Delegates, would have been cut down too. Ironically, an entirely new charter would only require a simple majority of the electorate to pass, while amending the old charter would have required a 3/5ths majority.[107]

Undoubtedly noticed by Tucker and Darst was suburban St. Louis County's move toward a home-rule charter of its own. It convened its own board of freeholders in November 1949, making this a case where the city needed to keep up with the suburbs.[108]

African American voters were split on the proposed charter. There had been proposed a civil rights section, which Tucker sent to the legal team for review. The freeholders' legal counsel, Sam Liberman Sr., concluded that he didn't think the freeholders had the constitutional authority to enact such a component. He feared that if a court were to decide the measure was unconstitutional, the judge could throw out the entire charter document. He said it would be better for the Board of Aldermen to enact such a law, and that way a court challenge would have far less impact.[109] As a compromise, the new charter authorized the Board of Aldermen to "enact ordinances in the interest of individual liberties."[110] This satisfied some African American voters but disappointed others. While some African American leaders supported the proposed charter, such as members of the Mayor's Council on Human Relations, others opposed it, such as R. L. Witherspoon, president of the local NAACP.[111]

Mayor Darst supported the charter, but his voice came in late and soft. "The proposed new charter represents a vast improvement [over the 1914 charter]. It streamlines the machinery of government. It forbids deficit financing…. I hope all of you will see fit to join me in [voting for the charter]. I am convinced that in so doing you will be serving your own best interests."[112] Darst had grown scared of all the opposition that had emerged. After all, this was a project he inherited from the Kaufmann years, and he had his own bold agenda that he needed to sell.

The new charter was put before voters on August 1, 1950. A simple majority was required to pass it—and it was overwhelmingly defeated in heavy turnout by greater than a 2-to-1 margin (roughly 117,000 against and only 51,000 for).[113] While the League of Women Voters supported it (as did church groups, the Chamber of Commerce, and the newspapers), the opponents were vocal and effective. The NAACP wouldn't support it due to the lack of a civil rights section. Some labor unions came out against it also, including the powerful AFL Steamfitters Union whose business agent was Lawrence Callanan—brother of Sheriff Thomas Callanan.[114] The most vicious opposition came from the political ward organizations, half of which Thomas Callanan dominated.

Both Republican and Democratic ward committees fought the new charter. Quite simply, it destroyed patronage jobs that had become their lifeblood. For them to support the new charter would mean sowing the seeds of their own destruction. Just as Mayor Darst said voting for the charter "will be serving your own best interests," the ward bosses said the same thing about voting against it. Obviously, the ward bosses were more successful in their messaging. Once again, party politics interfered with Raymond Tucker, undoubtedly bringing back memories of his father's experience.

GETTING INTO THE DRIVER'S SEAT

Joining the Darst Administration

After Tucker's charter defeat at the polls, Mayor Darst wanted to pull him into his administration to do a very specific job that only Tucker could accomplish. He was to become the city's Civil Defense Director in 1951 and be the brains behind a new Civil Defense plan. It was the Atomic Age, and the Cold War had begun. Soldiers were fighting communism on the Korean peninsula. The fear of atomic attack on the United States was real, and St. Louis could well be a viable target—given its prominent role in defense manufacturing.

Raymond Tucker took on the position and delighted in it. His meticulous style was exactly what was needed. The plan he produced by 1953 was a massive tome, filled with maps, illustrations, details, footnotes, and explanations as only a college professor could produce. The data were frightening: an atomic blast over the city would claim 90,000 victims; St. Louis was closer to Soviet bomber bases by air than New York or San Francisco; and a map was provided showing exactly the blast radius of various atomic weapons so that individuals can see if they were in the zone of destruction.[115] St. Louis was an attractive target psychologically, too. "If St. Louis could be hit," people across the US would believe that "we are vulnerable everywhere."[116]

In true Tucker fashion, his was the first one submitted to Washington DC and the first to receive federal approval.[117] He was quite proud of that fact. By the time he stepped down from the position, the plan was ready for the recruiting and implementation phase.

1953 Mayoral Primary Election: Settling on Candidates

Mayor Darst was slow to announce his intentions. By December 1952, many were convinced that the ailing mayor would not seek re-election.[118] Though Tucker's name was bandied about, there was no formal word, even as others were turning down any consideration. Darst announced he would not seek re-election on January 9.[119] The newspaper speculated that three candidates were in contention—Mark Eagleton, Mark Halloran, and Raymond Tucker. Eagleton was the favorite. Halloran's candidacy was considered a long shot, and Tucker was dismissed somewhat because he "aroused no enthusiasm" and was "not popular" among the ward bosses due to his work against patronage.[120]

Tucker formally threw his hat in the ring for mayor on February 1, 1953—for a March 13 primary. This was his greatest opportunity to effect the change he had long sought for the city. On the same day, Carl Stifel filed for the Republican nomination. After Tucker's announcement, Democratic political boss Thomas Callanan—the man responsible for the defeat of Tucker's 1950 charter proposal—said he was considering jumping in.[121] The next day, Callanan's home was bombed. Police suggested the motivation was union strife rather than his potential candidacy.[122]

Tucker's resignation from the Darst Administration took effect on February 5. He released his platform on February 7. There was a plank on Human Relations, where he said there needed to be "a better understanding of the problems and desires of everyone, and provision should be made for increased vocational opportunities in both public and private enterprise, regardless of race, color, or creed." He added, "there should be no second-class citizens." He said this before the country knew the name Martin Luther King. He said this before *Brown vs. Board*. He said this before the various Civil Rights Acts of the

1950s and 60s.[123] He placed himself on the cutting edge of Civil Rights.

Despite this early embrace of Civil Rights, his overture to the African American community—at least in the 19th Ward—was rejected. When Tucker planned to campaign there, he had booked a space at the Adams Hotel. However, committeeman Jordan Chambers (who endorsed Eagleton) "strong-armed" the hotel into canceling the event and replacing it with an Eagleton event.[124]

In his campaign talks, Tucker commended Darst's accomplishments. "We have made magnificent strides in public housing, urban redevelopment, airport development and in other fields of municipal endeavor." He called for improvement to neighborhoods as well as downtown.[125]

The Republican race largely was uncontested. Carl Stifel pulled ahead and stayed ahead. Former Mayor Aloys Kaufmann chaired his campaign, which drove away any serious competition.

Raymond Tucker received the Democratic primary endorsement of the *St. Louis Globe-Democrat* (the conservative paper) on Valentine's Day.[126] The *St. Louis Post-Dispatch* (the liberal paper) followed suit a week later. "It is no disparagement of Mr. Eagleton's past efforts for the betterment of St. Louis to say that they do not, in our opinion, come up to those of Mr. Tucker. The training, experience, and accomplishment which Mr. Tucker brings to the mayoral race are exceptional."[127]

Political Machine Makes One Last Grab for Power

The *St. Louis Post-Dispatch* observed that the outsider Tucker was not liked in the Democratic wards, but that he would enjoy considerable independent support—especially since there was no serious challenge from the Republican candidate. [128] Missouri's primaries, then as now, were "open" and there was nothing to stop a Republican from choosing to vote in the Democratic contest.

Going into the primary, Eagleton was winning the Democratic ward endorsements over Tucker nearly 2-to-1. In an editorial called "Pallid Primary," the *Globe* tacitly criticized Eagleton for not generating more excitement in the race. Tucker was running on his record, and the ward bosses hated that record and refused to support him. "Why would Mr. Eagleton change the quiet drift of the campaign when prospects look good?" the paper asked openly.[129] Independents, that's why!

The *Globe* wanted more excitement and in the following days, things started to change drastically. The primary election was about to be turned on its ear. The Democratic political machine run by Thomas Callanan publicly endorsed Mark Eagleton on stage at a ward meeting. (Tucker was invited to the meeting but did not show up.) On March 2, Clifford Haley, a Republican member of the city election board, abruptly resigned his post and filed for the Republican primary. The intention wasn't to thwart the leading Republican candidate, but rather to draw independent voters to a moderate Republican and away from Tucker. That would pave the way for an easy Eagleton victory on the Democratic side.[130] Tucker called it out for what it was: a ploy engineered by political boss Callanan.[131]

ST. LOUIS NEEDS A GREAT MAYOR!

VOTE FOR
MARK D. EAGLETON

Democratic Candidate for Mayor

AT PRIMARY, TOMORROW, MARCH 13

CITIZENS' COMMITTEE—MARK D. EAGLETON FOR MAYOR

DeBaliviere at Pershing   James J. Lee, Chairman
Telephone: DElmar 6202   Leland Jones, Treasurer

Eagleton campaign ad that appeared in the St. Louis Post-Dispatch, March 12, 1953. Newspapers.com

The *Post-Dispatch* spelled it out, too. Callanan's grab for power "was the most brazen and ambitious element in local politics." It called Callanan's machine "payroll-minded professional politicians" who were "more afraid of Mr. Tucker than of his opponent." [132]

The Tucker campaign started calling Eagleton the "Callanan-Shenker" candidate (referring to boss Callanan's associate Morris Shenker, a dubious defense attorney who worked in the circles of organized crime and engaged in backroom politics). Eagleton became enraged. Ed Dowd, a Tucker campaign leader, said publicly that Eagleton "could be handled by the politicians and the spoilsmen."[133] Eagleton slapped Tucker and his campaign with a $200,000 defamation suit, claiming they damaged his reputation. Eagleton said that he heard the Tucker campaign sought the Callanan endorsement, too. Tucker's team engaged one of the most prominent young attorneys working in St. Louis—Lon O. Hocker Jr., a Republican who would make a bid for governor and whose late father was a scion of the St. Louis Bar.

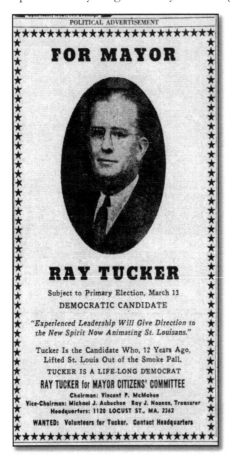

Tucker campaign ad, St. Louis Post-Dispatch, February 17, 1953. He had announced his candidacy on February 1st. Newspapers.com

Going to the Polls— and to Court

Ed Dowd, who was also the circuit attorney, noted "it is indeed strange for a man to solicit the support of Callanan and Shenker, and to consider it damaging to his reputation when it is pointed out that he has such support."[134] Tucker gave a blistering defense that was front-page news: "It is an irrefutable fact that Mr. Callanan did indorse [sic] Mr. Eagleton. It is also an irrefutable fact …that Mr. Eagleton appeared on the platform with Mr. Callanan on the evening of his indorsement. If he truly thought such an indorsement was detrimental, he should not have appeared at this [event] or accepted this indorsement. To the best of my knowledge to date, he has not repudiated this indorsement."[135]

Again, Eagleton became enraged and defensive. He offered a stammering string of explanations: that he didn't know this was Callanan's ward, that he didn't know the endorsement was coming, that he only knew Callanan by name, that he was endorsed by the ward not the machine.[136] Further, he said that Tucker campaign staff had "begged" Callanan for an endorsement. He asked the voters, "What sin have I committed?"[137]

The brouhaha brought out both retractions and endorsements for Tucker. The 25th ward committeeman withdrew his support for Tucker over the "tactics" of labeling Eagleton a machine candidate, while Mayor Darst (who had tried to remain silent) jumped in the day before the primary with his endorsement of Tucker and a blast at Eagleton's behavior.[138]

Going into primary day, Eagleton's statement in the press led with "Permit me to emphasize, I do not have the support of the Callanan machine." Even Callanan said that no one knows which lever he pulled in the voting booth. Tucker beat Eagleton in the primary election by only 1,679 votes out of 108,000 cast. [139] That total represents an 18,000-vote increase for Democrats from the last primary.[140] Eagleton dropped his suit in April.[141]

Becoming "Mayor" Tucker: The 1953 General Election

Tucker's primary victory was a big blow to the Callanan machine and a big endorsement of the Mid-Century Modern attitudes toward urban development. The ailing Mayor Darst had put the city on a path, a lot of it greased by former Mayor Aloys Kaufmann who brought along the business community (and who, by now, was leading the Chamber of Commerce).

Tucker's opponent in the general election was Republican Carl Stifel, a real estate man like Dickmann and Darst (and a cousin to the Stifel financial house founders). Stifel's most prominent position previously had been chairman of the St. Louis Housing Authority. Republican Mayor William Dee Becker appointed him in 1941, and his term extended into the mayoralty of Republican Mayor Aloys Kaufmann. By that time, Stifel was the Housing Authority's chairman. Real estate men like Stifel generally were not supportive of public housing or land clearance. When Kaufmann proposed two bills that would encourage public housing, Stifel resigned in protest. His term was ending anyway.[142]

There were divisions among Republicans when it came to embracing Mid-Century Modern attitudes, just like there were divisions among the Democrats. Both men agreed that the Chamber of Commerce's traffic plan should be implemented. This was a key want of former mayor Aloys Kaufmann. While Stifel embraced many changes and modernizations to the city, he did so on a smaller scale. He favored the construction of underground parking garages beneath the Aloe Plaza and Memorial Plaza zones, and the creation of a "Traffic Department" at city hall. He also favored completing the Arch. He was opposed to the earnings tax, and, in fact, opposed income tax anywhere in Missouri. He advocated that St. Louis should get more grant money from the state and national government.[143]

Tucker's plan, by comparison, was exceptionally bold. He advocated for creating a sewer district that would serve both city and suburbs, maintaining the earnings tax, issuing $100 million in bonds for a 10-year civic improvement plan, creating a public authority to operate mass transit, expanding parks and recreation facilities, as well as finishing the Arch.[144]

The general election campaign was rather uneventful compared to the primary. The *St. Louis Post-Dispatch* endorsed Tucker, while the *St. Louis Globe-Democrat* said both men were excellent and made no endorsement.[145] Tucker won by a landslide—142,000 to 82,000.[146] Democrats won 11 of 14 open seats on the Board of Aldermen as well. Even Callanan endorsed Tucker in the general election—an observation that did not escape the letters to the editor (it was bad for Eagleton, why not bad for Tucker?).

In selecting Tucker, though, St. Louis voters made a substantial departure from the past. The primary election shut out Callanan's old political machine, which would not rise again for a dozen years. The general election shut out the Republicans from power. There would never be a Republican mayor in St. Louis ever again.

The Republicans began to wonder what to do. Stifel returned to the community. He had once been the Grand Potentate of the Moolah Shriners Temple, and under his leadership started the annual Shrine Circus in St. Louis.[147] Another St. Louis Republican leader, Lawrence K. Roos, asked aloud "What's wrong with the Republican party in St. Louis?"[148] The answer might well have been visible in the actions of Roos himself. He was ensconced in the wealthy suburbs of St. Louis County, and from there built a large Republican organization that put him in the County Supervisor's office in 1962 (today called the "County Executive").[149] He was functionally the chief executive officer of suburbia, a jurisdiction that would become larger and wealthier than the City of St. Louis would ever be.

Raymond Tucker was now mayor of the City of St. Louis. He was now in charge of the government that he studied, that he criticized, and that he attempted to change. The voters, of whom he said in 1942 would need newfound respect for public officials before men of integrity would step forward, had ensconced him in Room 200 of city hall. With his victory was also delivered a sympathetic majority on the Board of Aldermen. The old political bosses would have to step back and lick their wounds for a while. The path was cleared for Tucker. His vision was big. The stakes were high. It was time to start moving, and he was in the driver's seat.

ENDNOTES

[1] Darst, Katherine. "Here and There," *St. Louis Globe-Democrat.* 24 Nov 1939, p. 1C.

[2] "Smoke Blankets City," *St. Louis Post-Dispatch.* 28 Jan 1907, p. 2.

[3] ibid.

[4] "Women Appeal to Housewives in Smoke War," *St. Louis Post-Dispatch.* 07 Apr 1912, PDF p. 19

[5] "One Little Street Car Journey…," *St. Louis Post-Dispatch.* 01 Feb 1902, p. 1.

[6] ibid.

[7] ibid.

[8] ibid.

[9] "New Smoke Bill Deferred After Public Hearing," *St. Louis Post-Dispatch.* 22 Mar 1934, p. 9A.

[10] ibid.

[11] ibid.

[12] "Aldermanic Group Approves Smoke Bill," *St. Louis Post-Dispatch.* 23 Jan 1935, p. 10A.

[13] "Citizens' Anti-Smoke League Dissolved," *St. Louis Post-Dispatch.* 04 May 1935, p. 3A.

[14] "New City Smoke Prevention Bill Is Being Drafted," *St. Louis Globe-Democrat.* 11 Feb 1936, p. 1B.

[15] "Anti-Smoke Bill Requires Washing of Low-Grade Coal," *St. Louis Post-Dispatch.* 11 Dec 1936, p. 20A.

[16] "Hearing Begins on City Smoke Bill," *St. Louis Star-Times.* 19 Jan 1937, p. 2.

[17] ibid.

[18] Allison 21

[19] ibid. 22-23

[20] Tucker, *A Smoke Elimination Program that Works*, 465; cited in Allison, 23.

[21] *St. Louis Post-Dispatch*, 12 Aug 1937; cited in Allison, 24.

[22] *St. Louis Globe-Democrat*, 12 Aug 1937; cited in Allison, 23.

[23] Allison 30

[24] ibid. 33

[25] ibid. 27

[26] ibid. 28

[27] ibid. 27

[28] ibid. 25

[29] ibid. 38

[30] *St. Louis Post-Dispatch,* 29 Nov 1939; cited in Allison, 47.

[31] *Minutes of Smoke Committee,* 30 Dec 1939; cited in Allison, 60

[32] Allison 56-57

[33] ibid. 58

[34] ibid. 182

[35] *St. Louis Post-Dispatch* editorial, 13 Nov 1939; cited in Allison, 45

[36] Allison 46

[37] *St. Louis Post-Dispatch,* 6 Jun 1939; cited in Allison 41.

[38] Allison 43

[39] ibid. 45

[40] ibid. 45-46

[41] *St. Louis Post-Dispatch,* 27 Nov 1939, cited in Allison, 46.

[42] ibid.

[43] *St. Louis Post-Dispatch,* 27 Nov 1939, cited in Allison, 47-48.

[44] Allison 59

[45] ibid. 72

[46] See NEA press photo caption, "The End of the Fight," 29 Apr 1941. Author's collection.

[47] Allison 129

[48] Lee 16

[49] Lee 24

[50] Lee 24, 199

[51] Lee points out that Taylor's private sector discussion is happening nearly a decade after Woodrow Wilson called for similar improvements in government (23).

[52] Described in Taylor, Frederick Winslow. *The Principles of Scientific Management.* New York: Harper and Brothers, 1911. P. 118 and elsewhere.

[53] "The Fact Hunters," *St. Louis Globe Democrat Sunday Magazine,* 02 Jun 1962, pp. 6-9

[54] Lee, in his methodology, makes certain to exclude research bureaus from his study (Lee 19).

[55] Lee 158

[56] Lee 198

[57] Lee 205

[58] "City Ignores 350 Changes…," *St. Louis Globe-Democrat.* 22 Nov 1946, p. 17.

[59] Mayor's Advisory Committee, 1941, 269

[60] ibid. 275

[61] ibid. 276

[62] ibid. 275

[63] ibid. 275

[64] ibid. 276

[65] ibid. 275

[66] ibid. 240

[67] ibid. 277-278

[68] ibid. 167

[69] ibid. 51

[70] ibid. 34

[71] ibid. 203

[72] ibid. 247

[73] ibid. 86

[74] "City Ignores 350 Changes…," *St. Louis Globe-Democrat.* 22 Nov 1946, p. 17. The exact number of changes was 939.

[75] Matherne 4

[76] Winn, Kenneth H. *It All Adds Up: Reform and the Erosion of Representative Government in Missouri, 1900-2000.* https://www.sos.mo.gov/archives /pubs/article/article.asp Some argue that Donald Trump embraced the Jacksonian style. See Barry Mitnick, "Trump Revived Andrew Jackson's Spoils System…," *The Conversation.* Posted 21 Jan 2021. Accessed 212 Sep 2021. https://theconversation.com/ trump-revived-andrew-jacksons-spoils-system-which-would-undo-americas-138-year-old-professional-civil-service-150039

[77] Myers 67

[78] Myers 69, 71

[79] "The Civic League to Mr. Citizen," *St. Louis Star*, 13 Jan 1914, p. 14.

[80] Hurd, Carlos. "Merit System for the City's Employes is the Aim of Charter Amendment No. 3," *St. Louis Post-Dispatch.* 23 Aug 1941, pp. 1C, 5C.

[81] ibid.

[82] Allison 180

[83] ibid. 181

[84] ibid.

[85] Tucker speech, 12 Oct 1942, cited in Allison, 181.

[86] ibid.

[87] Allison 181

[88] ibid.

[89] "Metropolitan Medley," *St. Louis Star and Times.* 24 Feb 1945, p. 10.

[90] "Charter Made," *St. Louis Daily Globe Democrat.* 4 Jul 1876, p. 3.

[91] Steffens 34

[92] Steffens v

[93] "GOP Members Walk Out...," *St. Louis Post-Dispatch.* 19 Apr 1949, p. 1A.

[94] ibid.

[95] ibid.

[96] "Democrats Take Control..., *St. Louis Post-Dispatch.* 20 Apr 1949, pp. 1, 6.

[97] ibid.

[98] ibid. p. 6

[99] "Charter Revision First," *St. Louis Post-Dispatch.* 06 Jan 1949, p. 2B.

[100] "64 Candidates in Race...," *St. Louis Star-Times.* 25 Feb 1949, p. 4.

[101] "Complete Unofficial Vote on Board of Freeholders," *St. Louis Star-Times.* 06 Apr 1949, p. 6.

[102] "Darst Appoints John J. O'Toole...," *St. Louis Post-Dispatch.* 21 Apr 1949, p. 3A.

[103] "Charter Board in First Meeting...," *St. Louis Post-Dispatch.* 21 Apr 1949, p. 3A.

[104] ibid. (both quotes)

[105] "Tucker Elected Permanent Head...," *St. Louis Globe-Democrat.* 29 Apr 1949, p. 2A.

[106] "New Charter for a Modern St. Louis," *St. Louis Post-Dispatch.* 16 Jul 1950, p. 1C.

[107] "Charter Board in First Meeting...," *St. Louis Post-Dispatch.* 21 Apr 1949, p. 3A.

[108] "Home Rule for St. Louis County," *St. Louis Globe Democrat.* 20 Nov 1949, p. 6F.

[109] "Labor Paper Urges Charter Support," *St. Louis Globe-Democrat.* 17 Jul 1950, p. 1.

[110] ibid.

[111] ibid.

[112] 7A, in "Extremely Heavy Vote...," *St. Louis Post-Dispatch.* 01 Aug 1950, 1A, 7A.

[113] "Still Needed," *St. Louis Post-Dispatch.* 02 Aug 1950, p. 2B.

[114] 1A, in "Extremely Heavy Vote...," *St. Louis Post-Dispatch.* 01 Aug 1950, 1A, 7A.

[115] See "A-Bomb's Toll Could Be 90,000 Here," *St. Louis Globe-Democrat.* 15 Mar 1953, p. 1; and St. Louis Office of Civil Defense. *Before Disaster Strikes: What to Do Now—A Family Handbook.* N.D. (probably 1954), pp. 6-8.

[116] ibid.

[117] "Tucker Resigns," *St. Louis Post-Dispatch.* 06 Feb 1953, p. 3.

[118] Trask, Herbert. "City Democrats are Looking for Darst Successor...," *St. Louis Post-Dispatch.* 07 Dec 1952, p. 1A.

[119] Noonan, Ray. "Callanan is Threat...," *St. Louis Globe-Democrat.* 10 Jan 1953, p. 1A.

[120] "McKenna Gains on Eagleton...," *St. Louis Globe-Democrat,* 16 Jan 1953, p. 3A.

[121] "Callanan Says He's Thinking of Filing for Mayor," *St. Louis Post-Dispatch.* 04 Feb 1953, p. 3A.

[122] "Intensive Hunt..., *St. Louis Globe-Democrat,* 07 Feb 1953, p. 3A.

[123] "Tucker Issues 10-Point Platform...," *St. Louis Globe-Democrat,* 08 Feb 1953, p. 2A.

[124] "Eagleton Names Tucker...," *St. Louis Post-Dispatch.* 05 Mar 1953, p. 1A, 20A.

[125] "Raymond Tucker Looks to Future...," *St. Louis Post-Dispatch.* 12 Feb 1953, p. 5A.

[126] "The Mayoral Race," *St. Louis Globe-Democrat.* 14 Feb 1953, p. 6A.

[127] "A Mayor to be Chosen," *St. Louis Post-Dispatch.* 18 Feb 1953, p. 2C.

[128] "Top Candidates...," *St. Louis Post-Dispatch.* 15 Feb 1953, pp. 1A, 4A.

[129] "Pallid Primary," *St. Louis Globe-Democrat.* 25 Feb 1953, p. 8A.

[130] "C. G. Haley Quits...," *St. Louis Post-Dispatch.* 02 Mar 1953, p. 4A.

[131] "Assails C. G. Haley...," *St. Louis Post-Dispatch.* 03 Mar 1953, p. 1A.

[132] "Callanan vs. Tucker," *St. Louis Post-Dispatch.* 02 Mar 1953, p. 2B.

[133] "Eagleton Names Tucker...," *St. Louis Post-Dispatch.* 05 Mar 1953, p. 1A, 20A.

[134] ibid.

[135] "Eagleton, Tucker Fight Continues...," *St. Louis Post-Dispatch.* 06 Mar 1953, p. 1A.

[136] ibid.

[137] ibid.

[138] "Darst Indorses Tucker," *St. Louis Post-Dispatch.* 12 Mar 1953, p. 3A.

[139] "Tucker Defeats Eagleton...," *St. Louis Post-Dispatch.* 14 Mar 1953, p. 8A.

[140] "Primary Election Results," *St. Louis Star-Times.* 12 Mar 1949, p. 3; and "Total Vote in City Primary," *St. Louis Post-Dispatch.* 14 Mar 1953, p. 8A.

[141] "Eagleton Drops His $200,000…," *St. Louis Post-Dispatch*. 30 Apr 1953, p. 3A.

[142] "Carl Stifel Quits…," *St. Louis Post-Dispatch*, 30 Jun 1945, p. 6A.

[143] "Information for Voters…Carl G. Stifel," *St. Louis Post-Dispatch*. 05 Apr 1953, p. 6, 7F.

[144] "Information for Voters…Raymond R. Tucker," *St. Louis Post-Dispatch*, 05 Apr 1953, p. 6, 7F.

[145] "Three Big Decisions," *St. Louis Post-Dispatch,* 06 Apr 1953, p. 2B; and "Tomorrow's Election," *St. Louis Globe-Democrat* 06 Apr 1953, p. 8A.

[146] Exact numbers are found at "Results of City Election," *St. Louis Post-Dispatch* 08 Apr 1953, p. 1.

[147] "Key Information…," *St. Louis Globe-Democrat*. 05 Apr 1953, p. 8B.

[148] "Panel to Discuss…," *St. Louis Post-Dispatch*. 26 Apr 1953, p. 22A.

[149] "Long, Roos, and Curtis Elected," *St. Louis Globe Democrat*. 07 Nov 1962, p. 1A.

1953 Mayoral Primary Campaign ad, St. Louis Globe-Democrat.

Chapter 2

The Needs of the Poor:
Poverty, Planners, and the
Mill Creek Valley

Mill Creek Valley Timeline

1908

1908: Housing Study targets inferior housing for action

1917: Slums are targeted for action in "Problems of St. Louis" report

1917

1947

1947 City Plan designates MCV for redevelopment; targets inferior housing

1948: Anti-Slum Committee targets Olive/Market area for redevelopment

1948

1950

1950: "Rockefeller Project" proposes hi-rise housing at Compton/Market, elsewhere in MCV

07/1954: Tucker convenes MCV advisory group made up of residents

1954

08/1954: Tucker announces MCV development plan

1955: City Plan Comm. disallows housing planned for MCV; cuts it by 70%

1955

1957

09/1957: STL NAACP endorses MCV development plan

10/1957: MCV advisory group endorses MCV development plan

1958

03/1958: Board of Aldermen approves MCV development plan 27-1

1959

02/16/1959: Demolition begins

1964: Congress investigates relocation problems of MCV

1964

JOSEPH DARST WAS DYING. He was experiencing heart failure. His doctors told him there was nothing more that could be done. Though he had only been mayor for a few years, Darst had launched a remarkable policy program on many fronts: he secured a commitment from the federal government for 5,800 units of public housing in St. Louis, he re-ignited talks on

Joe Darst signed his official portrait to this friend Ray Tucker, April 18, 1951. Block photo, 1951. Courtesy of the Tucker Family.

Gateway Arch construction, he strengthened the city's race relations committee, and he launched a new organization called Civic Progress that would bring high-powered corporate executives to the public policy table. He even endorsed an idea to bring the World's Fair back to St. Louis in 1953.[1] There was so much unfinished work. He could not entrust his work and legacy to just anyone—he reached out to his best friend and asked him to run. He could see the machine politicians preparing to run and he knew they were not up to the job. Only Raymond Tucker could replace him. He finished his term on April 21, 1953. He died on June 8. He was 64 years old.

The plans were in place for a massive program of land clearance and public housing. Those 5,800 new units of public housing promised to Darst in 1950 mostly materialized over the next decade under Tucker: Cochran Gardens, opened 1953, 704 units; Darst (named in Mayor Darst's memory), 1956, 645 units; Webbe, 1961, 580 units; Vaughn, 1957, 660 units; and the massive Pruitt and Igoe complex, 1955-1956, a whopping 2,870 units—one of the largest public housing developments ever built anywhere. Pruitt-Igoe had not opened yet before Tucker was planning to seek *even more* units (if the city could qualify).[2] The Blumeyer project, completed in 1967 after Tucker, at 789 units, topped out the 5,800 goal. [3] These projects were, charitably, short-term successes and long-term failures. The HOPE VI program demolished them all in subsequent decades.

Public housing in this era might be the best illustration of MCM attitudes of all, and in understanding the Tucker era. Pruitt-Igoe was a problem on multiple levels, and its failures are well studied and well known. The picture of the Pruitt-Igoe test implosion in 1972 may be the most recognizable photograph of St. Louis after the Arch. However, let's consider what was in the minds of leaders like Mayor Tucker in 1953. The attitudes of national and local government were quite different than the reality that showed up.

Understanding the Problems

Mayor Tucker was a pragmatist. He was not daunted by significant challenges. He always was a believer in what was possible. The debate was not "if" it was a good idea, but "how" it was a good idea. He was deeply intelligent and methodical in his approach to problem solving. He made lists. He was consistent, inclusive, and respected the roles of others. The *St. Louis Post-Dispatch* described him as making "no pretense that he is a miracle man," and admitting "quite frankly that he does not know all the answers," but he possessed "perseverance, without which no goal is reached."[4] He didn't see his policies as a finished product, but rather an ongoing and evolutionary force that, hopefully, learns and improves over time. That's big.

In a later speech to the Better Business Bureau at the Jefferson Hotel, he demonstrated that he understood the reality of impoverished neighborhoods. "[O]ur greatest problems today are not those of physical rebuilding, but social reconstruction of our community," he said. "...Some of the most important elements of leadership [on the issue] may be discovered or developed in the low-income neighborhoods themselves." He talked to those residents.

He noted that the urban poor were "a deprived group who do not fully receive the benefits of an expanding economy." Further, they experienced isolation in "the closed circle of under-education, undertraining, of underemployment, of broken families, of hopelessness, of constriction within the rubble housing of the ghetto."[5] He couldn't fix the decades of discrimination, but he could make a difference in the moment.

What Tucker indicated with those comments is that he viewed urban problems as having two separate components—a physical infrastructure problem and a social infrastructure problem. Government could address the physical infrastructure problem readily. The social infrastructure problem would require input from many elements. He continued, "[These social problems] do not lend themselves to quick and clear-cut, simple solutions. They are complex and will require time and the best brains available for their solution. Immediate and instantaneous cures should not be promised."[6]

He added, "As our affluence spreads, every segment of society shares in it in varying degrees with the exception of this hard core of unemployed. In fact, their numbers increase. What we are seeing now in a period of high economic activity is the clear fact that a significant segment of our society is not touched by 'good times' and high employment."[7]

Three Overriding Priorities

All major American cities in the post-WW2 era had some shared concerns. A new economic reality was setting in. The labor force had been stressed significantly: men were gone to war and women filled the factories—and suddenly men were returning. Housing developments were growing in the suburbs, not in the central cities that had been built-out for most of a century, and city revenues were starting to suffer as a result. Retail sales moved to new locations, meaning "downtown" was not the primary shopping district anymore, and the various social institutions no longer attracted the large pool of participants they once did.

In St. Louis, these changes meant that the city was on the verge of bankruptcy. Government services were clunky and inefficient (think of the justifications for 1950 charter reform) and its revenue streams were threatened. People of means were moving to the suburbs for a multitude of reasons. The City Plan Commission noted that half of the city's housing stock was substandard compared to what suburbia offered. As conditions and values declined, so did tax revenue. If nothing changed, the instrument of city governance would collapse (and voters already had shown a reluctance to enact large-scale change). The saving grace appeared to be the earnings tax, which was a way to tax suburbanites who worked in the city, but its legality was threatened through the mid-1950s.

Second, go big or go home. The city's problems were truly existential and required large-scale coordinated intervention. Voters were not keen on approving large-scale change, yet the small one-off projects that voters may approve would not help. The national government was investing billions of dollars in the moment and St. Louis was determined to grab its share. If there could be multiple lines of attack on the city's problems, then maybe some combined effect could result and give the city forward momentum.

There were several massive projects that didn't require much in the way of voter approval. The Army Corps of Engineers in 1950 began a $100+ million project to transform the Mississippi River with the Chain of Rocks Canal and flood protection walls. Interstate highway money was being awarded to states for a network of expressways to crisscross the country, estimated to be $150+ million in St. Louis.[8] The State of Missouri was aggressive. Land clearance programs offered the chance to get rid of properties that brought down the tax base and consumed far more revenue than they produced (a common justification). Even the Gateway Arch project that had been lingering since the 1930s offered promise of a new future. Tucker said in a statement to Aldermen that indecisiveness could mean that funds "earmarked for St. Louis" would be diverted to other cities "ready to use the money."[9] Tucker, like his predecessors, was not going to let this opportunity pass by.

Third, people would be disrupted in the short term, and would be made better off by this work in the long term. Displacement was a reality and could not be avoided. "If it were possible to construct [projects] in the city without demolition, I, of course, would support it vigorously. But that cannot be. [These projects] must be determined on the basis of service to the largest number of people, engineering feasibility and economics," Tucker said in 1957.[10] These projects were to do what was necessary in the moment to save the city in the future. Even in the 21st century, the City of St. Louis website reminds people of that: "In contrast to the negative connotations surrounding high-rise projects today, it is useful to remember some of the ethos surrounding these projects. By modernizing the conditions of the poorest dwellers, urban planners hoped the lives of people might change"—and then acknowledges that was not always the case.[11]

Everyone can acknowledge the long-term negatives of these programs, but that outcome was not visible from the moment. People cannot rely solely on a 21st-century lens to assess a mid-century decision. The view from mid-century (myopic as it may have been) looked promising and this was all that Mayor Tucker could have seen. Pruitt-Igoe was designed by one of the most brilliant architects in St. Louis—Minoru Yamasaki—and it was going to bring modern housing to people who needed it. Young families were going to live in "bedroom suburbs" and work downtown; expressways were going to facilitate that relationship, so the city needed to accommodate the automobile. Even with 1950s population loss, St. Louis was still a city of 3/4

61

million residents and a great number of workers commuting in daily. The city still possessed critical mass, and it needed to be leveraged for long-term success.

This was not a new idea. A generation earlier, Progressives saw the city as suffering ills that required intervention. Intervention in the moment would pay off great dividends in the long term. It started with awareness, and St. Louis Progressives pushed to make people aware. It all started with documentation and data. Those roots ran long and deep.

SEEING THE OTHER HALF

The Progressive muckraker Jacob Riis released a book in 1890 that shocked New York specifically and the country generally. *How the Other Half Lives* was a deep examination of life in the poorest districts of that city, especially the infamous Mulberry Street, and how immigrant families tried to eke out a living amid streets of crime, vice, drunkenness, and poverty. He purchased a camera and the latest flash technology to take nighttime images. His photographs are stunning and available today through the Library of Congress.

His work caught the attention of Theodore Roosevelt, who was then on New York's Board of Police Commissioners. Roosevelt asked Riis to take him to these corners of the city— where police behavior was scandalous. Roosevelt was shocked and a lifetime friendship developed between the two. Roosevelt wrote in his autobiography the following statement that could resonate with mid-century St. Louis.

> "It is very important to the city to have a businessman's Mayor, but it is more important to have a workingman's Mayor.... It is an excellent thing to have rapid transit, but it is a good deal more important, if you look at matters with a proper perspective, to have ample playgrounds in the poorer quarters of the city, and to take the children off the streets so as to prevent them growing up toughs. In the same way it is an admirable think to have clean streets; indeed, it is an essential thing to have them; but it would be

a better thing to have our schools large enough to give ample accommodation to all who should be pupils and to provide them with proper playgrounds." [12]

Cities are and have always been a juxtaposition of rich and poor. Cities generally seem to create separate living spaces, encourage lives that only modestly overlap with each other, and have some kind of rule structure that reinforces those separations. It is very easy to ignore *how the other half lives.* It was this way in New York. It was this way in St. Louis, too.

Bringing the Message
to St. Louis

In his first visit to St. Louis in 1903, Riis preached to the Wednesday Club about "better homes and better schools" as the solution to slums.[13] Quality of life in these neighborhoods, he said, required light, air, and privacy. "In New York now, millions of dollars are being spent along this line. That is, old tenements are being torn down and new ones built, giving these three greatly desired privileges to poor tenants."[14] Riis had not made an examination of the St. Louis slums and did not speak to them. His host, School Board President Dr. William Taussig, gave him a tour of the then-new Wyman School on Theresa Avenue, which impressed Riis.

MISS CHARLOTTE RUMBOLD.

Charlotte Rumbold, perhaps St. Louis' greatest Progressive Era leader, was featured in the St. Louis Post-Dispatch, June 2, 1914. Newspapers.com

One of the women in the audience for Riis's presentation was the Wednesday Club's Charlotte Rumbold, who lived at 3838 Olive Street. She was a Progressive Era powerhouse who transformed the conditions for young people in St. Louis and around the country.

She was a supporter of urban planning and sat on every Progressive Era council or committee she could (usually as the secretary). She was born in St. Louis in 1869, to a family that had relocated from Belleville, Illinois. Her father, a widower with two young children, was a prominent physician. She was the firstborn of his second marriage and was named after her mother. She became the supervisor of St. Louis's playgrounds and recreation in 1906—at the height of the playground movement, when city leaders were just beginning to appreciate the value of sunshine and fresh air for the proper development of children and young people. She never married.

Rumbold advocated after-hours school dances (chaperoned by parents) and the social use of school buildings in the evenings.[15] This was a new concept and part of a larger plan among some civic boosters for the "intensive use" of schools as a center for "all neighborhood activities."[16]

She advocated creating a School of Housekeeping to train domestic workers. In her view, it was problematic that many domestic workers lived in the home they served, and "her duties are never done."[17] Rumbold worked on a survey of girls laboring in St. Louis factories and found the factory environment appalling, but it allowed the girls to have their evenings free for home, social, or school activity. The School of Housekeeping would dispatch household help to employing households on a regular schedule, but that schedule would incorporate time off as well. One objection raised to the idea was that "it would lead directly to the formation of a servant girls' union, autocratic in its dictation and inflexible in its despotic sway over the housekeeper."[18] The school did not seem to take off.

Charlotte Rumbold's Report

One of Rumbold's greatest accomplishments in St. Louis was a 1908 study called *Housing Conditions of St. Louis*, which had been commissioned by the Civic League of St. Louis. The report had three distinct goals: examine existing conditions, suggest preventive measures, and **"recommend the abolition of the existing evils** so far as is possible within reason."[19] Even in 1908, the goal was to eliminate housing problems and prevent them from recurring.

The study examined the tenement zone that was near today's America's Center just north of the downtown core (bounded by Lucas Ave. on the south, O'Fallon St. on the north, 7th St. on the east, and 14th St. on the west). A team of social workers descended on the neighborhood and checked every block, yard, and building. The final report highlighted all that was wrong with urban life in general, and St. Louis in particular. One of Rumbold's colleagues on the housing committee was Roger Nash Baldwin, who would become a founder of the American Civil Liberties Union. At this time, he was the chair of the Sociology Department at Washington University.[20]

Back Yard and Porches of a Tenement on Tenth Street. Porches Only Means of Escape in Case of Fire.

Rumbold, Housing Conditions of St. Louis, 1908. Pg. 58.

Rumbold lamented the lack of fresh air and sunshine that would never reach the windows of rooms located on the lower floors of high buildings separated by narrow gangways. She observed the lack of fire escapes (or wooden ones) for these multi-story buildings. She noted the filth associated with toilets and drinking water, and the dangers of mixed-use spaces (e.g., residences alongside saloons). She would be a staunch advocate for zoning.

The report outlined the filth associated with the physical condition of the tenements.

- "No one is responsible for the cleanliness of the yard. Such things as are used by four or six families in common have a tendency to adapt themselves to the standard of the least clean. A total of 1,395 dwellings are served by 664 yards—an average of 2.1 dwellings for each yard." Each "dwelling" consisted of 2.76 apartments, each having both family and lodgers. More than 50% of the yards were evaluated to be "dirty," "very dirty," or "filthy." Janitors were few and were paid by giving free lodging in the least-rentable rooms.[21]

- "St. Louis, in common with some other Southern cities, has a vault known as the 'pier' or 'tier' vault." These outhouses would be constructed of brick and stand two to four stories high, with each level connected to a floor of a tenement by a catwalk. It is possible to keep them clean when well-flushed with water, but that seldom occurred and "where there is no water flush it is altogether unspeakable."[22]

- "The 1,818 vault compartments serve 2,892 families, an average of 1.6 families to each compartment. …In the Polish neighborhood, the average is 8.7 families. On O'Fallon Street there is a yard where 134 persons are using four compartments over a single vault." She ended this section with two words, "This, legitimately." "No one who understands the life of such a district thinks of this at all. It is a sad reflection on our municipality…."[23]

- "Many of the worst of the compartment privies are found in saloon yards, where families, for perhaps half a block, must share these closets with 'the saloon trade.'

Where several families share one compartment, the door cannot be locked and the 'saloon people' use one or the other indiscriminately until all are foul."[24]

- "Almost without exception urinals are without doors or screens. In all public and in many semi-public privies hang placards advertising patent medicines for and describing the diseases of men." "Children live and play in such yards."[25]

- "These conditions are not peculiar to this district, though they are aggravated by the congestion of population and the lower standards of cleanliness of the newly arrived immigrants." "It is hardly necessary to insist and insist that such conditions breed fevers, tuberculosis and hideous unnamable diseases, and that such things spread. In the democracy of the streetcar

A Typical Yard Hydrant and Drain.

Rumbold, Housing Conditions of St. Louis, 1908. Pg. 14.

jam we come in perilously close contact with it all. Is it safe? More, is it fair?"[26]

The report had quite a bit to say about the economic condition of the tenements. These buildings functionally warehoused the poor.

- "Low rents are the first attraction to such a neighborhood as this; 65.2 percent, nearly two-thirds of the apartments, rent under $10 per month [just under $300 in today's dollars]. The average monthly rental of a room is $4.36, about $1 per week.[27]
- "It is instructive to find, remembering what was said of the repair of their houses, that the Negroes pay higher rents than the whites, averaging $4.49 per room."[28]
- "As for the people who live below the margin of independence, the ill, the casual worker, or deeper still, the drunken, the criminal, it is not safe for a city to permit that any of its housing should sink to their rent-

Note the Typical Slop Sink in the Foreground.

Rumbold, Housing Conditions of St. Louis, 1908. Pg. 48

paying ability." She continued, "The fact that some people can pay but $2 per month for room-rent should not affect the demand that a landlord put his house into a condition that does not menace the city...."[29]

- She lamented the turnover in ownership for small profits, because "no owner, of course, is willing to make repairs except, perhaps, to add another layer of paper to some of the room walls." Some tenements changed owners three times in a year.[30]

She spent quite a bit of space speaking about the social impacts on young people, especially girls.

- "More than we realize, our expressions of friendship or acquaintanceship are determined by our means of showing hospitality, and this in turn by our house space. One room more or less makes a great difference in the way we entertain our friends. For a family crowded into two rooms, both of which must be used for sleeping rooms, all of this side of the pleasures of home must be cut off.[31]

- "If the daughter of the house wants to see one of her men friends, then since the children are in bed and the father is tired, she must go to a dance hall or to a theater, or, what is very popular, make a trip "down the pike," Franklin Avenue from Twenty-second Street east, and take in as many nickelodeons as the couple can afford.[32]

- "Among the families of the better class or tradition, there is a good deal of anxiety until the daughter has chosen her dance hall. The choice of the hall determines the character of her acquaintances, and, quite probably, the man she will marry."[33]

- "It is no coincidence that there are saloons in the district. The saloon affords cheap recreation. It is warm in the winter, cool in the summer—there is company of one's kind, light, and music—all for five cents. The saloon, besides, cashes checks which, to a person who has never been in a bank, is a great convenience. It is also the post-office of many laborers who, because work takes them here and there, have no permanent lodging.[34]

- "With the coming of the Jews, however, the saloon is replaced by the coffee house—which is often a misnomer, since there is served 'tea and philosophy in the Russian Jewish café, and wine and cards in the Roumanian.' In the Greek and Turkish cafés there is coffee, very strong and black, and the habitués drink twenty to thirty of the little cups a day."[35]

- "The St. Louis building code makes no distinction between cellar [underground storage room with external entry] and basement [ground or below ground level of a dwelling with entry from inside staircase]—neither do the tenants.[36]

- Living in these cellars, amid the building's storage, are old women. "She takes in washing. Yours?"[37]

The report laid out the direction of policy solutions. These included "ordinances controlling the water supply, the plumbing, sewering, light and air spaces in the shop and factory." She even notes that "the extension of the streetcar system" into these neighborhoods would help.[38] She advocated for urban planning and regulation, and improved city services.

Asking for a Raise

In 1915, Rumbold asked for a raise. She had been earning $1,800 per year running the recreation division and requested $2,400. When she asked the Board of Aldermen for this increase, she was denied—with the excuse that she was "not a voter."[39] The real truth was that she refused to hire assistants in the Recreation Division on political grounds, and ward politicians were determined to "take her scalp."[40] Though the public and the *Post-Dispatch* threw their support behind her, it was not enough. Not all attitudes in St. Louis were progressive. She resigned her position with the city on August 1, 1915, and remained in St. Louis throughout 1916, increasing her suffragist work and protesting voter discrimination along the route to the

Democratic National Convention that was held in the city that summer. [41]

Boston had tried to lure her away in 1914, and New York offered her a major political plum of an appointment earlier in 1915—as director of recreation paying $4,000 per year [over $100,000 in today's dollars], which she declined (but it motivated the pay raise discussion).[42] She wound up going to Cleveland in 1917, where she became secretary to the Cleveland Chamber of Commerce and the Ohio Commission on City Planning. She repeated her St. Louis efforts there, and the city embraced her.

A Cleveland newspaper editor, years later, called her the "tiny woman [who] never shrinks from storms," be they "winds off the lake or winds of civic acrimony." The old editor recalled that Cleveland's city council was dithering over details of some important issue and Rumbold said, "What you gentlemen need, what this city council and this city hall need, is a ton of dynamite placed right under it, and either you would be blown where you ought to be or you'd get down to business for your city."[43] She died there in 1960. She is buried in the family cemetery outside Belleville, Illinois.

Notes from Inspector Miller's cards (Rumbold, page 27):

> "O'Fallon Street—Filthy hydrant sink in brick shed. [hydrants were the shared source of drinking water]
> Biddle Street—Much rubbish and filth on roofs of sheds
> Carr Street—Large hole in yard where vaults are caving in
> Carr Street—Butcher pours blood in dirt yard, allowing it to soak in. Hydrant banked with feathers.
> Carr Street—Urinal drains through yard to hydrant sink.
> Wash Street—Yard almost covered with two feet of ashes, garbage, and rubbish. Stable under read house very bad-smelling and dirty. Fruit kept here. Dirty dog kennel. Very bad odor.
> Wash Street—Rotten fruits and garbage in stable lot. One seat in vault gone, leaving large opening in floor.
> Fourteenth Street—Air shaft between flats. Tenants complain of bad air.
> Fourteenth Street—Bad tier vaults without flush. Straw dumped about wooden ash bin [where hot coals would be dumped]
> Thirteenth Street—rear of house falling. Used for living purposes. Very dangerous."

The Juxtaposition of Rich and Poor

The place Rumbold described was one of the dilapidated areas that became the scourge of urban planners in the subsequent decades. It was the decay that later generations would say held back the city's progress. Yet at the time it was most active, the city never gave it much thought. Cities were Dickensian, and family stories and tragedies were akin to *A Christmas Carol* where the haves and the have-nots engaged in a sometimes ruthless, sometimes charitable coexistence.[44]

It was not until the World's Fair that the city began thinking much about its appearance. It was like a moment when a household realized that company is coming, and the place really needs a new coat of paint. Dichotomy—rows and rows of mansions, balanced by rows and rows of tenements; institutions of art and finery, balanced by saloons, dance halls, and brothels; it would be called in the 1950s "progress" and "decay," and they were in constant battle with each other. That was the juxtaposition that was seen in mid-century St. Louis: progress and decay. After WW2, it became a battle, and sides were being chosen.

THE RISE OF URBAN PLANNING

There is an illustration in the 1954 central city plan that showed what downtown St. Louis could be from the planner's perspective. It is a lovely and almost-dreamy image of a new space that is densely developed yet not overcrowded. It is simple and organized. It is uniform and uncluttered. It was a concept design by an architectural firm offered "as a civic contribution to stimulate citizen interest and to serve as a guide for future progress."[45] That it became a frontispiece to a public report shows how it resonated with leaders.

In it, there is almost no indication of the past (except the courthouses in the mall). This downtown seemingly is all new development. It is as if the slate was wiped clean and construction started anew. That was the planning perspective. Historic preservation was not part of it. Mid-century attitudes required that cities would grow, organically, and the new growth of the city—like that of a shrub—will look different, go in a different direction, and if the old growth had to be pruned to make room for the new, then so be it. Pre-existing conditions were not part of the discussion.

The 1947 comprehensive plan was the city's first, last, and only truly professional city plan for generations. In the Griffenhagen Report, Raymond Tucker and the Mayor's Survey Committee noted that the City of St. Louis had long had a City Plan Commission but never adopted a city plan. It urged the city to do so. The comprehensive plan was submitted to Mayor Aloys Kaufmann on January 14, 1947, approved by the Board of Aldermen on March 28, and signed into law by the mayor that same afternoon. In fact, the approving legislation contained an "emergency clause," which meant the plan became effective immediately upon signing.[46] The plan was now law, the legal guiding document for urban development.

Urban planners began eschewing the comprehensive plan in the 1950s, as city centers were being redefined by interstates and suburbia irreversibly shifted centers of commerce and wealth. Planning historian Mark Abbott noted that this environment made the plan even more important.[47] The plan was *the* vision for a city that was less recognizable each passing decade.

The 1907 Progressive Era Plan

In its era of (self-perceived) greatness around 1904, St. Louis was a powerful city with powerful ideas. It pushed the envelope and bullied its way to prominence. In an effort to get "to the front," as a 1909 slogan would later proclaim, the city embarked on a major effort to set its place among the world's great cities—the first comprehensive city plan. Other cities had made smaller plans, area plans, neighborhood plans, but St. Louis embarked on creating a plan that would encompass every square mile into a single plan. The Civic League of St. Louis in 1907 released *A City Plan for St. Louis*. It was full of dreams and wishes, ideals and justifications. It oozed of civic pride and boosterism, while embracing all the tenets of the "City Beautiful" movement that had begun with Daniel Burnham's work at the Chicago World's Fair in 1893 (for which St. Louis had competed). As urbanist Joseph Heathcott observed, the well-illustrated plan incorporated little in the way of action steps, strategies, or resource management to make the plan a reality.[48] The city had done something, though, that other cities had not—it laid out a formal vision of what could be.

These civic advocates managed to get a City Plan Commission established and populated it with some heavy hitters in the emerging field of city planning. One of the early appointees to the commission was George Edward Kessler—a powerful thinker in the field and a founder of the American Institute of Planners.[49] He came to St. Louis temporarily to do work around the 1904 World's Fair and stayed permanently starting in 1910. The city put a bold idea on the table that year: the Kingshighway Belt Boulevard, which would link the city with the surrounding parkland in the county suburbs. Voters rejected it.[50]

By 1912, Kessler had helped the Commission design the "Central Traffic Parkway" around today's Market Street and proposed amendments to the city charter to clear land, widen and landscape trafficways, and establish other public spaces. The plan had vision, structure, resource allocation, and legal authority attached to it. Voters rejected that one too. [51]

The City Plan Commission's 1916-17 *Annual Report* had an entire section on publicity. "It is absolutely necessary that the citizen should understand, first, what city planning is…. A wide campaign of education is essential." It also notes, "Recognizing the futility of attempting consistent city planning work without the assistance of a technical expert…. At the beginning of the fiscal year Mr. Harland Bartholomew, lately with the City Plan Commission of Newark NJ, entered the Commission's employ."[52]

A Man Named Bartholomew

Harland Bartholomew was an enterprising young man. He was born in Massachusetts in 1889, moved to New York as a teenager, and studied civil engineering at Rutgers. Though he did not finish his degree, he was technically minded and was able to gain employment in the field starting in 1912. He quickly rose to the top. Kessler's close colleague Henry Wright and St. Louis attorney and civic booster Luther Ely Smith recruited him to St. Louis with the idea of implementing the 1907 plan.[53]

Bartholomew was a pragmatic man. He was a technocrat. Urbanist Joseph Heathcott wrote that Bartholomew's "New England Protestant and agrarian origins must surely have placed him at odds with his rich, urbane patrons—many of whom were Catholic and harbored a living memory of slavery."[54] Bartholomew had a love-hate relationship with his benefactors, noting in a 1925 article that "leaders of civic thought and captains of finance" were, more often than not, the primary obstacle to the realization of…planning the ideal, efficient city."[55] Their involvement was a necessary evil, no doubt. His job with the city technically was part-time all along. He held a faculty position with the University of Illinois-Urbana/Champaign and ran the consulting firm that still bears his name.

HARLAND BARTHOLOMEW.

Harland Bartholomew, from a feature in the St. Louis Post-Dispatch on May 23, 1920. Newspapers.com

Bartholomew also held a board position in 1928 at the Mortgage Trust Company, led by one of his benefactors, J. Lionberger Davis. Part of his job there was to "[pass] upon each loan submitted to this company" and use "their care and caution" to safe-guard mortgage investments.[56] The man who was making decisions about housing location was also involved in the financing of it.

In a way, Bartholomew (a lifelong Republican) lived a life that had parallels to Raymond Tucker (a lifelong Democrat). Both were technocrats, from humble beginnings, with a vision for public service. Both had pragmatic minds and saw obstacles in the status quo—Bartholomew wrangling with moneyed interests and Tucker wrangling with ward bosses. They valued order and application. Bartholomew laid out the plan. Tucker implemented it.

One of Bartholomew's first major reports was *Problems of St. Louis*. In his introductory statement, Bartholomew speaks philosophically to justify the concept of planning: "The *welfare of the group* is therefore now generally considered to supersede the *rights of the individual* when questions of health, safety and general welfare arise."[57] He lays out all that he sees as evil in the urban environment, and it echoed Charlotte Rumbold: poorly ventilated/dark rooms, outhouses, dilapidated houses, horse stables, outside plumbing, fire traps, overcrowding, and the unregulated lodging house.[58] This list of evils would be the theme of his crusade for the balance of his time in St. Louis— and would mark his legacy.

He includes a large section on "districting," or what is today called zoning.[59] Back in the day, there was a real question over government's use of the "police power" to dictate land use to a private landowner. In fact, the earliest forms of zoning were struck down as being unconstitutional. Bartholomew discusses this constitutionality of the concept at length.

Bartholomew saw zoning as a means of control that was essential to a well-functioning city. He envisioned land uses being clustered and development being built to standards, especially regarding housing. In fact, he specifically quotes a pro-zoning use of the police power by legal scholar Ernst Freund (from 1904) that wonders aloud how reasonable it would be that *Plessy v. Ferguson* (1896) "might be carried to the length of assigning to black and white different quarters of the city for living...."[60] This is not to say that Bartholomew advocated this for St. Louis, but simply that he was aware of the possibility.[61]

Racism, Plain and Simple

Bartholomew likened African American residences as being a contributing factor to "blight"—the organic term that suggested deteriorating housing conditions would spread like disease. Though many have long suggested that St. Louis' urban planning documents were biased against African Americans, it is clearly shown in Bartholomew's 1942 report, *St. Louis After World War II*. It is a grim story of what lay ahead for the city if it did not act boldly on his planning ideas. He predicted that St. Louis' population would fall to 500,000 by 1980 (he only missed it by 47,000!). [62] Sub-standard housing conditions were associated with any housing that was 50+ years old, and St. Louis had an abundance of it.[63] The city had failed to consider large-scale redevelopment in the central city.[64] As new housing was built in the area's periphery, the center would become blighted and lose its "character and value."[65] Each new ring of development would cause the previous one to suffer. Local historian Harry Hagen described how the trend "resembled wave-like action" from east to west, with each district rising to a peak population and declining slowly, until the wave passed the western city limits into the suburbs.[66]

Bartholomew explicitly says that one of the forces that had been keeping blight under control indefinitely was "extensive use of private deed restrictions."[67] It was these private deed restrictions that silently enforced residential segregation in the metro area (declared unconstitutional by the Supreme Court case *Shelley vs. Kraemer* in 1948). Covenants in the deed document itself prohibited ownership of that particular property by persons of color, or certain religions, or gender, or any other specified group. Large swaths of urban and suburban property were "protected" by such agreements. It was an easy way to deny certain sales and keep racism subtle. St. Louis was infamous for the extent to which it used this tool.

Here is the evidence, plainly and simply, that racism was a key element in urban planning. It was not just in St. Louis, and it was not just at the local level, but it was there (and is still).[68]

Moving On

Bartholomew left St. Louis just before Raymond Tucker took over the mayor's office. His departure probably was not motivated so much by Tucker's arrival at City Hall as it was Eisenhower's arrival in the White House. President Dwight Eisenhower appointed Bartholomew to be the chairman of the new National Capital Planning Commission, with the authority to shape the development of Washington DC and surrounding federal infrastructure. Functionally, he became the federal government's urban planner. Bartholomew resigned his city position, turned over management of his firm to partners, and based himself in Washington DC for the next seven years. He and Ike became close friends.

There had been a time when he almost lost his job in St. Louis. In 1935, Bartholomew became the lead consultant to conduct a major slum clearance/public housing project in Chicago. Even though St. Louis was just starting slum clearance, Bartholomew had been doing this work a long time.[69]

Mayor Dickmann, the mayor at the time, was furious. Recall that Dickmann went out of his way (and probably violated the law) removing long-time Republican hires from their city jobs. Bartholomew was a holdover from the old Kiel Administration and had worked for all the Republicans since then.[70] There was tension between the City Plan Commission and Dickmann. The mayor was frustrated by lack of cooperation from the Republican appointees. The Commission claimed no cooperation from the Mayor's Office. The Commission boldly called for a "showdown" meeting with the mayor, and the press went to city hall to question the mayor about it. "The mayor had just removed his derby hat and hung up his overcoat" when news reporters asked if he "had anything to say" about the showdown. "'Yes,' he replied angrily."[71]

Dickmann called some of his advisors to the impromptu press gaggle, one of whom was Raymond Tucker. Mayor Dickmann launched into various criticisms of the commission, including how members are engaging in private business over the city's business. Regarding Bartholomew, the mayor said, "He should put in more time for the commission and not so much in boosting his private business...if he wants to stay on the payroll...." [72] Tucker chimed in, "I don't see how [Bartholomew] can give much of his time to the City Plan Commission when he has so much other work."[73]

Somehow the fences were mended by the time of the showdown. New appointees were added to the Commission's committees that could better coordinate with the Mayor's Office and Bartholomew stayed on the payroll for many more years.[74]

Sadly, he experienced a series of tragedies after leaving St. Louis in 1953. His wife Lillian died the following year while at their summer home in Michigan at age 65. His son Herbert died the next year in California, at age 43. Finally, his only other remaining family member, his second son Melvin, died the year after that at age 33. Melvin had been a residential client at the Woods School in Pennsylvania. Bartholomew remarried twice more, being widowed a total of three times. He died in St. Louis shortly after his 100th birthday.[75]

Bartholomew's vision culminated in the 1947 comprehensive plan. He presented "a vision—his vision—for how St. Louis could adapt to the next quarter century."[76] In a real sense, he desired to unclutter the city (he only saw buildings, not people).

THE MILL CREEK VALLEY

Understanding the Neighborhood

There has been a lot of conflicting information out there about the Mill Creek Valley land clearance project and the neighborhood. It is a passionate subject on many fronts, and deservedly so, especially since the Black Lives Matter movement. Sometimes numbers got transposed or rounded. Sometimes specifics got generalized. Sometimes the units of measure got shifted. Even official documents referred to the same thing with different numbers.[77] The oft-used descriptor "deterioration" seemingly implies something standing still while declining in the elements.

The Mill Creek Valley was a poor but dynamic neighborhood. It never stood still. There were comings and goings. Life took place there. Birthdays were celebrated around the tables. Laborers rested there after a long day. Friends met for drinks, perhaps at a bar or just on the front steps. People ran down to the corner shop for cigarettes or a can of soup or a newspaper. If the housing was bad, it wasn't because it was abandoned, rather it had been used to its useful capacity. It was just worn out. What was good there may have been very good; what was bad there may have been very bad…and there was a lot in between.

Author and entrepreneur Vivian Gibson poignantly recalled her childhood in *The Last Children of Mill Creek*. Her grandmother, Stella Hodges, purchased a home at 2649 Bernard Street for $1,400 in 1950, unaware of the city's plans.[78] She earned the down payment laboring in the houses of others as a domestic worker. She lived there with her son, his wife, and their eight children.[79] In recounting the story of her own parents, Gibson highlighted their love and consideration.

> "They didn't talk about the perils of what lay beyond the invisible walls of our community. But they tried to arm us with what they thought we needed to survive: resourcefulness, a positive self-image, and an understanding of the value of hard work."[80]

Dr. Malaika Horne told the story of *Mother Wit* at 328 South Garrison in her 2017 biography of her mother. "Hardship was [Mother's] constant companion" growing up the in South, she wrote.[81] There, her mother learned to appreciate anecdotes and mimicry. Her characterizations of people were keen as she was able to act out the people, events, and lessons of life. "Warm memories have sustained us, particularly of Mother regaling us with story after story…."[82] "Storytelling became an education in human values, a spiritual endeavor, and a way of connecting not just head-to-head but heart-to-heart and hand-to-hand."[83]

> "Every night, [Mother] had us get down on our knees with our hands folded in prayer alongside the bed (like birds nestled together) and we'd say the Lord's Prayer. But there was always a second prayer we recited: "God, bless mother, bless daddy, bless all my sisters and brothers and bless everybody in the whole wide world. Amen. Now…I can see that [this prayer] influenced us to think beyond our family with a worldview."[84]

Attorney Gail Milissa Grant spoke of her grandparents' home at 2620 Lawton Ave. Her grandmother, Lyda Franklin Hughes, was the driving force behind the family business, a mortuary that bore her husband's name. She was among the first African American female embalmers licensed in the state.[85] The funeral home occupied the first floor, her grandparents and mother lived on the second, and staff members occupied the third floor and basement (where the morgue was).[86]

> "And St. Louis had a nice social life. People entertained a lot in their homes because they couldn't go anyplace else," Grant's mother recalled. "There was Jordan Chambers' Club Riviera and the Club Plantation, which was owned by Jews. Cab [Calloway] played there a few times. We just had no nice places to go. There were a few restaurants, three or four little clubs, and a lot of Negro taverns."[87]

Fannie Cook was a white author who used her local prominence to advocate for the Black community. She wrote an award-winning novel in 1946 called *Mrs. Palmer's Honey* that described life in another Black neighborhood, The Ville.

She described The Ville this way: "Prosperous people lived in The Ville and let the people from the pretty fringe of the fabric believe what they pleased" [meaning there were no nice Black neighborhoods]. "The Ville remained obscure and lived secretly." "Once it had been called Elleardsville, a suburb."[88]

She described Mill Creek this way: a "betaverened crisscross of shabby streets near Union Station" and "observing that region's slatternly ways, [household employers] would at times consider sending their dark-skinned cook to a clinic for tests and

Fannie Cook press photo from Doubleday, Jepsen photo, 1945. Author's Collection

treatment." However, the hotel there was "a model of Christian respectability"[89] in her story.

Cook compared the prosperity of The Ville to the poverty of Mill Creek. "To [Ville residents,] the black folks near Union Station were 'immigrants.' Newly come north from Mississippi or Louisiana. A few were Ville folks fallen from grace, but more were sharecroppers with the dust of cabin floors still beneath their toenails, dreams of northern freedom still in their eyes, snuff still in the mouths of the women as well as the men." She added, "Their ways slowed a climb for other Negroes. Because of that, The Ville bore them a grudge."[90]

In fact, the influx of unskilled labor migrants that Cook writes about was flagged as a statistical concern by the St. Louis Urban League in 1954. The organization conducted a study about African Americans in the local labor force. The purpose of the study was to create a policy framework for business and industry to better utilize this pool of labor. It found that out-migration of African Americans from St. Louis was "a younger and more skilled" labor group than those arriving, so the training and "resource cost to the community is relatively high."[91] It should not be surprising that Mill Creek Valley would be a home to newly arriving migrants looking for a better life. This is consistent with the anecdotal evidence from the Mill Creek Valley and Fannie Cook's story.

St. Louisans noted that African Americans were growing in number following the Great Migration in the 1910s and 20s, and they were purchasing homes on street blocks owned by whites. Fearful white residents called it "negro invasion," and even then, it was challenged. One letter to the editor noted that African Americans were only buying property that was being offered for sale. Lewie R. May, president of the Elleardsville Civic League, wrote that the organization (which dated to about 1900, but referring to it in 1924) was "to serve all of the negro residents in the district bounded on the east by Grand Boulevard, on the south by Enright Avenue," and without limit to the north and west.[92] He continued by saying there is no organized effort to buy property in white neighborhoods, but only "buying property when and wherever you can get the best values for the money."[93]

When the population of Mill Creek Valley scattered in the 1950s, many were forced to go to The Ville, as there were very few places where African Americans could live. The once-prosperous neighborhood began filling up with new arrivals—overflowing, really—and over time the neighborhood lost a good amount of its prosperity and cohesion.[94]

Implementing the Plan

When it came time to *do something* about the long-explored problems of St. Louis, the institution of government already had its decision. Jacob Riis spoke of tearing down the tenements in 1903. Charlotte Rumbold wrote of the abolition of the existing evils in 1908. Harland Bartholomew called slums a problem in 1917 and called for their removal one way or another every decade thereafter.

The fate of the Mill Creek Valley zone may have been determined in 1940, when much of it was left out of the city's new zoning map. It was, simply, "unrestricted."[95] This was due to the dominance of railroad ownership and industrial activity in the old creek bed. It was not a place for residential use. Newspaper articles described it as noisy, filthy, and—in an era when St. Louis was trying to clear the smoke from the air—polluted. There was talk of building a new farmers' market there, due to its central location in the city and its transportation connections.[96] Even the idea of an airplane landing strip was floated.[97] The name "Mill Creek Valley," then, was synonymous with industrial and commercial endeavors. To be certain, there were residences adjacent to and among the industry, but it was not commonly thought of as being a residential neighborhood. Planners marked all adjacent areas (including those with residences) "to be reconstructed," implying their current land use had no planning value.[98] That's what became law.

In 1948, Mayor Aloys Kaufmann's Anti-Slum Committee had proposed clearing an area between Olive and Market Streets—territory that would be added to the Mill Creek Valley project eventually. Gloster B. Current, an NAACP official from Detroit, spoke at the Pine Street YMCA in the neighborhood. Overall, he favored the project. He said the work was "important for redevelopment, and the [Olive-Market area] certainly needs it badly."[99] Current also demanded, though, that there be African American representation on the commission "to look after the interests of colored persons who would be displaced," and pushed St. Louisans to ensure better housing conditions, better school facilities, and equal job opportunities for African Americans.

After Congress passed the Housing Act of 1949, the situation changed abruptly. William Zeckendorf, who represented "Rockefeller interests" in New York and owned the landmark Chrysler Building there, came to St. Louis in 1950 and met with Mayor Darst. They started focusing on building high-rise housing between Jefferson and Grand Avenues, and between Laclede Avenue and the Mill Creek Valley railroad tracks.[100] Darst, who served as an FHA administrator after leaving the Dickmann Administration, admired the sleek dense housing towers of New York. The plan was to start developing a mix of multi-story buildings, duplexes, and even some single-family dwellings on already-vacant land in the area—2,500 units in total—so that people displaced by other activity could be moved there.[101] This "Rockefeller Project," the *Post-Dispatch* noted, was taking place almost exclusively in an African American neighborhood. "Families now living in the area," said Zeckendorf, "unable to afford [the $40-45 monthly rent], would be relocated to public housing or in homes vacated by families moving to the Rockefeller Project."[102] So even before there was any land clearance authority created at all, the neighborhood that became the "Mill Creek Valley" as known today had been targeted for re-development a decade before.

The plan as first speculated would start with housing specifically for African Americans of "various income levels" and would be located near the Vashon Community Center at Market St. and Compton Ave. This clearly illustrated who was about to become displaced. The multiple-income-levels in the plan spoke to segregation. Because people were being assigned to housing by the color of their skin, they would include a wide variety of earners: professionals, skilled workers, and laborers. In segregated places in St. Louis and East St. Louis, it was not uncommon to have highly trained professionals, such as dentists, living in the same block as truck drivers. The City Plan

Commission already targeted this area for potential slum clearance.[103]

When the city did create a land clearance authority, and hired Charles Farris to lead it, and when Congress started to put money behind it, St. Louis started thinking big. Harland Bartholomew had been pushing this for a long time, and in a sense, had moved on (at least metaphorically) to places that were implementing his ideas, not just thinking about them.

Targeting the Mill Creek Valley

In the vein of "go big or go home," the Mill Creek Valley land clearance project was the largest such project ever in the United States to that time. The historic Mill Creek Valley itself was primarily industrial railroad land bordering the southern edge of downtown from the Mississippi River to Grand Avenue. Adjacent to Mill Creek's industrial uses was a rather large residential tract between 20th Street and Grand, between Olive Street and Scott Ave. Large parts of the housing stock were dismal by most modern measures of quality of life.

Bartholomew's 1947 Comprehensive Plan, which was codified into law, outlined the 10 goals and provisions for the control and correction of blighted areas. Nearly all these issues had been cited in Rumbold's 1908 housing study. They were:
1. elimination of overcrowded conditions through prescribed occupancy standards
2. standards for the number, area, and functionality of windows permitting fresh air and light
3. screens on doors and windows to restrict flies and mosquitoes *Author's Note:* Surely these planners recalled the summer of 1933 and the emergence of "St. Louis Encephalitis" transmitted by mosquitoes.
4. elimination of non-standardized basements as residential units
5. elimination of hopper water closets and outhouses
6. standards for the location of water closets and the number of persons using them
7. keeping dwellings clean, sanitary, habitable, and free from infestation

8. maintaining dwellings tight from the weather and to allow reasonable heating
9. installation of flues to allow operation of heating equipment and maintain adequate temperature in each habitable room
10. adequate daylight or light fixtures in halls, bathrooms, and other habitable rooms.[104]

By these measures, the housing of the Mill Creek Valley failed miserably. The conditions of the dwellings paled in comparison to what the modern high-rise public housing apartments could offer. Urbanist Neal Peirce, a generation ago, was only half-joking when he called the site 465 acres containing 5,000 outhouses.[105]

The housing conditions were deplorable and overcrowded. Ron Fagerstrom states in his examination of Mill Creek that officials did not properly analyze the *causes* of deterioration.[106] The 1947 plan simply stated that homeowners leaving and the remaining homes being allowed to deteriorate caused it all.[107] Fagerstrom noted that the real causes were: inadequate income for Blacks to maintain housing (due to discrimination), absentee landlords, insufficient code enforcement, and redlining preventing loans that would benefit this area.[108] This was all true.

One of the first contracts signed before the demolition work was for rat control, so as not to displace the vermin into the surrounding areas. The amount was $935 to treat 373 buildings planned for the initial demolition.[109] Four years before the full demolition, but just a year after demolition was announced, there were offers to move residents into new public housing if they had rat infestation. This move came after a high-profile case of a 2-month-old who suffered from rat bites in his crib on South 23rd Street, despite an existing law requiring landlords to abate rats.[110] Obviously, landlords were ignoring the law, and the city was not enforcing it.

Calculating the Numbers

The statistical reality of Mill Creek Valley bounced around in any given month, and measuring population, dwellings, families, and businesses necessarily shifted over the twenty-year period it was studied and re-studied (and for the twenty, forty, sixty years since). For purposes of this work, the Fagerstrom study and primary source documents from the Land Clearance Authority will guide the analysis.

Sometimes, the Mill Creek numbers reported in media included the Kosciusko Redevelopment Area as well, since they were executed at the same time, with the same funding blocks, and a similar agenda. Kosciusko (ko-SHOOS-ko) was a riverfront district located between Broadway and the Mississippi River, adjacent to the Soulard neighborhood and across the river from Sauget, Illinois. Though often combined, tiny Kosciusko was less than a fifth of the scope of expansive Mill Creek.

The attention paid to Kosciusko seems odd in the big picture. The Nooter Corporation for industrial expansion desired large segments of the land. However, a motivating or justifying factor must have been the plans for a Cahokia Bridge across the Mississippi River. The bridge that ultimately was the Poplar Street Bridge was, in 1955, intended to cross the Mississippi at the industrial suburb of Sauget (then Monsanto), Illinois, and attach to US Highway 66, called Chippewa Street. Though approved by the Board of Aldermen in 1955, the plan was foregone when the Arch-adjacent idea took hold in 1958. Nooter began buying up the cleared land, and both state and local planners started focusing on the present path of the Poplar Street Bridge.[111]

Studies go into little detail about the density of the neighborhood. However, using the numbers from Ron Fagerstrom's examination, the challenges of living in Mill Creek Valley become apparent. There were 19,700 people living in about 5,600 families.[112] The number of families often gets morphed into the number of dwelling units, and the number of dwelling units gets morphed into the number of structures—hence decades of confusion.

People maximized the occupancy of structures, living in basements, garages, and third floor attics (places not always meeting the technical definition of a "dwelling unit").[113] Therefore, 20,000 people (rounding the number up, as city documents did) may equate to 5,600 families, but 5,600 families do not equate to 5,600 dwellings—or even if they did, 5,600 dwellings to not equate to 5,600 structures (e.g., one apartment building may have multiple dwelling units). If that were true, the average structure would have occupancy of 3.5 people per— hardly overcrowded, as the historical record clearly showed Mill Creek Valley to be.

Fagerstrom defines 839 commercial or institutional enterprises, which this study will assume to be an independent structure—and some rather large (e.g., hotels, churches, and schools). Based on the dimensions in Fagerstrom's map, the project site from Olive/Lindell Boulevard between 20th Street and Grand Avenue is 1.37 miles, and from Grand Avenue to Scott Avenue is .53 miles.[114] Therefore, the occupied space of the Mill Creek Valley is .7261 square mile, or 464.7 acres, which is consistent with published acreage for the project. That gives a population density of 25,118 people per square mile—very high for St. Louis. A visual count from an aerial photo in Fagerstrom's book showed an average of 11.7 structures per street block, with two street facings per block for a total of 23.4 structures per square block, for 104 blocks, gives an estimated total of 2,434 structures.[115] An official publication of the Land Clearance Authority states there were 2,200 parcels in the project area, which is consistent with the structure estimate.[116]

If 839 of the 2,434 structures are commercial, then 1,595 structures are residential. From there, we can calculate occupancy as follows: 19,700 people divided into 1,595 structures give 12 people per structure. That is a realistic number and is consistent with the stories Fagerstrom reports of people living in all available spaces. Further, 5,600 families living in 1,595 structures means three and a half **families** are living per structure on average. Some of these structures were apartment buildings, some of these structures were four-family flats, and some of these were single-family dwellings.[117] The ownership rate was low; the official city report noted that 501 families (less than 10%) owned their own homes (and that 484 of those owners were Black).[118] Of those families that owned their own homes, 217 of them relocated to newly purchased homes (less than 50%).[119]

The argument that inadequate income prevented property maintenance did not apply to the vast majority of the families there. Absentee landlords were problematic then, as now; and the behavior of renters is suspect.[120] Slums are profitable for their owners, in the sense that no money is spent on upkeep and the occupants have little choice about moving away.

Fagerstrom faulted poor code enforcement as a key cause of Mill Creek's demise and suggests that more enforcement would have saved the neighborhood. Code enforcement is a double-edged sword. On the one hand, the housing code revisions put forward in the 1940s helped keep living conditions tolerable; on the other hand, it opened the door to condemnation or eviction of unmaintained homes. A similar outcome may have resulted, just one or two at a time instead of all at once.

The Decision to Move People

The mass dislocation of people might have been imposed on the project, rather than planned. There is a very interesting document among Mayor Tucker's papers at Washington University. William H. Coibion, the City Plan Commission's Director of Planning (he replaced Harland Bartholomew), issued a long response to the Land Clearance Authority's plan for Mill Creek Valley, and proposed (perhaps dictated?) changes to it. Keep in mind that the City Plan Commission's job was to take the individual projects being pursued by various city agencies and mold them into conformity with the comprehensive plan. The Plan Commission, which had a record of looking at buildings instead of people, said the following:

"In the development of [the City Plan Commission's] land use plan, we are deeply aware of the fact that 20,000 persons now live in the area, and we have been apprised by the staff of the Land Clearance Authority that your Authority's objective is to accommodate as much of the present population as possible in any redevelopment proposal. Hence, it is not surprising that the [Authority's] plan prepared in August 1955, [intended] to rehouse 20,000 people [on site].

"We of the Plan Commission believe that the redevelopment of the area should achieve the highest degree of land utilization in accordance with the overall needs of the community and in accordance with the general city plan [for design and density...].

REDEVELOPMENT PLAN

FOR

MILL CREEK VALLEY

ST LOUIS MISSOURI

PROJECT MO R-I

LAND CLEARANCE FOR REDEVELOPMENT AUTHORITY

Cover Page of the 1958 MCV Redevelopment Plan that was presented in February of that year and approved by constituent groups over the summer. Revised 1960. Theising image.

"This necessarily concludes that only about 80.5 acres of the total Project Area should be redeveloped for residential reuse. This will provide a total of approximately 1,610 dwelling units or accommodate about 5,367 persons [or 3.3 persons per dwelling]. **Admittedly, this will [aggravate] the relocation problem which will confront the Land Clearance Authority.**"[121] (emphasis added)

The land that the Authority wanted to use for residential became industrial by the City Plan Commission. "It is a well-known fact that St. Louis faces a serious shortage of industrial tracts of 5 acres or more. It is even more acute whenever you attempt to find a 5-acre industrial tract with rail facilities. In view of the central location of the Mill Creek Valley project and its proximity to the rail facilities in the Valley, it is believed the area south of Market Street has an extremely high market for industrial reuse."[122] The City Plan Commission had spoken, and the Land Clearance Authority had a massive new task on its plate. (There is no evidence that the LCA fought the decision.)

William H. Coibion, successor to Harland Bartholomew's lead planner role, in 1957 when he left his city job, complaining to Mayor Tucker that "the city is not able to pay top level personnel." Tucker openly disagreed. Globe-Democrat, November 15, 1957, p. 6. Newspapers.com

Frank Sengstock, in his team's analysis of the racial tensions of the 1960s, was blunt when it came to clearing the land: the people "who tolerate slums are the people who own them and make a profit from them. They are oblivious to the cause-and-effect relationship between the conditions they themselves create and their frequent comments: 'Look how the colored people live, I'm glad I'm not one of them.'"[123] He continued, noting, "When the primary bankers, investment firms, civil and labor leaders decided that there were no more profits to be wrung from these tired and sick dwellings, they found it necessary to do some new 'pump priming,' made possible through public subsidy—the same source relied upon by welfare recipients."[124]

Sengstock said the average displaced resident found that "in his new neighborhoods, new slums are in the making. For him, the planners have failed to provide the promise of improved municipal services, better schools, and the like. And he has no reason to believe that such promises will be kept in the future. On the contrary, it may be far more reasonable for him to believe that they will not."[125] Less than half the displaced persons from the Mill Creek Valley went into the new public housing complexes that were rising around the city thanks to the groundwork laid by Mayor Joseph Darst. The other half scattered to other African American neighborhoods—especially The Ville, a functioning upper-middle-class African American neighborhood. These impoverished families brought with them the problems of Mill Creek. "[City officials] pushed the deterioration elsewhere, rather than relieving it; and they destroyed a functioning neighborhood," said Robert Powers of the city's decision to relocate families in places like The Ville.[126] That was exactly the concern Mill Creek Alderman Archie Blaine had when it all started years before.

Mayor Tucker's Position

Tucker valued civil rights. Tucker understood the plight of the poor (at least intellectually, if not emotionally). He followed the law. The law said to tear down slum housing, and he supported that. ...But the law also said to provide for them, and he thought he was doing that too—those ideas were not separated in his mind.

In a draft letter responding to a constituent complaint about public housing being linked to slum clearance and deviant behavior, Tucker wrote his opinion succinctly: "public [housing] is (my opinion) not the answer to slum clearance. Slums do not mold a person nor should it in any way injure his character." (emphasis Tucker's)[127]

Slum housing was a weakness in the eyes of city planners in several respects. First, the poor neighborhoods consumed more dollars in city services than they generated. In tight budget times, it was a challenge to maintain such arrangements. Second, they believed that slums spread. As people of means left for the suburban periphery, poorer persons moved in— paying an inordinate amount of their income for rents and, therefore, not having additional dollars for maintenance. Third, there were funds available for what—at the time—seemed to be a perfect fix: land clearance, land re-use, and public housing. The city needed only to put-up essential matching funds. Voters had shown their willingness to approve such bonds.

Tucker felt it was the financial burden that must be addressed. In a letter to Missouri Governor Phil Donnelly, Tucker lamented that "no other city [in Missouri] has to cope with as much over-crowding, as many slums, as much traffic."[128] He continued, "Our biggest producer is the property tax," and slums were a threat to that revenue stream. He described the problem of slums as "staggering" and described his city as "rapidly drifting toward municipal bank-ruptcy."[129] Tucker's letter to Donnelly was around state authorization for the earnings tax, which would enable a major bond issue. Once the legislature secured St. Louis' earnings tax in 1954, a massive $110 million bond issue was put on the ballot that included $7 million for the local portion of the Mill Creek redevelopment project.

Despite the differences in opinions on the merits of the project, the land clearance project did have support from within the African American community. The project had the support of the African American alderman of the Sixth Ward, Archie Blaine, at least at first.[130] The local NAACP endorsed the Mill Creek Valley proposal, too, though one national official termed urban renewal as "Negro removal."[131] (The great writer and activist James Baldwin famously used the phrase in an interview, in 1963.) The other African American aldermen voted to support it. Tucker respected formal authority. When an individual, organization, or institution provided an endorsement—as Blaine, the NAACP, and the Board of Aldermen did—Tucker moved forward. There wasn't a lot of room to turn around.

Ernest Calloway, NAACP President. His wife, DeVerne Calloway, would become the first Black woman elected to the Missouri House. Post-Dispatch, Newspapers.com

Support for the Project

Substandard housing has long been a concern for the African American community. At a conference in 1951, a string of speakers addressed the effects of discrimination. Norman Seay, then the chairman of the Urban League's Federation of Block Units, said "without pleasant up-to-date homes, at reasonable rentals, the colored person has no chance to succeed or live a full life."[132] Chester Stovall, also of the Urban League, pointed to the "flagrant violation" of anti-discrimination clauses in government contracts by defense contractors. These violations, of work and housing, combined to ruin the quality of life for African Americans.

The local NAACP endorsed the Mill Creek Valley project, and this support is noteworthy. In its organizational newspaper, an editorial stated that the project "promises to become one of the most encouraging practical examples of a city determined to stop the spread of its slums."[133] The group acknowledged that nearly 10% of the African American population in the city resided there. The local NAACP held a public meeting on the subject at the Union Memorial Methodist Church, at Pine and Leffingwell, in the Mill Creek Valley neighborhood so residents could attend.[134]

In March 1953, on the same ballot that voters chose Tucker over Eagleton for mayor, voters defeated the Plaza Bond Issue—a land clearance project downtown near the Central Library. Tucker resurrected the bond issue immediately and put it on a September ballot. The local NAACP opposed the Plaza

Bonds both times. That summer, the national NAACP held its convention in St. Louis and the new Mayor Raymond Tucker welcomed them. However, the NAACP locally still withheld its support of the Plaza Bond Issue because there were no guarantees that African Americans would get jobs (or even be allowed to rent an apartment in the resulting buildings).[135] To the supporters of the project, 1953 St. Louis NAACP President Henry Wheeler asked a damning question: "Do you place property values above human values?"[136]

When it came time to endorse the Mill Creek Valley project, the organization pursued exactly the same goals of employment and desegregation. This time, though, there was higher confidence in the city's ability to deliver results. Ernest Calloway, the local NAACP president at the time of Mill Creek, said that slum clearance would be part of the organization's priorities, in addition to a "long overdue" public accommodation ordinance and tackling employment opportunity problems.[137] It stood firm in its support until 1962, when the many construction jobs there were not inclusive of African American laborers.[138] It threatened a lawsuit to stop the work "as a last resort." Arthur Kennedy, chair of the local NAACP's labor committee, said, "St. Louis is on the road to becoming one of the most progressive cities in the nation, and citizens wouldn't stand for a halt to this progress because of bias by unions and employers." Kennedy added that African American voters helped ensure passage of the bond issues and had justification for a share of the skilled jobs— "not just the ditch digger jobs."[139]

Meet Archie Blaine

Archie Blaine was a burn-no-bridges kind of politician. His high level of flexibility made him a friend to many, but it frequently put him on both sides of a single issue. He was the alderman for the sixth ward, where the Mill Creek Valley was located. He was one of the few African American voices on the board, having been elected in 1955.

There is an article about him from 1929 that was carried in newspapers across the Midwest, when he got into trouble as a youth for stealing some money from his landlady. The theft of

$56 (over $800 in today's dollars) was used to buy gifts for the kids of his neighborhood. He admitted that he took the money. "There are lots of poor people around here and I wanted to be Santa Claus for them," he said. "I spent all the money, but I didn't get anything for myself."[140]

He was the lone dissenting vote on the bill to raze the Valley in 1958, despite favoring the concept early on.[141] He was pressured by fellow aldermen to change his vote, but he resisted. His reason for voting against the bill was not the decimation of his ward, but rather "moving slums to other parts of the city" while providing housing in Mill Creek "for people who don't need housing [help]." [142] (Remember the high-rise housing discussions.)

Alderman Archie Blaine, Argus 1962, provided by SHSMO. Newspapers.com

Despite being opposed to the Mill Creek Valley bill specifically, he was a proponent of urban renewal generally. He introduced the clearance bills that made way for the Mansion House towers and the downtown Busch Stadium (which obliterated "Hop Alley"—the center of commerce for the small St. Louis Asian community). The latter bill had trouble getting out of committee. A disappointed Blaine said he had sympathy for the people who would be disrupted, but that the stadium overall "would be good for St. Louis."[143]

But then urban renewal came to his own front door. He had lived for years near the corner of Jefferson Ave. and Walnut St., which was right in the heart of the Mill Creek Valley land clearance area. The people affected were his friends and constituents, the businesses being moved were the ones he patronized and knew. His was the lone vote opposing the project, but he then rolled up his sleeves and worked to make sure the project unfolded in a way that was fair to his constituents. He attended the groundbreaking. He set up and chaired an oversight/coordinating committee on the Board of Aldermen. He opposed it but since it was going to happen anyway—he wanted to make sure it happened correctly.

Americanist scholar Dr. Maire Murphy suggested he must have been aware at the time that his electoral base was being destroyed and the project jeopardized his political future.[144] He won re-election in 1959, but his legislative career came to an end in 1963. It was not a surprise. The large African American constituency that kept him and his predecessors in power was gone. The influx of white residents into the new housing development at Plaza Square tipped the electoral scales away from his favor. He lost his primary election to a white candidate, former City Marshal David "Babe" Lohr—close friend of the ward committeeman. The *Post-Dispatch* estimated that only 250 African American voters remained in the ward of 2,300 registered voters.[145] [146]

Engaging the Community

About a month before the first Mill Creek Valley plans were to be formalized, Mayor Tucker reached out to key African American leaders in and around the affected area. He invited them to a meeting with him, and subsequently to join an ongoing advisory committee, regarding the redevelopment plans. "I'm most anxious," Tucker wrote, "to have the advice and suggestions of representative Negro leadership about this possibility *before* any formal action is taken by the City Plan Commission or the Board of Aldermen to declare this area 'insanitary' or 'blighted.'" (emphasis Tucker's)[147]

Tucker's letter of invitation spoke to his vision for the area. He saw an opportunity to development modern housing, modern commercial and industrial establishments, as well as parks and other civic improvements that would lead to "a balanced and integrated community."[148] Not everyone invited accepted the invitation to join, but those who accepted positions on the committee were:

- Mrs. Valla D. Abbington, 4361 Enright Ave. (committee secretary)

- Mrs. Edward Bell, 2901 Laclede Ave.
- Dr. J. Owen Blache, Urban League President, 4924 Lotus Ave.
- Mr. Archie Blaine, 2601 Walnut
- Rev. G. Wayman Blakely, Pastor, St. Paul AME Church, 15, N. Leffingwell
- Mr. Leo Bohanon, Executive Director, Urban League, 3017 Delmar Ave.
- Mr. Ernest Calloway, President, NAACP, 11 N. Jefferson
- Bishop Matthew W. Clair, Jr., 2731 Pine
- Dr. Mason D. Cloyd, President, United Negro Organizations, 4733 Labadie
- Mr. James Cook, Executive Director, Pine Street YMCA, 2846 Pine St.
- Mr. Harold Garner, Russell Undertaking Co., 2732 Pine St.
- Rev. Herman Gore, Pastor, Southern Mission Baptist Church, 2966 Market
- Rev. John J. Hicks, Pastor, Union Memorial ME Church, 208 N. Leffingwell
- Mrs. Edith Johnson, Deluxe Restaurant, 10 N. Jefferson
- Mr. DeWitte Lawson, 2738A Franklin Ave., Alderman 19th Ward
- Mr. Robert Mack, Executive Secretary, NAACP, 11 N. Jefferson
- Mr. T. H. Mayberry, 4864 Easton Ave., Alderman 4th Ward
- Mr. Malcolm Myers, 3424 Clark
- Mr. Isaac Newman, President, Federation of Block Units, 2811 Clark
- Mr. Sidney R. Redmond, 2103A Market (committee chairman)
- Mr. Lamar Smith, Principal, Johnson School, 2841 Laclede
- Mr. Wayman Smith Jr., 4456 Easton Ave., Alderman 18th Ward (committee vice-chairman)

- Mr. Chester Stovall, Executive Secretary, Council on Human Relations
- Mr. Nathaniel Sweet, *St. Louis American*, 11 N. Jefferson
- Mr. Howard Woods, Executive Editor, *St. Louis Argus*, 2314 Market
- Mr. Bige Wyatt, President, New Age Savings and Loan, 1523 Whittier
- Dr. Walter A. Younge, MD, 2337 Market Street
- Rev. F. L. Zimmerman, St. Malachy's, 2904 Clark[149]

Committee members rightfully expressed concerns, a number of which were published in the *St. Louis Argus* by committee member Howard Woods prior to the committee's first formal meeting. Would African Americans be included in the demolition and construction jobs? Would African Americans be allowed to return to the new middle-income housing, if they desired? Could whites move to the area if they desired or would it be marked "for colored only"? These were well-founded concerns and paralleled the concerns that were expressed during the Plaza Development project the previous year.[150]

The city responded immediately and in writing. All Land Clearance for Redevelopment Authority employees are to be hired without discrimination. Every LCRA contract for demolition would carry a clause prohibiting discrimination in hiring by the contractor. Any of the land sold would be without any kind of deed restriction. Private companies doing development work independent of the LCRA would be notified of the LCRA's anti-discrimination stance. The middle-income housing planned would be offered first to families being displaced who could afford it (estimated to be 40% of families). Those who could not afford it would be offered public housing choices (estimated to be 60% of families), and in all cases everyone displaced "*must* be offered decent, safe and sanitary housing for relocation." (emphasis theirs)[151]

The committee voted to hold a hearing for the property owners in the area. The records were written in such a way that decisions were not unanimous and opposition to the project existed. Members came and went. Eventually, after the ever-evolving plan became finalized and went forward for funding, the committee voted to support the Mill Creek Valley redevelopment project.[152]

Wielding Spades in Mill Creek Valley

Alderman Archie Blaine (far left) participates in a development project groundbreaking ceremony in 1961. Mayor Tucker is second from right. Newspapers.com

"Mistakes Were Made"

Tucker announced the planned demolition on August 7, 1954. Chaos ensued. Speculators began working the neighborhood, trying to trade properties with owners so that high valuations could be negotiated in government buyouts.[153] Aldermen, including Archie Blaine and Clinton Watson, urged residents "not to be stampeded into selling their property to land speculators" and ensured "they would get a fair price for their property."[154] About 400 residents attended the meeting, and that was nearly the number of people who were resident landowners in Mill Creek Valley.

Additionally, half the population left. Gone! Moved out. This was five years before demolition began. According to the congressional GAO report, in 1958 there were 4,212 families to be relocated—a number already lower than the 5,600 identified in the 1950 Census. By 1961, the total project relocation was 2,072 families with only a handful of that number remaining.[155] More than half the families took off rather than wait and see what was coming.

In its own advertising brochure, the city's housing agency noted "1,050 of the 4,200 families displaced from the project were relocated in decent, safe and sanitary housing."[156] This begs the question: what happened to the others?

The relocation of thousands of people did not go well, understandably. Complaints reached all the way to Washington DC and Congress made an investigation. Farris and the relocation committee were accused of moving people from one substandard situation into another.

Federal authorities investigated 31 dwelling units to which people were relocated and found 30 of them substandard.[157] Farris acknowledged that "some mistakes were made," but still asserted that the Land Clearance Authority lived up to the rules and worked carefully with the Urban Renewal Administration in doing its work. "It could well be that some units that were up to standard in 1958 and 1959 when they were first occupied became substandard several years later when the GAO made its investigation."[158] This explanation by Farris rang ironic, since it spoke to the quality of public housing construction (which was suspect all along) and it spoke to how homes deteriorate over time—precisely what justified the destruction of Mill Creek Valley in the first place.

Archie Blaine's coordinating committee stated that "housing has been found for 3,000 families, plus 1,000 individuals" between May 1958 and June 1960.[159] He also said that attempts were unsuccessful to get the Housing Authority to change its rule prohibiting "unmarried women with illegitimate children," which applied to 19 women looking for relocation assistance.[160]

The Relocation Plan reported that there were 4,212 total

families affected by the Mill Creek Valley redevelopment project, along with 1,331 individuals. Of those, 3,776 families and 250 individuals were eligible for public housing. The breakdown of the 3,776 families eligible for housing was 1,294 2-person households, 1,187 3-4 person households, and 1,295 5+ member households.[161]

This allows a basic calculation of population based on these figures. Depending on how one tabulates the possibilities, these families and individual occupants total between 16,000 and 17,000 people. The overall population estimates were between 19,000 and 20,000 people. Where did those 3,000 people go? These residents likely were those "staying with" friends or family, occupying attics or basements.

Charles Farris argued in 1961: "The [Land Clearance] Authority frankly acknowledges that not all dislocated businesses and families substantially improved their surroundings. Some voluntarily moved into sub-standard structures. In some instances, they moved before the Authority's relocation service could be introduced. In other cases, relocation assistance was refused. …Some displacees chose not to pay somewhat higher rents for standard housing. The Authority counsels against this, but it cannot completely forestall this."[162]

"Mill Creek Owners"

We can work out your deal now before you sell your property. We will advance your down payment. St. Louis Co. R.E. PA 7-08 I 8 We have many other properties available. We will trade. (*)

Real estate firms such as the St. Louis County Real Estate Company actively sought to buy out MCV owners before they settled with the City of St. Louis. Post-Dispatch, March 5, 1959. Newspapers.com

Doing the Deed

Mayor Tucker addressed the United States Senate's Housing Subcommittee of the Banking and Currency Committee (that reviewed grant programs) on November 5, 1957. He made a plea for better funding of physical and social infrastructure. He remarked that the "total cost of re-building our city is simply beyond our present financial re-sources." He continued, "The future of all social welfare pro-grams is uncertain in our present political climate. Yet the need for such programs was never

102

greater. The American people are moving by the millions each year from rural to urban centers. Despite this, there are indications of a de-emphasis of federal programs designed to alleviate the problems resulting from this migration."[163] Tucker felt that federal funding streams were threatened in the moment they were most needed.

The long planned demolition of this long loved neighborhood began on February 16, 1959—over three years after the bond issue passed—and redevelopment of the Mill Creek Valley was delayed for years beyond that. "For several years, about the only movement in the mile-long Mill Creek area was the waving of tall weeds in the summer breezes."[164] The site sat vacant for so long that many called it "Hiroshima Flats," a name that was only about a dozen years after the actual Hiroshima destruction. How ironic that the sitting mayor, just prior to taking office, had developed the Civil Defense plan to respond to an atomic attack in St. Louis.[165]

Various small projects emerged. St. Louis University expanded its campus in the five-block area along Grand and Laclede Avenues.[166] In 1961, the University Heights Village apartments were begun near present-day Harris-Stowe State University. [167] It was not until 1964 that the major redevelopment opened.

The project that eventually rose up was LaClede Town, a creation of I. E. Millstone—the builder who had developed the first public housing project in the country (St. Petersburg, Florida, in 1937-38) and had constructed over $100 million worth of public housing since [including Pruitt-Igoe].[168] Scholar Eugene Meehan criticized these projects as being substandard in their construction due to cutting corners to save money— something I. E. Millstone denied to the end of his 100+ year life.[169]

LaClede Town was the nation's first integrated community with a diversity of people. People there "do their thing" and "in doing their thing, get along together." "LaClede Town must be seen to be believed, visited to be understood.[170] It is a feeling, a fun place to live, a new way of life, a model that can and probably will be duplicated by energetic and concerned developers in other parts of the country. It may not solve one social problem in the world today, but it has proven that people, regardless of background, religion, politics, or hopes, can live together harmoniously."[171]

LaClede Town was probably the most diverse, hip neighborhood St. Louis has ever known. Though its success would not last beyond the 1970s, and it too would be demolished in 1995, it was wildly successful in its early years while Tucker was mayor. Subsequent investment by A. G. Edwards (now Wells Fargo) in a new headquarters complex, Teamsters Plaza, and high-rise apartments brought new construction to the Mill Creek Valley. Financially, the city would quadruple its investment over the 20-year life of the bonds. [172]

Ada Louise Huxtable, architecture critic, noted in *The New York Times* that another hip place had opened in St. Louis— Gaslight Square, "a profitable, appealing and highly successful example of spontaneous private renewal, done without public sponsorship." Ironically, she noted, its buildings were all rehabbed with fixtures and trimmings salvaged from the Mill Creek Valley demolition.[173] Gaslight Square faded by 1972, after a high-profile crime and seedier storefronts diminished the area's "appeal."[174]

The Mill Creek Valley has been cleared for generations now. Subsequent reports and articles about the Mill Creek Valley can disagree on specifics of what had been there and what was lost there. What was most irreplaceable, though, were the culture and bonds that existed in the neighborhood, not to mention the old architectural styles of pre-Civil War St. Louis. With hindsight, St. Louisans see the shortcomings of these choices, but at the time, it was seen as a state of crisis that required the radical solutions of land clearance. One former resident said on record, "there was nothing wrong with the Mill Creek Valley. They saw this land, they wanted it, and they took it."[175] This statement shows the difference in perspectives that existed. Tucker and other civic leaders saw the negative. Residents knew the positive.

ENDNOTES

[1] See "Mayor Darst Throws Administration Weight Behind World's Fair Here in '53," *St. Louis Star-Times.* 06 Jan 1950, p. 3.

[2] "City May Apply for Additional Public Housing," *The St. Louis American.* 13 Jan 1955, p. 3.

[3] Two low-rise public housing projects existed prior to Mayor Darst's tenure. Carr Square Village (658 units) was built on the near North Side and segregated for Black residents. Clinton-Peabody (657 units) was built on the near South Side and segregated for whites. Both developments opened in the summer of 1942 and exist today in different forms. For more information, start with the blog *The Symbol of Failure in Public Housing...* https://52193861.weebly.com/st-louis-housing-authority.html Posted: N.D. Accessed: 28 Jul 2024. The data largely are based on the work of Eugene Meehan (e.g., *The Quality of Federal Policy-Making*).

[4] "Three Big Decisions," *St. Louis Post-Dispatch.* 06 Apr 1953, p. 2B.

[5] This speech was given after Tucker left office, but he was a consistent man and this attitude did not represent a change. Tucker, 1968, pp. 1-12.

[6] ibid.

[7] ibid.

[8] Naffziger, Chris. "In 1951, City Planners Plotted...," *St. Louis Magazine.* Posted: 11 Nov 2020. Accessed: 02 Feb 2022. https://www.stlmag.com/history/highways-interstates-st-louis/.

[9] "Quit Stalling...," *St. Louis Post-Dispatch.* 14 Dec 1956, p. 1A.

[10] "Misunderstandings and emotions have clouded the real basic issue in debate...," *St. Louis Globe-Democrat.* 24 Mar 1957, p. 6.

[11] "Carr Square Neighborhood Overview," *St. Louis Mo. Official Website.* Posted: n.d. Accessed: 02 Feb 2022. https://www.stlouis-mo.gov/live-work/community/neighborhoods/carr-square/carr-square-overview.cfm

[12] Roosevelt 352

[13] "Hark!...," *St. Louis Post-Dispatch.* 04 Feb 1903, p. 13.

[14] ibid.

[15] "Dances in School Buildings Planned," *St. Louis Globe-Democrat*, 23 Sep 1914, p. 12.

[16] ibid.

[17] "The Wednesday Club Plan for Settling the Servant Problem," *St. Louis Post-Dispatch*, 27 Oct 1901, PDF p. 43.

[18] ibid.

[19] Rumbold 4, emphasis added
[20] "How 'Big Brother' Reforms…," *St. Louis Post-Dispatch.* 21 Nov 1909, p. 1B.
[21] ibid. 13
[22] ibid. 18
[23] ibid. 19
[24] ibid. 20
[25] ibid. 19-20
[26] ibid. 20
[27] ibid. 59
[28] ibid. 59
[29] ibid. 59
[30] ibid. 62
[31] ibid. 70
[32] ibid.
[33] ibid. 71
[34] ibid.
[35] ibid. 70
[36] ibid. 35
[37] ibid.
[38] ibid. 59
[39] "Women to Attend Hearing on Raise for Miss Rumbold," *St. Louis Globe-Democrat.* 20 Jun 1915, p.7.
[40] "Miss Rumbold's Work," *St. Louis Post-Dispatch.* 23 Jun 1915, p. 12.
[41] "Supervisor of Recreation Not to Be Chosen…," *St. Louis Post-Dispatch.* 31 Aug 1915, p. 2.
[42] "Miss Rumbold Ordered…," *St. Louis Post-Dispatch.* 18 Feb 1915, p. 1.
[43] Seltzer, Louis B. "Tiny Woman Never Shrinks from Storms," *Cleveland Press*, 1945. Case Western Reserve University Archives.
[44] Dickens himself did not care much for St. Louis when he visited there in 1842. See his *American Notes* from that year.
[45] "A Study for a Comprehensive Plan for Redevelopment of the Central City Area of St. Louis." St. Louis City Plan Commission, January 21, 1954. The firm was Russell, Mullgardt, Schwarz, and Van Hoefen.
[46] "Mayor's Signing Clears Way for New City Plan," *St. Louis Star-Times.* 29 Mar 1947, p. 1.
[47] Abbott 2009, 6
[48] Heathcott 327
[49] Toft

[50] ibid.

[51] Heathcott 327

[52] City Plan Commission 1917, 2-3

[53] Heathcott 326

[54] Heathcott 329

[55] Bartholomew, cited in Heathcott 329

[56] "The Judgment of Fifteen Men," Real Estate Mortgage Trust Company advertisement, *St. Louis Globe-Democrat* 03 Oct 1928, p. 3.

[57] Bartholomew et al 1917, xv; emphasis Bartholomew's

[58] ibid. 98-101

[59] ibid. 64-76

[60] ibid. 72

[61] Mark Benton, in a 2018 essay, called this "administrative evil," where an immoral outcome is delivered under the mask of study, betterment, or other public legitimacy. See his article " 'Saving' the City: Harland Bartholomew and Administrative Evil in St. Louis," *Public Integrity* 20:2 (2018) pp. 194-206.

[62] Bartholomew et al 1942, 13

[63] ibid. 16

[64] ibid. 23

[65] ibid. 13

[66] Hagen 557

[67] Bartholomew et al 1942, 36

[68] Flint 103, f1. Barbara Flint has written an outstanding dissertation examining zoning's use of racial bias. (See the bibliography to locate a copy near you!) She notes that Bartholomew gave an address at the Chicago Association of Commerce on October 9, 1919, where he said that "where values have depreciated, homes are either vacant or occupied by colored people...." This is just a snippet from the whole speech, but it links race and property values in an early year. She said this speech is reported in Charles M. Nichols' *Zoning in Chicago* from 1919, but this author was unable to locate an original copy of that work in time for publication.

[69] "Bartholomew Gets New Job," *St. Louis Post-Dispatch.* 16 Jan 1935, p. 3A.

[70] "Mayor Assails City Plan...," *St. Louis Star-Times.* 16 Jan 1935, p. 1.

[71] ibid.

[72] ibid.

[73] ibid.

[74] "Groups Named to Further City Planners' Objectives," *St. Louis Post-Dispatch*. 02 Feb 1935, p. 3A.

[75] Bartholomew's family is buried at the Oak Grove Cemetery in St. Louis County. This family history was compiled by this author and has been added to the free public database *Findagrave.com*, and the entry for Harland Bartholomew (1889-1989).

[76] Abbott 2007, 113

[77] The author acknowledges that this study may be no different, and apologizes if the accuracies of any sources are later disproved.

[78] Gibson 14

[79] ibid.

[80] ibid. 16

[81] Horne 2, 4

[82] ibid. 2

[83] ibid. 4

[84] ibid.

[85] Grant 46

[86] ibid.

[87] Grant 75. The Club Plantation was for whites only, but brought in big names of Black entertainment.

[88] Cook 1-2, part of a longer quote

[89] ibid.

[90] ibid.

[91] Sobel et al 24, f10, f11

[92] "Everybody's Column: Negro View of Segregation," *St. Louis Star-Times,* 25 Jun 1924, p. 14.

[93] ibid.

[94] As will be shown later, this was not necessarily formal government relocation, but rather informal self-relocation.

[95] "New Zoning Plan...," *St. Louis Globe Democrat.* 17 Jan 1940, p. 4A.

[96] "Commission Row," *St. Louis Star-Times.* 21 Aug 1941, p. 9.

[97] "Test Air Strip Asssailed...," *St. Louis Star and Times.* 23 Aug 1944, p. 3.

[98] Bartholomew et al 1947, plate 10

[99] "Officer of Negro Group Backs Plan...," *St. Louis Post-Dispatch.* 01 Mar 1948, p. 8A. A later article on October 4th spelled his first name "Gloucester" and said he was from New York.

[100] "Multi-Story Housing Units...," *St. Louis Post-Dispatch.* 15 Jun 1950, p. 1A; and also "Zeckendorf to Hold Onto Chrysler Building," *St. Louis Globe-Democrat.* 20 Aug 1957, p. 1A.

[101] "Multi-Story Housing Units...," *St. Louis Post-Dispatch*. 15 Jun 1950, p. 1A.
[102] ibid.
[103] "Darst Announces Plans...," *St. Louis Post-Dispatch*. 18 Mar 1950, p. 1A.
[104] Vexler 115
[105] Peirce 52
[106] Fagerstrom 55; emphasis added
[107] ibid.
[108] ibid.
[109] "Rat Treating Job in Mill Creek Area Awarded," *St. Louis Post-Dispatch*. 14 Jan 1959, p. 10C.
[110] "Relocation Plan in Rat-Infested Area Is Offered," *Neighborhood News (St. Louis)*. 16 Jun 1955, p. 2.
[111] See "Cahokia Bridge Approved by St. Louis Board," *St. Louis Post-Dispatch,* 31 May 1955, microfilm p. 3; [Poplar Street Bridge] Brickley, Michael. "The Bridge Between St. Louis and East St. Louis," *NextSTL Policy and Commentary: Transportation*. 06 Apr 2012. www.NextSTL. com; and [Nooter] "Ground Broken for New Building," *St. Louis Post-Dispatch*, 06 Jul 1958, microfilm p. 64.
[112] These were the 1950 Census numbers, and they show up in many of the official planning documents and subsequent reporting.
[113] Fagerstrom 21
[114] There is a bulge in his diagram that follows rail lines, which is omitted from this analysis since there are no dwellings in this rail-only zone.
[115] Fagerstrom p. 8 is the base source of the block photograph used for this measurement.
[116] St. Louis Housing Authority... 1-2
[117] These can be identified in photographs.
[118] Watson and Farris 5
[119] "Relocation Job in Mill Creek...," *St. Louis Post-Dispatch*. 28 May 1961, p. 1.

[120] See the interviews in Fagerstrom p. 45.
[121] Coibion p. 4, emphasis added
[122] ibid. 5
[123] Sengstock et al 110
[124] ibid. 111
[125] ibid.
[126] cited in Perald, 15

[127] Letter draft to Genevieve Pullis, 05 Aug 1960. Raymond Tucker Papers, Series 2, Box 16, Folder "Land Clearance and Housing Authority June 1, 1960-Dec. 31, 1960"

[128] Tucker, 1953, 8

[129] ibid. 4, 18

[130] Fagerstrom 61

[131] O'Neil, Tim. August 9, 2009. "A Look Back: Clearing of Mill Creek Valley Changed the Face of the City," *St. Louis Post-Dispatch*. Posted 09 August 2009. Accessed 05 March 2015. http://www.stltoday.com/news/local/a-look-back-clearing-of-mill-creek-valley-changed-the/article_04738cde-b0f8-5688-a20e-6fd86266d1ac.html; and also Primm 497.

[132] "Housing Most Important Problem...," *St. Louis Post-Dispatch*. 13 Feb 1951, p. 14A.

[133] "St. Louis NAACP Backs Mill Creek Slum Project," *St. Louis Post-Dispatch*. 29 Sep 1957, p. 14A.

[134] "Mill Creek Plan to be Explained at Meeting," *St. Louis Post-Dispatch*. 08 Dec 1957, p. 8G.

[135] "Plaza Bond Issue Vote on Tuesday [head]...NAACP Against It [subhead]," *St. Louis Post-Dispatch*. 27 Sep 1953, p. 13A.

[136] "Letters from the People: As to a Bond Issue," *St. Louis Post-Dispatch*. 24 Sep 1953.

[137] "NAACP Here Outlines 1958 Legislative Targets," *St. Louis Post-Dispatch*. 05 Jan 1958, 24D.

[138] "NAAACP Says It May Sue to Tie Up Building Projects Here," *St. Louis Post-Dispatch*. 02 Apr 1962, p. 1A.

[139] ibid.

[140] "[Negro] Boy Plays Santa...," *Kirskville Daily Express and Daily News* (Kirksville, MO), 19 Dec 1921, p. 1)

[141] "Aldermen OK 2 Mill Creek Bills, 27-1," *St. Louis Globe Democrat*. 22 Mar 1958, p. 1.

[142] "Aldermen Pass Measures on Mill Creek Plan by 27 to 1 Vote," *St. Louis Post-Dispatch*. 21 Mar 1958, p. 1A.

[143] "Blaine is Disappointed," *St. Louis Post-Dispatch*. 19 Feb 1960, PDF p. 24.

[144] Murphy 87

[145] "Archie Blaine Loses Support of Organization," *St. Louis Post-Dispatch*. 14 Dec 1962, p. 3A.

[146] Blaine's personal life seemed to get destabilized as well during his last term. His wife of six years and the mother of his children filed for divorce. Judge Michael Scott granted the divorce, gave custody to the mother, along with a monthly alimony/child support

payment of $332. They attempted reconciliation and remarried a year later, but she filed for divorce again within months, citing "general indignities." He decided to join the ministry and invited fellow aldermen to hear his trial sermon.

He operated a cleaning service in the Plaza Square Apartments (which had been the first slum clearance project in his ward), for the people who displaced him, where he took up residence in an apartment that probably would not have rented to him when built. He would go on to work in a mayoral administrative position for future Mayors Cervantes and Poelker. See "Archie Blaine to be Minister," *St. Louis Globe-Democrat,* 22 Apr 1960, PDF p.50.

[147] *Memo on Mill Creek Advisory Committee.* N.D. (summary document of its work back to 1954; written late 1957 or later) Raymond Tucker Papers, Series 1, Box 13, Folder "St. Louis Convention Board" [this specific folder seems inappropriate for this document, and so it may be misplaced], Washington University in St. Louis. There is duplicate information found in Series 1, Box 14, Folder "Land Clearance for Redevelopment Authority (Minutes of Meetings)."

[148] ibid.

[149] ibid.

[150] ibid.

[151] ibid.

[152] ibid.

[153] "Mill Creek Area Co-ordinators' Office to Open," *St. Louis Post-Dispatch.* 13 Jul 1958, PDF p. 26.

[154] "Don't Sell Fast, Mill Creek Land Owners Warned," *St. Louis Post-Dispatch.* 28 May 1958, p. 3A.

[155] Comptroller General… 10 (GAO)

[156] St. Louis Housing Authority… 2

[157] "Mistakes Made in Relocating Families, Farris Acknowledges," *St. Louis Post-Dispatch.* 18 Jun 1964, PDF p. 27.

[158] ibid.

[159] "3000 Families Moved from Area," *St. Louis Globe-Democrat.* 30 Jan 1960, p. 2A.

[160] ibid.

[161] Watson and Farris 5

[162] Farris 1+

[163] Tucker 1957, 1

[164] Hagen 560

[165] See St. Louis Civil Defense Commission. *The St. Louis Civil Defense Plan.* St. Louis: Office of Civil Defense. January 1953. A

copy can be found in the St. Louis collection at the St. Louis Central Public Library.

[166] Kirschten 440
[167] O'Neil, 2009
[168] Hagen 560
[169] See Eugene Meehan's *Quality of Federal Policymaking.*
[170] Hagen 560
[171] ibid. 562
[172] Primm 498
[173] Huxtable, Ada Louise. "St. Louis and the Crisis of American Cities," *The New York Times.* 20 Jun 1964, PDF p. 297.
[174] O'Neil, Tim. "Gaslight Square Burned Brightly…," *St. Louis Post-Dispatch.* 01 Nov 2021.
[175] Fagerstrom 58

Press photos of Mayor Tucker speaking at an unidentified development project. About 1957. Courtesy of the Tucker Family.

Citizens Committee for a Better St. Louis, 11 Dec 1961. From left: Mayor Tucker, Harry F. Harrington, David R. Calhoun Jr., Margaret Bush Wilson, Daniel L. Schlafly. (uncredited photo) Courtesy of the Tucker Family

Chapter 3

Confronting Discrimination:
The Emergence of Civil Rights
in St. Louis

St. Louis Civil Rights Timeline

1945

St. Louis University admits Black students, 1944

Archbishop Ritter desegregates Catholic parishes, 1946

CORE is formed, 1947

Supreme Court decides Shelley v. Kraemer, 1948; racial deed covenants end

NAACP declared 1948 its "best year ever"

1950

CORE conducts sit-ins at segregated lunch counters, 1948-52

Washington University desegregates, 1952

Tucker names first woman to mayoral cabinet, 1953

Brown v. Board decision, 1954; Tucker desegregates city institutions

1955

Tucker signs Fair Employment Practices Ordinance, 1956

Tucker appoints African American to School Board, 1955

MLK makes first visit to STL, praises city's progress, 1957

Tucker negotiates desegregation of six restaurant chains, 1960

1960

Theodore McNeil becomes MO's first Black state senator, 1960

City passes Public Accommodation Ordinance, 1961

Tucker appoints first African American to mayoral cabinet, 1961

DeVerne Calloway is 1st Black woman in MO House, 1962

Jefferson Bank Protest, 1963

Tucker signs the Fair Housing Ordinance, 1964

1965

Percy Green creates ACTION, 1965

MULTIPLE SCHOLARS HAVE DESCRIBED Raymond Tucker as being difficult to pin down regarding his Civil Rights attitudes (for example, see Stein's *St. Louis Politics: Triumph of Tradition* or Lang's *Grassroots at the Gateway*). However, this study clarifies Tucker's attitudes by examining the different elements of Civil Rights happening in St. Louis and placing Tucker within those elements, allowing us to focus clearly on the contributions made within his scope.

Tucker had several personality traits, explored elsewhere in this work, which affected his approach to any task.

- He was fastidious and detail-oriented.
- He was pragmatic, choosing to work within existing frameworks and making those structures produce the best possible outcome. He could take the theoretical and make it implementable.
- He was a by-the-book man. He obeyed the rules (perhaps his Catholicism is showing), and if the rules were broken then he advocated fixing the rules.
- He was an institutionalist. He believed in codifying rules and relationships; in having institutions that worked in a professional and apolitical manner.
- He had little use for politicking, deal making, grandstanding, and backroom bargains. He recognized that these dynamics were a necessary evil in some circles and that politicians needed space to maneuver, but he rejected them because such arrangements were inconsistent, unreliable, and—in the end—not in the broad public interest.

Above all, he was consistent. His position on anything was solid and reliable, unless research and inquiry indicated the need for change. And this, perhaps at a level, was his weak spot when it came to Civil Rights. He was consistent and reliable, and the Civil Rights Movement simply outpaced him.

Raymond Tucker's character is discernable through his public and academic service. He was professional (vs. political) in his public life. He embraced knowledge, process, and rational decision-making (all professorial traits expected of someone in the academy) and he took those elements to city hall. The desired end was to make the right decision, the best decision—not for himself—but for the city and its people.

His character is discernable through his pragmatic approach to problems. While he was capable of lofty thinking, as most professors are, he placed value on being practical, which meant meeting goals and commitments in a measurable way. The desired end was doing his best and honoring his obligations to public trust.

As is shown throughout this work, Tucker believed in institutions. He played by the rules, and the rules applied to everyone equally. If the rules did not serve the purpose of the institution, then the rules should be changed (and there was a process for that). The desired end was to make institutions work well for all people by honoring, maintaining, and amending the processes for the benefit of all. Here, though, we consider what shaped his sense of right and wrong, good and evil.

Tucker's disdain for politics reflected this sense. Tucker's respect for fairness did too. He was remarkably consistent in his behavior—showing that his moral compass indeed was the product of an iterative process. His desired end was to live and model a personal life that was honest, and to do honest work each day.

There is plenty of room for criticism of mid-century St. Louis. It was a city of segregation, injustice, and racism—both institutionalized and personal. It was on display everywhere. For purposes of this study, let's consider how Tucker navigated the travails of leading a city steeped in traditionalistic ways. This analysis is not to put him on a pedestal, but rather to consider what may have had meaningful impact on his character development and how he employed it.

DESEGREGATION—Catholic Style

Raymond Tucker was part of a Roman Catholic family, active parishioners at SS. Mary and Joseph Church in the Carondelet neighborhood. While we cannot know the degree to which his Catholicism shaped his political points of view, the broad strokes of the church's progressive direction in the postwar era and Tucker's own political behavior show important parallels. Tucker was a product of Jesuit education at St. Louis University during his formative years (SLU high school class of 1913, and SLU college class of 1917), and it is clear that he held the Jesuits in esteem and maintained friendships there. They shaped his moral compass and he seemingly embraced their structural tenets.

Relic of the Past

On Christmas Eve 1945, St. Louis Archbishop John J. Glennon received a very special surprise. Word arrived that he had been elevated to the rank of Cardinal within the Catholic Church. He had served St. Louis Catholics since Theodore Roosevelt was president and traveled the following March to and from Rome (via his native Ireland) to be installed in the College of Cardinals. The elderly shepherd at first deemed himself too frail to make the trip to Rome, but he reconsidered and took the flight to Europe with two other Cardinals-elect.

On the flight, however, he caught a cold. He couldn't shake it. He was installed as Cardinal and, on the return trip, stopped in his native Ireland. He died in Dublin on March 9, 1946, and the Cardinal's body was returned to St. Louis for interment in the crypt of the grand new cathedral he had built—dressed in the red robes he had never worn while in St. Louis.

Historian Msgr. Michael Witt told of the blatant racism that existed in some parishes under Glennon's reign. A Catholic African American couple went to the Most Blessed Sacrament Church at North Kingshighway at Northland Ave. to join the parish. The pastor confirmed that they were indeed in the boundaries of the historically white parish, but advised them that they would be "more comfortable" at neighboring Visitation Parish near (what would become) Martin Luther King Drive and North Taylor, which already served an African American population. In parting, the pastor reminded them that they indeed lived in Most Blessed Sacrament Parish and had a duty to support it financially—as he handed them a package of contribution envelopes.[1]

The *Post-Dispatch* carried an article on Sunday April 28, 1918, about a fiery sermon given at St. Ann's Church, corner of Page and Whittier. The pastor called out to the full congregation that if there were any African Americans in the audience, "they should know that they are not welcome and, in the future, to stay away from [this] church." The Reverend Father Walsh told the *Post* reporter, "There had always been Negro residents of the parish, but only along the boundaries, never in the heart of the parish." He then went on to say how boys were throwing rocks at windows, how "white women are afraid to venture out after night," and that petty crime had increased. He lamented that in seven years, his parish had dwindled from 400 families to 250, and now for-sale signs were popping up because of the "further encroachment."[2]

Glennon had opposed integration of parishes, rather preferring to support the large number of African American parishes already formed and working in St. Louis. Mrs. Jane Aileen Kaiser, an African American woman with very light skin, paid a visit to Archbishop Glennon (he accepted the meeting presuming she was white). She spoke up about pursuing racial integration and Glennon retorted, "Blacks…are violent, irresponsible, ungrateful, and undeserving of any greater generosity than they already received." He further stated that he feared "integration would lead to [miscegenation], which," in a happy tone according to Kaiser, "was forbidden by law."[3] The conversation showed that even Servants of God were steeped in the area's racism.

The children's hospital that bears his name today opened a decade after he died—then the only free-standing non-profit Catholic children's hospital in the country. It had been a dream of Cardinal Glennon to open such a facility and so its founders chose to honor him in that way.

Glennon's death meant that the Pope then appointed a new archbishop for St. Louis. The man chosen was Joseph Elmer Ritter, a 54-year-old prelate from Indianapolis. Archbishop Ritter would be a great force in St. Louis and on Mayor Tucker.

A Bold New Path

Ritter was shocked at the open racism in St. Louis. Immediately, Ritter desegregated the Archdiocese—its churches, schools, and institutions—in the City of St. Louis, St. Louis

County, and the surrounding counties in Missouri. When the lawsuits started and the outcry from whites rang out, Ritter reminded them of their duties to love as Christians and threatened to excommunicate any who would openly defy their bishop on this matter. Protests to the papal representative in Washington DC were rebuffed. "The policy of admitting Negro children to Catholic schools with white pupils is one which [I] consider [my] duty as chief pastor of this archdiocese, regardless of race or nationality."[4] The opposition stopped, but it resulted in what scholar Sarah Siegel called "passive liberalism," where there is embracing of a social ideal without a demand for personal commitment.[5]

Undoubtedly, Tucker admired Ritter's actions and the authority to carry out decisions that were in the best interests of the flock. Ritter himself said "I've taken part in civil rights protests and if a priest in the archdiocese wishes to take part in such protests, it is up to him. I definitely support civil disobedience for a just cause."[6]

Ritter would continue to prove himself to be radically different from his predecessor and force-fed progressivism to his flock. He avoided some of the finery of his office. He rejected life in the old Walsh Mansion on Lindell Boulevard by the Cathedral—which had been donated to the church in 1924 to serve as the archbishop's residence. Instead, he opted to live with his Labrador Retriever named Bonus in a modern ranch house on Ladue Road surrounded by three acres, where he spent time quietly tending his greenhouse and rose garden a good distance away from Lindell Boulevard.[7]

The house had been owned by Mr. and Mrs. Martin Lammert, CEO of an old St. Louis furniture firm and sold for $80,000 (about $950,000 in today's dollars, which did not come from regular donations). In order to separate himself from criticism of moving to the wealthiest suburb in St. Louis, Ritter was careful to stress that, "I live on Ladue, not in it—please."[8] His area was unincorporated at the time, and he signed a petition to prevent the area from being incorporated by Frontenac in 1949. It later became part of Creve Coeur.[9]

The Church in Suburbia

At the same time Ritter was forcing St. Louis Catholics to play together in the same sandbox, he was also enabling white flight. Ritter went on a spree of establishing new parishes in the growing suburbs. In a sense, his desegregation order may have given white Catholics another reason to move to suburbia. (Recall that he himself chose to live in the suburbs.) He ordered the sale or demolition of many landmark structures in old parts of the city and county, and similarly ordered the construction of new (technically desegregated) parishes in predominantly white suburbs. "I'd say I've established 50 new parishes. We constantly have $8 million to $10 million worth of building going on."[10]

Msgr. Michael Witt added more detail to the story. Ritter closed (the technical word is "suppressed") St. Elizabeth Church in the Mill Creek Valley, 2721 Pine Street, a thriving Jesuit parish built to serve African Americans. The great African American priest, the Venerable Augustine Tolton, had given a sermon there on December 6, 1891.[11] Ritter's instructions were for the parishioners to join the neighboring parishes of St. Malachy (which also would be destroyed in the Mill Creek Valley urban renewal), St. Nicholas in downtown, or St. Bridget adjacent to Pruitt-Igoe—thereby integrating those churches.[12]

North County was especially active. Florissant was the fastest growing suburb in the United States between the 1950 and 1960 census periods—over a 900% increase in population. Sacred Heart Parish there alone grew by 1,500 parishioners, and St. Ferdinand Parish grew by 3,700[13] (prompting Ritter to close the historic 1821 church building in the city's Old Town and construct a new one on Charbonier Road; he was ready to demolish the landmark until Rosemary Davison, Mary Kay Gladbach, and other Florissant residents successfully demanded—and funded—its preservation).

He saw suburbanization with clear eyes. "The...population shift from city to suburban life must be faced and met. It means constant planning and building out from the city."[14] The archdiocese's expansion fund by 1964 netted $72 million, (over $600 million in today's dollars).[15]

Ritter was elevated to the rank of Cardinal in 1961, and played an important role in the Vatican II council of 1963. Just as he brought St. Louis Catholics into more modern times, he helped transform the modern Catholic Church around the world. One of the big changes was for parishes to use the local language rather than Latin. On August 24, 1964, he arranged the first English-language Catholic Mass ever in the United States, before 12,000 St. Louis Catholics at Kiel Auditorium.[16]

Ritter was described in 1960 as a respected administrator, a "tough cookie," and a "good Dutchman"—and though his rulings are not always popular, they were "by the book." About this, he said "I didn't lay down the law, I interpreted it."[17]

While Ritter's words were powerful, he himself was unimposing, standing 5'6" and weighing about 150 pounds. The *New York Times* described him as not being "a powerful speaker" and "lacking a booming voice that could thunder from the pulpit." Rather, "he possessed administrative and persuasive skills that helped him to wield authority well."[18] ("Hard-headed holiness" was how one of his secretaries described him.) Notice the parallels with Tucker. He was a bookish man who did well as a lecturer, though not dominating in size or voice. His administrative capacity was deep, and he used logic and reason to make bureaucracy effective.

Ritter eschewed the archbishop's luxurious residence on Lindell for a quiet home in the suburbs, just as Mayor Tucker eschewed the high-end neighborhoods most other mayors enjoyed (Dickmann lived on prestigious Portland Place, Darst lived in an apartment building he owned at Maryland and Newstead Aves. in the Central West End—and future mayor A. J. Cervantes lived on ritzy Westmoreland Place). Tucker remained in his childhood home in Carondelet—a neighborhood that had a small African American presence.

"Racial Injustice is a Sin"

On April 1, 1954, more than a month before the United States Supreme Court handed down its *Brown v. Board* decision, Archbishop Ritter wrote to the coordinator of Catholic hospitals for the Archdiocese. "For some time, the thought has come to me that you should give consideration in your hospital work

...to [lay] down a uniform policy in regard to the admission of Negroes."[19] By the next year, Catholic hospitals in St. Louis were desegregated. "Catholic hospitals, along with the whole Church, have a most serious obligation to carry out courageously the teachings of Christ and to put aside their policies and practices and end all discrimination because of race, color, or religion."[20] Mayor Tucker followed suit, (after the Supreme Court decision) signing an order desegregating city hospitals in 1955, requiring admissions regardless of race, color, or religion.[21]

At the same time the March on Washington was happening, and that the Jefferson Bank Protest was happening in St. Louis, Archbishop Ritter was further changing the archdiocese. On Sunday, August 11, 1963, a letter from Ritter was read to all Catholics in St. Louis. He was establishing an archdiocesan Commission on Human Rights, the function of which would be to "advise and recommend procedures which will bring about a reign of justice and charity in the community; to initiate a program that will enable all to understand the principles involved in the current civil rights issue; and to formulate activities that will overcome the obstacles that now impede the use of God-given rights."[22] On August 28, he announced a three-day pastoral Institute on Human Rights at the Park Plaza Hotel, instructing every pastor, assistant pastor, and teacher to attend. "I ask that you schedule your calendar so as to be present."[23]

At the Institute, Ritter made a tremendous declaration that left no doubt where the local Catholic Church stood on the matter: "**Racial injustice is a sin**, and it is a serious violation of charity, which is the essence of Christianity." He continued, "For anyone to go to the altar and receive [Holy Communion] with bitterness in his heart, with hatred in his heart for his fellow man—this certainly would be considered a sacrilege and a great insult to Christ."[24] These words made every Catholic parish and every Catholic individual engage in an examination of conscience. Mayor Tucker, a devout Catholic, would not have excused himself lightly from the archbishop's pronouncement.

Jesuits Pushing Desegregation

Archbishop Ritter didn't start from zero when it came to desegregating holy institutions in St. Louis. One brave Jesuit had greased the skids for him already.

Saint Louis University (SLU) already was considering desegregation in January 1944, and there was a small article buried on page 13 of the *Globe-Democrat* stating that Father Halloran was making inquiries.[25] The Very Reverend Patrick Holloran, S.J., the SLU president, was investigating the matter by sending out letters to a "very restricted group of friends." Father Holloran continued, "The weight of the appeal has stressed the position of the Negro in the Catholic Church and

A snapshot of Cardinal Ritter with Mayor Tucker, about 1962. Courtesy of the Tucker Family.

the serious challenge of discrimination by a Catholic university against colored Catholics who find it impossible to obtain a Catholic education." He assured, "There will never be any lowering of academic standards in the admission of colored students" and that there would be "no more than 20 such students in as many years would be involved...."[26] Clearly, he was trying to be quiet and make the effort seem small and non-threatening.

He had sent out a letter to alumni and other key Catholics that asked a simple question: "Would you be less inclined to send a son or daughter to Saint Louis University if Negro students were admitted?"[27]

Holloran was tiptoeing through deep waters. He deserves credit for engaging in a tough conversation that was sure to draw heat from several directions. Archbishop Glennon was opposed to the idea "to the point of bigotry."[28] The Sisters of Loretto wanted to admit an African American Catholic woman, Aloyse Foster, to their Webster College (then an academic unit of Saint Louis University) the previous semester and Glennon personally blocked it.[29]

The blocking of Foster's application was, according to Rev. Donald Kemper, "straightforward deception." [30] Glennon refused to approve the application, but *asked that his decision be kept secret*. Kemper noted that this was how Glennon operated and it allowed his quiet power to reach far and wide, while not subjecting it to criticism.

A local committee of the Midwest Clergy Conference on Negro Welfare was behind Foster's application. When word reached them that Glennon quietly scuttled the application, the conference wrote him a letter trying to get his decision into public view. Glennon summoned Father Patrick Molloy, only two years a priest and a signatory to the letter. Is this a "Jesuit ploy?" Glennon asked. Molloy said no. Glennon told him to go back to his parish and listen to his pastor. Molloy chuckled and noted that his pastor was a signatory too. Molloy then reminded Glennon of the principles involved. Glennon ended the meeting and had Molloy transferred to a parish far away from his African American parishioners.[31]

Glennon's denial of Aloyse Foster's application for fall semester 1943 gained national attention. The *Pittsburgh Courier*, a major national African American newspaper, made Foster a front-page story on February 5, 1944.[32] The newspaper reached the St. Louis conference and the hands of a young Jesuit priest.

Knowing that the University was considering the subject, a brave young archaeologist named Rev. Claude Herman Heithaus, S.J., Ph.D., also a member of the St. Louis conference, saw an opportunity to force the issue. He was still new on the faculty of SLU, having been in place only a few years. Father Heithaus was an early proponent of desegregation and was considering making a bold move—one that would bring the leadership of the local church down upon him and would, for a time, end his career here. He was OK with that. He was about to take on a human rights issue that was more important.

Father Heithaus received his doctorate in London and worked archeological sites in Syria, Lebanon, and elsewhere in the Middle East in the 1920s. By 1940, he was back in his hometown and back at his undergraduate alma mater, Saint Louis University. Father Heithaus had been trained around the world, and had seen the shortcomings of the United States. He was quoted in the *St. Louis Globe-Democrat* in 1941 as saying "We of America demolish our past to make a desert, then go to Europe to see what we have destroyed."[33]

"Even the Pews Stood Up"

On February 11, 1944, Heithaus challenged the status quo. He challenged his school, his employer, his church, and his order of priests to a new and higher calling—that of integration. He knew his remarks would be controversial and that people would try to silence him, so he made plans. He gave the text of his homily to the school newspaper in advance (it helped that he was the newspaper's faculty advisor). He invited one of the editors from the *Post-Dispatch* to be in the choir loft of the St. Francis Xavier church. After sacred readings, it was time for Father Heithaus's homily to a church filled with 500 students. He did not hold back.

He started off by denouncing racial intolerance and injustice. "[To] some followers of Christ, the color of a man's skin makes all the difference in the world." He noted that SLU admitted Protestants, Jews, Muslims, pagans, and even atheists in the spirit of "teach all nations," yet would seemingly "slam our doors in the face of Catholics because their skin complexion happens to be brown or black." He exhorted the students in attendance to commit themselves to ending the injustice and do all in their power to prevent it from happening further. The crowd jumped to its feet and "even the pews stood up," in favor of his words. His superiors were stunned.[34]

President Holloran reprimanded him and told him never to speak publicly on the subject again. Archbishop Glennon was furious, and called both Holloran and Heithaus to his office for a scolding. But it was too late—the dye was cast. A week later, Heithaus was invited to speak to the department store workers union at the Kings-Way Hotel on the same topic, where he encouraged other institutions to follow suit.[35]

Heithaus's plan had worked. Several weeks after the February homily, President Holloran received a call from the US Jesuit Superior's office. He was instructed to integrate Saint Louis University.[36] By mid-April 1944, five African Americans were admitted to Saint Louis University—three public school teachers for summer coursework in the Graduate School and two men as undergraduates in the College of Arts and Sciences.[37] Heithaus pleaded with students to reject prejudice and "never again to have any part in the wrongs white men have done Negroes."[38]

The Pine Street YMCA awarded Father Heithaus a scroll to honor his work in desegregating the university.[39] In October, Saint Louis University was nominated for a "St. Louis Award," a cash award of $1,000 and endorsed by a blue-ribbon commission of the city's elite along with the Mayor Aloys Kaufmann. It remains the city's highest honor. It was to honor SLU for its decision to admit African Americans.[40]

Segregation Ended, Racism Didn't

Despite the praise being heaped on SLU for its decision, it was not going well for President Holloran. He had instructed Father Heithaus to quit speaking publicly about integration, and clearly was feeling pressure about the decision to desegregate. He was caught between his Jesuit superiors (who favored integration) and the Archbishop Glennon (who did not).

Holloran's relationship with Heithaus was tense ever since the homily in February 1944 that started it all. The tension climaxed over the Student Conclave, a formal prom held at the Hotel Jefferson on April 13, 1945.

Holloran allegedly instructed the hotel's management that the African American students were not to be admitted if they were to attend the event. Further, he arranged for a police detail to be present just in case some kind of student demonstration formed outside. Further, he had instructed Heithaus, who was also the faculty advisor for the SLU newspaper, to publicize the event in the *University News*. Heithaus said that, in good conscience, he could not call anything a student dance when the students of color were not included. He refused to insert the publicity. Fr. Holloran

Father Claude Heithaus, S.J. St. Louis Post-Dispatch staff photo, 1944. Newspapers.com

reminded Heithaus that, as a Jesuit, he had no choice but to obey the orders of his superiors. Father Heithaus asked to be relieved of his duties.[41]

Father Heithaus then traveled to St. Mary's, Kansas, where he reported to Father Joseph P. Zuercher, S.J., leader of the Missouri Province of Jesuits (which included a much larger territory than just Missouri, and to whom Holloran reported in the Jesuit hierarchy). Father Zuercher took up the matter with his provincial advisors and reported to Holloran that he could not support the decision to keep African American students from the prom. As a result, Holloran withdrew his restrictions and four African American couples attended the evening. Once again, Father Heithaus's actions of conscience undermined President Holloran's social conformity.[42] Heithaus would not be welcome at Saint Louis University for more than a decade.

Holloran's heart health began to decline shortly thereafter, and he stepped down from his leadership role in September 1948 to recuperate in Texas. Father Paul Reinert, S.J., then vice-president of the university, took on the presidency in an acting capacity. In the spring of 1949, Reinert took on the permanent role and Holloran returned for a time to a faculty position in philosophy and as the director of the very alumni association that he had written earlier to discern if integration was a good move.[43]

In the 1957-58 school year, Father Holloran was sent to a Jesuit high school in Kansas, and later went into parish work in Illinois.[44] That same year, Father Heithaus was recalled to St. Louis University—after a 14 year absence—and installed as a professor of classical languages, and curator of the St. Stanislaus Museum in Florissant upon his retirement.[45]

Holloran had been only 36 years old when he took on the presidency. Archbishop Glennon at the time described him then as "a young president with an old head."[46] Upon Holloran's death in 1969 at age 62, his successor Paul Reinert was generous in describing Holloran's leadership on the matter of integration: "The young leader took a bold step when he opened the university to all interested young people, making her the Missouri pioneer in the march toward equal rights and educational opportunity."[47]

SLU was the first segregated university in a former slavery state to desegregate. It was Heithaus who forced the hand, who was the internal voice of dissent, who was the moral conscience. There was never an apology for his banishment from SLU and he was never thanked or acknowledged by the institution during his lifetime.[48] The priests of the St. Louis conference showed bravery right alongside Heithaus.

Gail Milissa Grant noted that others had worked to pressure SLU to open its doors to all students. Charles H. Anderson, an African American teacher at Sumner High School, was denied admission because "his presence would be resented by the student body."[49] Anderson saw through the thinly veiled disguise and called out the racism. He was determined to find out if a majority of students really objected to his presence. Grant noted that Anderson continued his protest regularly and publicly.[50] After SLU opened its doors to all students, Anderson wrote a glowing letter to the *Post-Dispatch*, praising SLU for its action: "commissions can meet and meet, and talk and talk, but…it's action that counts."[51]

When Holloran was pressed on how his letter writing project about desegregation went, he could only say that the responses "varied," but acknowledged "the student body was found to be entirely favorable" thanks to Father Heithaus. Charles Anderson must have been gratified to read that, since that was the excuse made to him for denial of his application just a few years earlier.[52]

There is a pattern here, with a distinct lesson for St. Louis. There are many St. Louisans, regular folks as well as people in positions of power, people who profess goodness and godliness, that have a blind spot when it comes to human rights—having witnessed tumult their whole lives but not calling it out for what it was. Change in this case (then and now) requires a firm hand, guided by a moral conscience, prepared to drag the population kicking and screaming to its new reality. It's not quite how the great scholar Thomas Kuhn meant "paradigm shift" to happen, but at least it happened.

A PIECE OF THE PIE

As St. Louis moved into mid-century, there was a man who desired to unclutter some of the politics that he saw. He was OK with the larger societal process being whatever it was, but he intended to consolidate the African American part of power in his own organization. He did it well.

The "Negro Mayor of St. Louis"

African American power in mid-century St. Louis was centered around one man—Jordan W. Chambers (1896-1962). He was the political boss of the 19th Ward and he never endorsed Raymond Tucker in a primary.

Chambers was an "old-style paternalistic boss" who wielded an "iron fist in a silk glove."[53] He believed in delivering material things to Black voters. He saw Civil Rights as being an "individual" thing and saw little reason to help someone who was capable of helping himself. "His more successful and educated friends" knew this and didn't rely on him. Chambers championed the underdog—"as long as the underdog stayed on his leash."[54]

Disliking Raymond Tucker

Right off the bat, the civic-minded college professor who eschewed bargaining wasn't going to be Chambers' friend. Chambers in this sense was a shrewd politician. He leveraged the need he saw in the Black community and would occasionally push the boundaries of Black employment of the day.[55] By and large, though, he built his power on patronage jobs.

He took an "ombudsman/employment agency approach" to patronage.[56] If an employment slot existed for a man, Chambers would "try his darndest" to make it happen. If it did not exist, Chambers would try to get it created. A key goal was to help the worker maintain his self-respect.[57]

Think back to the merit system that emerged in 1941 during Chambers' reign. The man who drafted that charter amendment was Raymond R. Tucker—whose "do the right thing" attitude could be grating against ward politicians like Chambers.

Lana Stein notes that Joseph L. McLemore, an African American attorney, said that the merit system would protect employees from being dismissed "as long as he is efficient."[58] Furthermore, "any plan that classifies people on the basis of merit should appeal to Negroes who are seldom given the consideration they merit." This was not the position of Jordan

Chambers. Chambers wanted political assurances that he could deliver jobs, and the merit system did not give those assurances.

In fact, Chambers already had a grudge against Tucker over clean coal. Recall that it was Raymond Tucker who devised the mandate to burn expensive hard anthracite coal instead of the cheaper high-sulfur soft bituminous coal that was readily available across the river in Illinois. Chambers was furious at the economic injustice of such a move.

Chambers blamed Tucker for inflicting extra costs on the poor. "Most of those who still used coal were poor, and anthracite coal cost almost twice as much per ton as bituminous."[59] The burden of clean air was hitting the poor— and Jordan's constituents in the 19th Ward—harder than other groups in the city. Tucker tried to counter these criticisms with explanations that anthracite has more BTUs for the money, and bituminous contains a large amount of inert slate, which only makes the coal heavier and does not add to its BTU value. The technical explanation was lost on ward politicians like Chambers, who only focused on the bottom line. The coal issue was a big victory for environmentalism, but made life more difficult in the city's working-class neighborhoods. Though Chambers grudgingly supported the Democrats in the 1941 election, and Dickmann endorsed Chambers' candidate for 19th Ward Alderman, the Democrats were crushed—not only losing the mayoralty, but also 16 seats on the Board of Aldermen (a majority of the board's 28 seats).[60] It was a political disaster.

Influencing Higher Office

Chambers focused on influencing higher offices as well. In 1934, Chambers (as well as Mayor Dickmann) put his effort behind Congressman John J. Cochran to be elected to the U. S. Senate. While Cochran won St. Louis, he lost statewide to Harry Truman. In 1940, Chambers got behind Truman's Senate campaign and let him know it.

Truman's opponent in 1940 was Governor Lloyd Stark, a nurseryman from Louisiana, MO who was the inventor of the Golden Delicious apple. Stark did not employ any African Americans at his nursery 90 miles north of St. Louis, and Chambers took aim at him. Stark had a fundraiser aboard the

S. S. Admiral on the St. Louis riverfront (segregated at that time). Chambers had 100,000 political cartoons printed, depicting Stark standing at the boat's entrance under a sign "No Negroes Allowed."[61] Truman carried the 19th Ward and was re-elected statewide.

A Singular Force for Success

Jordan Chambers was a force to be reckoned with. In some ways, he was an old-fashioned politician who worked through existing means to deliver patronage to his constituents. In other ways, he was groundbreaking leader of "Black is Beautiful" long before it was a popular slogan. He was "more akin to a Black Power advocate than to [organized interests]" said one scholar, placing him more in the camp of assertives rather than pragmatists. Yet, Chambers was pragmatic. Aldermanic President Don Gunn (a Tucker ally) said "Chambers would probably go to the white man and offer to withdraw in exchange

This Paul Monroe postcard from the 1940s shows the excursion boat Admiral with the description of how these groups of people, "colored as well as white," enjoy watching the river roll by. Persons of color would not be allowed to enjoy the Admiral until after 1962. Theising image, Author's collection.

for practical considerations."[62] The end for Chambers was delivering the goods.

The case of Herbert Duckett, a black chemist, exemplified Chambers' technique in handling patronage jobs.   Duckett wanted a job with the Municipal Testing Laboratory. Chambers got Duckett the job, but his Republican boss threatened to have him fired as incompetent. Jordan Chambers and a friend went to the boss's office and tossed a series of questions back and forth. "Is this guy Duckett's boss?" "Is he a holdover from the old administration?" "Have we appropriated the money for his salary?"[63] Duckett kept the job. In a sense, Duckett was atypical, for Chambers usually championed the unskilled underdog—as long as the underdog stayed on his leash.

Gail Milissa Grant noted that the chemist Duckett was process-minded and, like Tucker, helped abate the smoke and enforce the ordinance. [64]   In 1942, he was credited with discovering (and helping arrest) a coal dealer who had smuggled seven tons of dirty coal to a rooming house on Page Avenue.[65]

Chambers was a successful man, politically and materially. He controlled the 19th Ward specifically and Black politics generally. He was referred to multiple times as the "Negro Mayor of St. Louis," as early as 1931 and certainly into the 40s, 50s, and 60s.[66] He was a successful labor organizer, undertaker, constable, and nightclub owner (Club Riviera). He was always well dressed in a white Stetson and a string tie. He wore a diamond ring, smoked expensive cigars, and drove a fine Cadillac. He owned racehorses and sponsored a boxer named "Kid Riviera" after his nightclub. He loved hosting big bands at his club on Delmar. He knew everything and everyone in the 19th Ward—the good and the bad. He enjoyed a wide circle of friends, but made sure their hands were clean ("if too many worms got into the apple, there would be no apple left").[67]

The scholar Mary Welek, who wrote a thorough academic piece on Chambers in the 1960s, describes him as a complicated subject. He was a successful businessman, "but his methods were not always commendable;" he campaigned hard for his candidates and made issues simple to understand, but "he was not always above using smear tactics or twisting the facts;" and he lived by the lesson he learned early on— "he must either be a

135

leader or a loser."[68] He was on the losing side almost as often as he was on the winning side, but he was always a leader.   And, Welek noted, he remained consistently opposed to Raymond R. Tucker's administration and its emphasis on "good government."[69]

THE FISSURES WITHIN THE MOVEMENT

There always has been a great juxtaposition within the Civil Rights movement—perhaps better described as two sides of the same coin. On the one side is realism or pragmatism (working through existing rules, boundaries, and structures) and on the other side is idealism (focusing on larger issues of justice without concern for existing arrangements).   This has been on display for nearly two centuries.

There were the early arguments around the abolition of slavery, even at the constitutional convention.   Some were willing to compromise on the matter to achieve an end, others would not even consider it.   Booker T. Washington, a pragmatist, spoke of ways to maximize quality of life within the existing social boundaries.   At the same time, W.E.B. DuBois, an activist, advocated tearing down the boundaries altogether and rebuilding them anew.

Martin Luther King Jr., an activist, used nonviolent civil disobedience to challenge boundaries and force communities to make decisions on integration (which certainly entailed violence on the part of the oppressors).   Malcolm X, a militant by comparison, criticized King's approach and goals, pushing for the exercise of Black Power and autonomy apart from mainstream society.

This same juxtaposition appeared in the Civil Rights movements in St. Louis.   There were circles that wanted to use existing structures to achieve their ends, while other circles wanted to challenge those structures and tear them down in order to build anew.   Both of these elements worked to achieve a measure of racial justice in St. Louis (granted, the "measure" achieved remains small).

The Splintering of Black Power:
NAACP Goes beyond Chambers

While Jordan Chambers consolidated political power and patronage, he was not necessarily fighting in the trenches in the larger battle of Civil Rights. That was the work of W. E. B. DuBois's NAACP. Patronage jobs were important because there was often a "lug" associated with them—a 1% or so "tax" on income to the machine for the courtesy of getting the job.[70]

The NAACP in St. Louis was powerful and proud of its heritage. It counted powerful people among its leaders, especially attorney Margaret Bush Wilson. Mrs. Wilson would become a towering figure within the NAACP, serving on its board and eventually leading the national organization (though not without controversy) from 1963 to 1983.

When attorney David M. Grant was the chapter's president in the mid-1940s, he began to challenge racial discrimination using the courts, coming up with clever approaches in a time when court decisions did not lean in favor of Civil Rights. In the summer of 1945, a year after Saint Louis University desegregated, the NAACP under Grant made a move to challenge segregation at Washington University in St. Louis. "This is a white school and always has been," said Grant to the *Post-Dispatch*.[71] The legal challenge was to its tax-exempt status on downtown buildings it owned. The City of St. Louis had already brought suit, stating that these were not educational buildings and were, therefore, taxable. However, Grant applied to the court to intervene with the city and adding the argument that being tax-exempt meant that all taxpayers were forced to support the institution yet the institution did not serve all taxpayers.[72] The suit was unsuccessful.

The NAACP nationally declared 1948 to be its best year ever, making "slow but steady" progress through the courts and legislatures.[73] The national organization's Executive Secretary told the *Post-Dispatch* that he was gratified by the numbers of students, churchgoers, labor unions, and others who "are slowly forming an effective bloc against bigotry."[74] To be certain, the St. Louis chapter was playing its role well.

Washington University board president Harry Brookings Wallace (nephew of famous philanthropist Robert S. Brookings, who had also been board president) responded to the press was that the institution was chartered by the State of Missouri and merely was following the example of that state's educational institutions. The 1927 Nobel Prize-winning chancellor Arthur Holly Compton—who had just arrived at Washington University—at first made no comment, but later noted that "local social attitudes" prevented the school from integrating.[75]

In its early years, William Greenleaf Eliot's university did admit and graduate African Americans. This practice fell away in 1892, later supported by the *Plessy v. Ferguson* (1896) decision. When the Medical School accidentally admitted an African American to the ophthalmology program in 1947, it allowed integration of that unit.[76] The George Warren Brown School of Social Work followed later that same year.

Chancellor Compton finally desegregated the entire campus for the fall term of 1952, and resigned soon afterward.[77] He stayed around for the university's centennial celebration in January 1953 and submitted his resignation to the board that April.

The Splintering of Black Power:
CORE Goes beyond NAACP

The NAACP was *the* voice of Civil Rights in St. Louis for decades. In 1947, though, the Committee *of* (sometimes "*on*") Racial Equality (CORE) was formed. It was later re-named the Congress of/on Racial Equality, and started independently of the Chicago-based 1942 national CORE movement.[78] It grew out of the NAACP's Youth Council and was populated with younger working-class people "that the NAACP had been unable, or unwilling, to mobilize" said historian Clarence Lang.[79]

CORE included leaders like Norman Seay, husband-and-wife team attorney Charles R. Oldham (who was white) and Marian C. O'Fallon Oldham (who was Black), as well as the man who was a rising political force: William L. Clay. Their protests challenged the status quo with sit-ins and "passive resistance"— where participants were to "show no anger, no matter how...provoked." [80] Their work was done without much attention, in the sense that the major St. Louis newspapers coordinated a "black out" of stories—fearing any publicity of their work would encourage lawlessness.[81] The *Post-Dispatch* later acknowledged this to be true.

CORE was more aggressive than the NAACP, though with the same goals. CORE was more proactive, seeking out offending institutions rather than responding to plans and opportunities, or relying on courts. It had a more in-your-face quality that made white residents open their eyes to racism in their daily routines (banks, theaters, lunch counters), rather than the institutional approaches of lawsuits, panel appointments, and research reports.

Still, CORE was not active enough for rapidly changing times. Some members became disenchanted with CORE. After scoring a big victory at Jefferson Bank (discussed in a following chapter), the group rested on its laurels according to some. Most notably, Percy Green II (discussed in the following section) and Richard Daly (a white man) climbed the Gateway Arch under construction and pushed the Civil Rights movement into a new chapter by forming the Action Committee to Improve Opportunities for Negroes (ACTION). When asked why ACTION was necessary in St. Louis, Green was blunt: the white power structure had coopted the NAACP (and the Urban League), and CORE lost interest in civil disobedience after the Jefferson Bank success.[82] It cost Green his job. The region needed an aggressive pursuit of Civil Rights and an open challenge to barriers, and ACTION filled that role.

The Man of ACTION

The great Percy Green II has proven to be a giant force for Civil Rights. He had grown impatient with the "tea and cookies" approach to Civil Rights—which honestly included Mayor Tucker and the local NAACP.[83] Green was at the forefront of the Civil Rights Movement in St. Louis, under the banners of the NAACP, CORE, and ACTION. The latter was founded in January 1965—just a few months before Mayor Tucker left office.

When the rest of St. Louis's Civil Rights leaders agreed that "protest measures are less necessary or no longer adequate" thanks to the Civil Rights Act of 1964 (including Bill Clay), Percy Green was the only holdout. He valued "militant" action and lamented that corporate funding streams for such work "were channeled to the groups that do little."[84]

He was the activist of all activists. Notably, he organized the unmasking of the Veiled Prophet at St. Louis's highest social ball, he climbed the leg of the Gateway Arch to protest a lack of jobs for African Americans, and sat himself down in Mayor Tucker's City Hall to keep the issues of Civil Rights fresh in the minds of leadership. He protested Missouri's participation in the New York World's Fair, noting the spending was a lower priority than addressing African American unemployment in St. Louis.[85] He sat silently in the City Treasurer's Office to protest city funds being held in banks that discriminate, and was carried out by police.[86] He even attempted to get a marriage license with a white woman, and was turned away. Green was told that interracial marriage violated an 1851 Missouri law and was considered "a felony punishable by imprisonment in the State Penitentiary for a period of two years."[87]

He protested the lack of legal protections for African Americans inside the U.S. Attorney's Office in St. Louis, leading to a telephone conference between the Green, the U.S.

Percy Green II lays down to protest the unfair hiring practices in the construction of the Gateway Arch. Rackwitz photo. St. Louis Post-Dispatch, July 15, 1964. Newspapers.com

Attorney, and the Deputy Attorney General in Washington DC, who agreed to inform the President of the demonstration.[88] Three months later, that same U.S. Attorney requested that charges be dropped against Green for his action at the Gateway Arch.[89]

He protested the hiring practices at McDonnell Aircraft, one of St. Louis's major employers and his own—and from which he was terminated. He led a group to have a "stall-in" of cars blocking key intersections near McDonnell's production facility and led a picket in front of James McDonnell's house in Ladue.[90]

He did more than protest in the streets and offices. He wrote letters to the editor, calling out bad behavior.[91] He called out labor union practices that excluded African Americans.[92] He even filed legal action against discriminatory business, filing the first formal complaint in St. Louis under the Civil Rights Act of 1964.[93] His case against McDonnell-Douglas went all the way to the United States Supreme Court and, in 1973, the court forever shifted the burden of proof in certain labor disputes.[94]

He led a boycott against Anheuser-Busch products when the brewery's main distributor would not hire more African American truck drivers. The firm responded that it had "received no application from qualified Negroes...."[95]

He had a falling out with the NAACP by 1965, after Tucker's term had ended. He said, "The NAACP was part of the 'white power structure' that controls St. Louis and had 'sold out the Negro community.'"[96] He had moved along a very different path.

Process vs. Protest

At the 1961 annual meeting of the National Baptist Convention in St. Louis, president Dr. Joseph H. Jackson noted that he would not criticize protesters, but favored the approach of the NAACP and fighting in the courts as being "by far the strongest and most effective" path, being "a more wholesome approach, more fruitful."[97] He continued, "Protest alone is not enough. The next step forward for the Negro race in America will be beyond protest. ...It will come by our own efforts...to use the resources at our command" to build a better community for all.[98]

Both paths were valuable: protest and process. Someone needs to keep the issue front-and-center so that voters do not grow apathetic, and someone else needs to keep the pressure on courts and legislatures. There was room for both and both performed admirably in the face of blatant opposition.

MAYORAL EFFORTS

Early Hopes for Racial Equity

The first real discussion of a public accommodation law in St. Louis came after the State of Missouri convened a new constitutional convention in 1944. Basically, the law would require private places "open to the public" to be open to ALL of the public. The old document was a relic from 1875 that had only been amended modestly since then. Civil Rights proponents, including the Mayor Kaufmann's new St. Louis Race Relations Commission, endorsed a public accommodation provision in the new document (that would render St. Louis's segregation null and void). When that failed at the state level, greater attention was paid at the local level.

Kaufmann's Commission was important, in that it was an official vehicle for change at a time when there were very few choices. He had convened the commission in 1943. Among the commission's leadership team was Edwin Meissner, a highly active civic and religious leader who was president of the St. Louis Car Company (the country's largest maker of streetcars and railcars). Among the commission's membership was Fannie Cook, author and outspoken advocate for civil rights. The two had a terrific clash in 1946. When Cook learned that members of Meissner's leadership team had given backroom assurances to downtown department stores that their tea rooms and lunch counters would not be desegregated by the commission, she exploded. She publicly condemned the actions of the commissioners involved.

Meissner called her "a starry-eyed housewife, bright and sweet, but totally inexperienced in the affairs of the world."[99]

He called for her resignation. Cook, however, was already there. She submitted her resignation to Mayor Kaufmann. He begged her not to leave, but she refused to participate in the hypocrisy. The press release Meissner gave was a short and sweet cover-up. "Mrs. Cook resigned solely because of the press of other duties and expressed her willingness to continue to cooperate with the commission in improving race relations here."[100]

In 1946, an anti-discrimination amendment to the city's charter was passed, but it only applied to public services not private entities.[101] Rewriting the city charter could achieve a similar outcome in the private sector, too, and Raymond Tucker was leading the Board of Freeholders that was doing just that in 1949.

Attorney Eugene H. Buder, representing the St. Louis Civil Liberties Committee (different from the mayoral commission), offered the Freeholders an enabling clause that would allow local Civil Rights legislation to be passed by the Board of Aldermen (recall that the State of Missouri still had segregation laws in effect, so the City of St. Louis would need permission to go around state laws). The Board of Aldermen had let a public accommodations bill die in its 1947-48 session, and would do the same in 1948-49.[102] The *Post-Dispatch* noted in a lengthy pro-Civil Rights feature in 1950 that St. Louis was the only city in the major leagues where African American baseball players are barred from the hotels where their team plays.[103]

A special committee of Tucker's Board of Freeholders, consisting of four lawyers, held a hearing on the matter in December 1949.[104] More than two-dozen supporters from civic groups, church groups, labor unions, the Mayor's commission, men's groups, and women's groups outlined the benefit of public accommodations. The four attorneys were not swayed. "It appears that the special committee did not even submit the matter to the full board" for a vote, said the chairman of the Interracial Commission of the Metropolitan Church Federation in a letter to Tucker. "If you don't like the bills [we] offered, [then] do it your own way, perhaps in some covering statement like a preamble..." said the Federation leadership.[105] There would be no Civil Rights section of the proposed charter.

It could have been purely a legal interpretation by the lawyers—no Missouri city had such authority to enforce public accommodation, no matter how appealing the idea was. It was rejected as part of the state's 1945 constitution and there was no enabling legislation from Jefferson City. Missouri was still a segregated state.

What must have helped quash the idea of pushing boundaries—though no one would admit it—was the fresh memory of the race riot at Fairground Park on June 21, 1949. When the St. Louis Director of Public Welfare deemed there was no justification for denying African Americans access to city swimming pools, the gates were opened to one and all. The resulting riot by whites against African American swimmers forced Mayor Darst to reinstate the segregation policy after only one day.[106] This glimpse of racial violence from beneath the city's sludge showed to all—even the pragmatic Tucker—that white voters were at their limit regarding Civil Rights. [107]

The Early Attempts at Public Accommodation

The demand facing leadership at mid-century was for "public accommodation" rules—that any place "open to the public" is indeed open to "all" the public, be it in the public sector or the private sector. Theaters, restaurants, hotels, transportation, and even churches adhered to the social norm of segregation. When Mayor Tucker took office in April 1953, St. Louis still did not have a public accommodation ordinance that would regulate discrimination in the private sector, though there had been action on public sector protections.

In 1946, Alderman Jasper C. Caston, a Republican from the 6th Ward and one of two African Americans on the Board of Aldermen, introduced an amendment to the city charter that would prohibit racial discrimination in city hiring. (He had also proposed one for private sector hiring, but the city counselor's office said that it was illegal.)[108] He worked with the local branch of the NAACP to devise the amendment. Voters narrowly approved the amendment (receiving just 1,000 votes over the minimum 3/5 threshold, with over 85,000 votes cast).[109] The Board of Aldermen, then-Mayor Aloys Kaufmann (Republican), and several African American groups had endorsed its passage.

The legal concern over the city's ability to enact a public

accommodation ordinance rested with the tenet laid out in *Dillon's Rule*. This philosophy, created by Judge John F. Dillon of Iowa in an 1868 case, is still respected today. Simply stated, cities can exercise only the powers given them by the state.[110] By this rule, St. Louis did not have authority either from the state legislature or in the state's constitution to start exercising such power over the private sector.

The Changing Landscape: *Shelley v. Kraemer* (1948)

It is unclear what changed in the 1950s that cities felt empowered to take on Civil Rights activity. Perhaps it was the pressure from activists at street level. Missouri did not even convene a commission on the subject until 1957, and produced no legislation until 1965 (at the behest of Washington DC).[111] The Congress did not take any action until 1957, and again in 1964. What may have given some legal wiggle-room to cities was the landmark US Supreme Court case *Shelley v. Kraemer* (1948)—a case that originated in St. Louis.

This was the decision that ended the enforceability in court of racially restrictive deed covenants. Missouri state courts had upheld the ability to enforce such covenants, but on appeal the Supreme Court disagreed. Such enforcement was a violation of the equal protection clause of the 14th Amendment to the Constitution because it denied ownership or occupancy to citizens based on race.[112]

J. D. and Ethel Shelley, an African American couple, purchased a home at 4600 Labadie in October 1945. Shortly thereafter, Mrs. Louis Kraemer who lived at 4632 Labadie sued to prevent them from moving in, since the property was covered by a restrictive covenant. The initial judgment from Circuit Judge William K. Koerner was in favor of the Shelleys, but Mrs. Kraemer appealed to the Missouri Supreme Court that reversed Koerner's decision. The Shelleys appealed to the United States Supreme Court, which ruled that such covenants violated the Constitution and were unenforceable in any court.[113] The Shelleys lived in the house throughout the legal challenge. A variety of church and professional groups helped fund the case.

Mrs. Shelley noted that she and her husband just wanted a safe place to raise their children. "Riding around, we saw this

Ethel Shelley reads about her successful court case in the Post-Dispatch. Post-Dispatch photo. May 8, 1948

house with a 'for sale' sign on it, and on the sidewalk there was a colored youngster playing. We didn't have any idea about the restrictions," she told news reporters. She added, "For land's sake, if I'd known all the court fight that was coming, we'd have run like rabbits."[114]

The Shelleys lived on the first floor of the house they owned; the second floor was rented to Mr. and Mrs. George Edelen, a white couple who were content to stay where they were.[115] *Amicus curiae* briefs were filed on behalf of the Shelleys by several prominent names: Eugene H. Buder, the Civil Liberties attorney who tried to get public accommodation into the 1950 charter; Luther Ely Smith, considered to be the "founder" of the Jefferson National Expansion Memorial; and, somewhat surprisingly, Alger Hiss on behalf of the American United Nations Association—he would be put on trial during the 1950s as a spy for the Soviet Union.[116] The restrictive covenant itself was created in 1911 and was to last 50 years—so an expiration date of 1961.[117]

A lesser-known provision of the *Shelley* ruling is that people could voluntarily enter into such agreements. This was interpreted at the time meaning that a group of white property owners could themselves voluntarily collude to restrict their home sales.[118] The Supreme Court later declared even this discriminatory behavior unconstitutional in another St. Louis area case as a violation of the 1964 Civil Rights Act's public accommodation provision—*Jones vs. Mayer* (1968). Samuel Liberman II argued that case. He was the son of Tucker's city counselor, Samuel H. Liberman, who raised the *Dillon's Rule* issue back in the 1940s.[119]

George L. Vaughn argued the *Shelley* case before the Supreme Court (among others, including the great jurist Thurgood Marshall). He was a longtime ally of Jordan Chambers and an executive with the local branch of the NAACP. He died the following year (age 69) and was buried at the Washington Park Cemetery near the St. Louis Lambert Airport.[120]

This was an important case on many levels, but for the case of public accommodation it had special relevance. This ruling basically said that discriminatory agreements in the private sector could not be enforced in court. Therefore, if St. Louis were to enforce public accommodation and it were challenged, there now was legal precedent that state courts could not participate in enforcing the private-sector discrimination. Any challenge would have to be on other grounds.

Armed with this new legal precedent and after the defeat of the proposed new city charter, a public accommodation ordinance was introduced to the Board of Aldermen—again.

A Proposal for the Aldermen

Sam Liberman, the same attorney who advised the charter commission that it did not have authority to enact a public accommodation clause in 1950, speaking as City Counselor in Tucker's first term, advised the mayor that the city indeed did have it by 1953.

The Board of Aldermen took up the matter in its 1953-54 session, and the bill died in committee. The Board took it up again in the 1954-55 session at the urging of Tucker's Council on Human Relations, and the bill made it out of committee, but was sent back for further study.[121] The Council pushed the bill again in the 1955-56 session, to no avail.[122] The bill never got out of committee and the surprised Human Relations Council sent a sharply-worded rebuke: "We believe the Board of Aldermen has a clear responsibility to act now on this matter and not to permit further delay!"[123]

Liberman's office continued to indicate that the city had such authority and drafted what would become the first public accommodation ordinance for St. Louis.[124] Earlier versions of the public accommodation ordinance were introduced in 1948 and 1953. Aldermen, including Alfonso Cervantes at first, defeated Liberman's bill in 1955, and again in 1956, 1958, 1959, and 1960.[125]

In the 1956-57 session, two bills emerged—one from the Human Relations Council and another from the four African American aldermen, including Archie Blaine. Mayor Tucker personally addressed the Board. He rejected the Blaine bill out of hand because it did not include or incorporate the Human Relations Council, to which the city had given authority on the matter. Tucker spoke on the Council bill's importance and pleaded for its passage. Cries of "boo" were heard from the gallery after he finished. Board President and Tucker ally Donald Gunn said, "it would take courage to vote for it, but I remind you the price of freedom is never cheap."[126] The full board voted both bills down.

A different strategy was employed in the 1957-58 session. The public accommodations bill would establish a new branch of the Human Relations Council that would be in charge of enforcement and manage complaints. The legislative committee noted that it could not reach a decision at its first debate, and would "continue studying the matter" after the holiday recess—which functionally killed the bill.[127]

Yet another attempt was made in the 1958-59 session. This version of the bill made it to the full board for a vote, but once again could not get a majority of support.[128] Tucker personally vowed to resubmit the bill in the next session.[129]

For the 1959-60 session, Tucker called on the aldermen to pass the bill this time. The bill "[was] needed for a forward-looking St. Louis," he said.[130] It fell on deaf ears, again.

Hopes were high for the 1960-61 session. Ten aldermen came together to sponsor the bill this time. It laid out the law and set up the measures by which the Human Relations Council would enforce it, along with time frames and legal referrals.[131] Finally, the Board passed it in the spring! On a 20-4 vote, the bill was approved (four were absent).[132] Mayor Tucker proudly signed the long-sought bill. Then the lawsuits started, from restaurants, bars, and one prominent riverboat.

Strekfus Steamers Inc., owner of the whites-only *Admiral* excursion boat, filed suit to block the ordinance's enforcement against the boat and have the law declared unconstitutional.[133] The company argued, "the admission of Negroes in large numbers could result in disturbances while the vessel is out on the Mississippi River with no police protection available."[134] It added that it operated on the water, which was outside of the city's jurisdiction. Further, it said the ordinance was an "improper" use of the city's power and amounted to "undue interference" with a private business. [135] In making its jurisdictional argument, Strekfus gave the city grounds to get the case dismissed. Federal anti-discrimination law already applied to interstate river carriers and Strekfus now was in violation of that.

A major concern (that never materialized) was the status of Homer G. Phillips Hospital, which had been built under Mayor Dickmann's administration to serve the African American population of the city. Mayor Tucker already had desegregated the hospital system by executive order in 1955. Homer G. Phillips was a high-quality hospital that played an integral part in the education of generations of minority doctors and nurses. When a public accommodation complaint was filed because the hospital sent *white* patients to City Hospital #1 (the historically white hospital), fear popped up that Phillips would be closed. It earned a mention in the nationally distributed *Jet* magazine. Alderman William L. Clay claimed the complaints were being fueled by "officials [who] did not want to see the institution remain open."[136] While it was just a rumor, the NAACP leader Ernest Galloway said "giving up the hospital may be the price we have to pay for an integrated community."[137] The hospital remained open for another 25 years, but the rumor of impending closure was persistent.

The attorney George L. Vaughn, who represented the Shelleys' case before the United States Supreme Court. Theising image; Author's collection.

TUCKER'S RECORD ON CIVIL RIGHTS

Raymond Tucker was consistently in support of Civil Rights, from the Human Relations plank in his 1953 mayoral campaign to his advocacy and tenacity in supporting public accommodation for eight straight sessions of the legislature. He made several bold statements in favor of the rights of minorities and women.

Only weeks after becoming mayor, Tucker appointed the first female department head ever. He chose Virginia Brungard, a colleague from the 1949 Board of Freeholders, as the city's Director of Public Welfare—the city's largest department in terms of budget and employees.[138] She served admirably in the position until 1959, when Tucker appointed her director of the newly formed Department of Parks, Recreation, and Forestry.[139] While it made the front page of both daily newspapers, the *Globe-Democrat* (the conservative paper) treated it as major news and plastered the headline in large bold letters: TUCKER NAMES WOMAN TO CABINET.[140]

He declared December 9, 1955, as Human Rights Day in St. Louis—mirroring the national Human Rights Day championed by Eleanor Roosevelt and the United Nations. [141] Tucker believed in human rights, in human relations, and in equality—including between the races. He was consistent in these.

Tucker understood the call of the Supreme Court in the *Brown v. Board* (1954) decision. St. Louis had been changing long before *Brown*, though slowly and sometimes reluctantly. Tucker's own classrooms at Washington University began desegregating in 1949, and were completed across the board by 1952. His Jesuit alma mater had been desegregated by then, as had his church. An Anti-Defamation League study from 1956 praised Mayor Tucker in his level-headed response to the *Brown* decision: "The people of our community should accept calmly and intelligently the ruling of the Supreme Court, which holds that there must be no discrimination in the public schools of our nation." [142] He did not fight it; rather, he encouraged his fellow citizens to embrace it thoughtfully.

Tucker realized the public would still need some prodding. Dr. Walter Younge, an African American physician and professor at the Saint Louis University Medical School, lost his election to a school board seat by only 2,000 votes in the April 5, 1955, municipal election. On April 19, Mayor Tucker took the opportunity to appoint him to a board vacancy instead. In a sense, Tucker was willing to override the will of the voters to add diversity to the school board, and in doing so assured an important voice was added in the critical period after the *Brown vs. Board* (1954) decision. [143]

Tucker made local Civil Rights history again in 1961, when he appointed the first African American to a mayoral cabinet. He promoted Chester Stovall, who had been executive secretary of the Council on Human Relations and previously an Urban League executive, to the position of Director of Welfare. [144]

Tucker began a campaign in the summer of 1962 to rid Forest Park of the Triple-A tennis club, a private club that did not allow black members. Parks Director Virginia Brungard attempted to evict the club from its long lease with the city, and had the backing of an ordinance passed by the Board of Aldermen that gave the club 25 months to vacate (it had been in this place since 1919). [145] Club president Frank Thompson said that Tucker was using the club as "whipping boys" to secure the black vote in St. Louis—though the election was two years away and Tucker was then not a candidate for re-election.[146] The Club survived only by tying up the eviction in court until Tucker was no longer in office. His successor, Alfonso Cervantes, dropped the eviction.

Tucker was a leader in the United States Conference of Mayors. In the summer of 1963—the very same time the Jefferson Bank protest in underway—Tucker chaired a committee that put forth 26 resolutions, much of which was on civil rights topics. It would be the first time the conference took a stand on civil rights—even though it had prior opportunities to do so.[147] First, Tucker's committee endorsed President Kennedy's five points:

1. that bi-racial human relation committees be set up
2. care be taken to review local ordinances to ascertain their conformity with constitutional protections
3. municipal employees be hired and promoted in accordance with non-discriminatory practices
4. equal opportunities be provided for all people
5. school dropouts, which contribute to unemployment and other social and economic problems, be discouraged through positive action with juveniles

Tucker's committee, however, added a sixth item:
"That all citizens be encouraged to recognize the correlation of responsibility and duty with right, and that equality of responsibility be encouraged along with equality of opportunity."[148] Tucker believed in these principles.

Tucker was an imperfect man and there certainly were Civil Rights blunders (like the appointment of Harry Pope to the Human Rights Council, which is addressed in a following chapter.) His actions are not beyond reproach, but when he had a decision to make that would advance Civil Rights, he favored Civil Rights more often than not. The St. Louis Civil Liberties Committee honored him with the group's "Civil Liberties Award" for his long advocacy for public accommodation and improving the climate of St. Louis.[149]

In remarks to the first meeting of his Equal Employment Opportunity Commission, Mayor Tucker said that there must be "purposeful discussion" that "must welcome the most candid exchange of ideas and attitudes without personal rancor." He called on the commission to identify and describe specific practices of discrimination. "Further, the Commission's discussions must be systematically geared to an action program," noting that it would be a waste of time to be "a mere debating society."[150]

While it may be easy with hindsight to criticize Tucker for missing the memo where equality shifted to equity, he was a pragmatic man with a moral compass who believed in Civil Rights. He did more than talk the talk—he walked the walk. Tucker embraced Civil Rights before Congress passed the Civil Rights Act of 1964. Tucker embraced Civil Rights before the Supreme Court ruled in *Brown v. Board of Education.* Tucker embraced Civil Rights before Martin Luther King emerged on the scene at the Montgomery Bus Boycott. Tucker embraced Civil Rights from his first day in office.

Tucker did not place himself of the same opinion as those elected officials in more southern cities who openly opposed civil rights—and whose vitriolic antics had played out on news stories throughout the civil rights movement. "Civil rights leaders should adapt their tactics to the specific local situation," Tucker said. "Methods which are necessary in some localities where community leadership is opposed to their goals are surely not appropriate for St. Louis."[151] Tucker truly felt he was a friend of civil rights. He truly believed that breaking laws "debase[d] the serious principles involved" with Civil Rights. His greatest Civil Rights challenge was yet to come—the Jefferson Bank Protest. How will he react? He will react in his consistent, law-abiding, pragmatic, moral manner.

A listing of other items that add to Mayor Tucker's Civil Rights Record, in addition to the community engagement processes associated with these outcomes:[152]

- signed the first Fair Employment Practices Ordinance, July 10, 1956
- signed the public accommodation ordinance, June 1, 1961
- signed the second Fair Employment Practices Ordinances, including the prohibition of discriminatory practices in employment and training, November 29, 1962
- negotiated the desegregation of six restaurant chains, October 1960
- credited by State Senator T. D. McNeal for helping to secure Missouri's fair employment practices law, 1961 session
- called for (April 16, 1963) and signed (January 31, 1964) the city's Fair Housing Ordinance

ENDNOTES

[1] Witt 3:223

[2] "Priest Denounces Negroes' Moving into His Parish," *St. Louis Post-Dispatch*, 28 Apr 1918, PDF p. 34.

[3] Witt 3:225

[4] "Joseph Cardinal Ritter, 74, Dies; Liberal Archbishop of St. Louis," *The New York Times*. 11 Jun 1967, pp. 1, 86. (Spencer Tracy died the same day, and the two obituaries were front-page features in the *Times*.)

[5] Siegel dissertation, cited in Witt 3:227

[6] "Joseph Cardinal Ritter, 74, Dies; Liberal Archbishop of St. Louis," *The New York Times*. 11 Jun 1967, pp. 1, 86.

[7] "Archdiocese seeks to buy county home," *St. Louis Post-Dispatch*. 10 Apr 1947, PDF p. 23.

[8] Start, Clarissa. "New Cardinal Has Won Respect and Admiration as Administrator and Man of Deep Spirituality," *St. Louis Post-Dispatch*. 18 Dec 1960, p. 3A.

[9] "71 File Protests to Frontenac Annexation," *St. Louis Star and Times*. 01 Oct 1949, p. 4.

[10] Start, Clarissa. "New Cardinal Has Won Respect and Admiration as Administrator and Man of Deep Spirituality," *St. Louis Post-Dispatch*. 18 Dec 1960, p. 3A.

[11] "The Only Colored Priest," *St. Louis Post-Dispatch*. 06 Dec 1891, p. 10.

[12] Witt 3:213

[13] ibid. 3:214

[14] Schneider 73

[15] Witt 3:214

[16] "First English Mass in US Offered in St. Louis; Protestant Hymns Open and Close Rite before 11,000 in Kiel Auditorium," *The New York Times*. 25 Aug 1964, p. 21.

[17] Start, Clarissa. "New Cardinal Has Won Respect and Admiration as Administrator and Man of Deep Spirituality," *St. Louis Post-Dispatch*. 18 Dec 1960, p. 3A.

[18] Joseph Cardinal Ritter, 74, Dies; Liberal Archbishop of St. Louis," *The New York Times*. 11 Jun 1967, pp. 1, 86.

[19] Schneider 21. A bit of Catholic hierarchy explanation is needed here. While technically all religious in St. Louis have a reporting line to the archbishop, many institutions (universities, schools, hospitals, etc.) are special operations affiliated with the "order" of priests or sisters running them, and not the main-line operations of the archdiocese. St. Louis University, founded and operated by the

Jesuit order, desegregated independent of the local bishop. Various Catholic hospitals fell into this category as well.

[20] ibid.
[21] Toft (Phillips)
[22] Schneider 22
[23] ibid. 23
[24] ibid., emphasis added
[25] "St. L. U. Considers Accepting Negroes," *St. Louis Globe-Democrat* 28 Jan 1944, p. 13.
[26] ibid., all quotes in paragraph
[27] "Even the Pews..." *Policy and Commentary*. Posted Feb 2013. Accessed: 02-02-2022. https://nextstl.com/2013/02/even-the-pews-stood-up-the-forgotten-history-of-the-racial-integration-of-st-louis-university/
[28] ibid.
[29] ibid.
[30] Kemper 11
[31] Kemper 10-11, whole paragraph
[32] Kemper 11
[33] Darst, Katherine. "Here and There," *St. Louis Globe-Democrat*. 15 May 1941, p. 3.
[34] "Even the Pews..." *Policy and Commentary*. Posted Feb 2013. Accessed: 02-02-2022. https://nextstl.com/2013/02/even-the-pews-stood-up-the-forgotten-history-of-the-racial-integration-of-st-louis-university/
[35] "Rev Heithaus Praises Lowering of Racial Bars," *St. Louis Globe Democrat*. 20 Feb 1944, p. 8.
[36] "St. L. U. Considers Accepting Negroes," *St. Louis Globe-Democrat*. 28 Jan 1944, p. 13.
[37] "St. Louis University Accepts Five Negroes as Students," *St. Louis Star-Times*. 26 Apr 1944, p 3.
[38] *St. Louis Globe-Democrat* 26 Apr 1944, p. 1A
[39] "Two Workers in Education of Negroes Given Scrolls," *St. Louis Post-Dispatch*. 08 Jan 1945, p. 3.
[40] "12 Nominations Made for St. Louis Award," *St. Louis Post-Dispatch*. 13 Nov 1944, p. 17.
[41] "Two on St. Louis U. Faculty Out Over Negro Students," *St. Louis Post-Dispatch*. 20 Apr 1945, p. 3.
[42] ibid.
[43] "Father Holloran to teach Philosophy at St. Louis U.," *St. Louis Post-Dispatch*. 12 May 1949, p. 43.

[44] See "Rev. Fr. Patrick James Holloran Jr." Posted: 31 Oct 2010. Accessed: 21 Sep 2021. https://www.findagrave.com/memorial/60921560/patrick-james-holloran

[45] "The Heithaus Homily," *SLU Legends and Lore.* Posted: 26 Feb 2020. Accessed: 21 Sep 2021. https://www.slu.edu/news/2020/february/slu-legends-lore-heithaus-homily.php

[46] "Fr. Patrick J. Holloran Funeral Mass Tomorrow," *St. Louis Post-Dispatch.* 10 Feb 1969, p. 13.

[47] "Lady of Lourdes Pastor Rev. Patrick Holloran, Once Educator, Dies," *Decatur [IL] Daily Review.* 09 Feb 1969, p. 3.

[48] "Even the Pews…" *Policy and Commentary.* Posted Feb 2013. Accessed: 02-02-2022. https://nextstl.com/2013/02/even-the-pews-stood-up-the-forgotten-history-of-the-racial-integration-of-st-louis-university/

[49] "Negro Charges St. Louis U. Barred Him on Ground Students Object," *St. Louis Globe-Democrat.* 25 Sep 1942, p. 1A.

[50] Grant 188

[51] "Civic Award Nomination," *St. Louis Post-Dispatch.* 16 Nov 1944, p. 2B.

[52] "Negro Students to be Admitted to St. Louis U.," *St. Louis Post-Dispatch.* 26 Apr 1944, p. 3.

[53] Welek 357

[54] ibid. 360, whole paragraph

[55] ibid.

[56] ibid.

[57] ibid.

[58] Stein 56

[59] Welek 363

[60] ibid.

[61] ibid. 364, whole paragraph

[62] ibid. 367-368, whole paragraph

[63] Welek 43

[64] Grant 54

[65] "Charged with Illegal Coal Sale," *St. Louis Globe-Democrat.* 10 Sep 1942, p. 5A.

[66] "Negro Buried, Row Over Body Goes On," *St. Louis Post-Dispatch.* 24 Apr 1931, p. 14D.

[67] Welek 367

[68] ibid. 368

[69] ibid. 365

[70] "Housecleaning Urged…," *St. Louis Post-Dispatch.* 11 Feb 1958, p. 1A

[71] "Negroes Plan Tax Fight Against Washington U.," *St. Louis Post-Dispatch.* 19 Jun 1945, p. 3.

[72] ibid.

[73] "Negro Equality Gains Called Slow but Steady," *St. Louis Post-Dispatch.* 22 Aug 1948, PDF p. 28.

[74] ibid.

[75] Sargent, Davis. "Civil Rights and Washington University—A Complex History," *Student Life.* Posted 11 Sep 2011. Accessed 21 Sep 2021. https://www.studlife.com/ scene/2011/09/01/civil-rights-and-washington-university-a-complex-history/

[76] ibid.

[77] "Arthur Holly Compton," *Chancellors.* Posted n.d. Accessed 21 Sep 2021. https://wustl.edu/about/history-traditions/chancellors/compton/; and "A University Unlocks Its Doors," *Student Life*, reprinted in *St. Louis Post-Dispatch.* 18 May 1952, p 2B.

[78] Joiner, Robert. "The Battle with Jim Crow," *St. Louis Post-Dispatch*, 04 Feb 2001, p. F8.

[79] Lang 2004, 733

[80] Joiner, Robert. "The Battle with Jim Crow," *St. Louis Post-Dispatch.* 04 Feb 2001, p. F8.

[81] ibid.

[82] Christian, June C. "Percy Green, Interview 2," *American Lives Project*; transcript by David Walsh. Posted: 31 Jan 2022. Accessed: 02-02-2022. https://libguides.wustl.edu/ c.php?g= 46953&p=529254

[83] O'Shea, Devin Thomas. "The Prophet's Bane: How Percy Green's Activism Changed St. Louis," *Slate.* Posted: 21 Dec 2021. Accessed: 14 Jan 2022. *https://slate.com/news-and-politics/2021/12/percy-green-st-louis-activism-veiled-prophet-ball-ellie-kemper.html*

[84] "Demonstrations Fading Here as a Rights Weapon," *St. Louis Post-Dispatch.* 01 Aug 1965, p. 1A, 23A.

[85] "City Demonstration Against Part in Fair," *St. Louis Post-Dispatch.* 23 Apr 1964, p. 19A.

[86] "Sit-Down Protester in City Hall Jailed," *St. Louis Post-Dispatch.* 07 Nov 1963, p. 8A.

[87] "Pair Denied Right to Wed in St. Louis *The Pittsburgh Courier.* 20 Jun 1964, p. 1.

[88] "St. Louis CORE Demonstrates…," *St. Louis Post-Dispatch.* 27 Jun 1964, p. 3A.

[89] "Gateway Arch Climber is Free; Charge is Dropped," *St. Louis Post-Dispatch*. 23 Sep 1964, p. 16A.

[90] "Civil Rights Action Group Formed Here," *St. Louis Post-Dispatch*. 10 Jan 1965, p. 3A.

[91] "Race at the Arch," *St. Louis Post-Dispatch*, 04 Jun 1964, p. 2E.

[92] "CORE (cont.)," *St. Louis Post-Dispatch*. 20 Jun 1964, p. 7A.

[93] "First Case in Area Under Rights Law," *St. Louis Post-Dispatch*. 07 Jul 1965, PDF p. 27.

[94] Excellent detail of the case's path is found in "4 Pair Empl. Prac. Cas. 577, 4...," *Justia US Law*. Posted n.d. Accessed 02 Feb 2022. https://law.justia.com/cases/federal/ appellate-courts/F2/463/337/83407/

[95] "CORE Begins Campaign to Boycott Busch Beer," *St. Louis Post-Dispatch*, 25 Jun 1964.

[96] "Two Groups Here Split over Phone Job Data," *St. Louis Post-Dispatch*, 02 May 1965, p. 13A.

[97] "Achieve Objectives Legally, Negroes Told," *St. Louis Globe-Democrat*. 21 Jun 1961, p. 10A.

[98] ibid.

[99] Tabscott, Robert. "Two Women, One Fight," *St. Louis Post-Dispatch*. 26 Mar 2001, p. 19A.

[100] "Quits Race Commission," *St. Louis Globe-Democrat*. 28 Nov 1946, p. 3A.

[101] "Civil Liberties in St. Louis—A New Appraisal," *St. Louis Post-Dispatch*. 10 Dec 1950, p. 3B.

[102] "Anti-Race Bias Section Offered for City Charter," *St. Louis Post-Dispatch* 04 Oct 1949 p. 12A.

[103] "Civil Liberties in St. Louis—A New Appraisal," *St. Louis Post-Dispatch*, 10 Dec 1950, p. 3B.

[104] "Civil Rights Provisions Urged in Proposed New City Charter," *St. Louis Star-Times*, 06 Dec 1949, p. 3.

[105] "Freeholders Are Asked to Change Civil Rights Stand," *St. Louis Post-Dispatch*. 15 Jan 1950, p. 2A.

[106] "Civil Liberties in St. Louis—A New Appraisal," *St. Louis Post-Dispatch*, 10 Dec 1950, p. 3B.

[107] Homes had been bombed over this. Back in 1927, a widow who owned the home at 1411 N. Vandeventer received a phone call: "Are you renting to colored people?" the caller asked. "Yes," she replied. "Well, you ought to be ashamed of yourself. I'll fix you!" A bomb was thrown in through the vacant house's front window, blowing out all the windows, destroying the plaster, and demolishing the ceiling—even blowing a small hole in the roof.

In 1957, it happened again. An occupied house at 5011 Parker Ave. was listed for sale with an African American agent. A bomb was placed on the back porch while the owner was in the back bedroom. The blast was so great it shattered windows on the two adjacent houses, but did not injure the owner. He had been asked to reconsider selling to African Americans. See "Bomb Demolishes House…," *St. Louis Globe-Democrat.* 16 Feb 1927, p. 9; and "Civic Leaders Deplore Home Bombing Here," *St. Louis Post-Dispatch.* 10 Mar 1957, p. 3A.

[108] "Alderman Proposes Charter Amendment Against Discrimination," *The St. Louis Star-Times.* 25 Jan 1946, p. 10.

[109] "4-Million Rubbish Plan, Amendments to Charter Voted," *St. Louis Star-Times.* 07 Aug 1946, p. 3.

[110] Moore, Travis. "Dillon Rule and Home Rule: Principles of Local Governance," *LRO Snapshot.* Posted: 01 Feb 2020. Accessed: 21 Sep 2021. https://nebraskalegislature.gov/pdf/reports/research/snapshot_localgov_2020.pdf

[111] March 1558

[112] "Shelley v. Kraemer—334 U.S.1, 68 S. Ct. 836 (1948)," *Law School Case Brief.* Posted n.d., Accessed: 9-21-21. https://www.lexisnexis.com/community/casebrief/p/ casebrief-shelley-v-kraemer

[113] "Court Ruling on Realty Race Restrictions Potentially Affects 500 Blocks in St. Louis," *St. Louis Star-Times.* 04 May 1948, p. 1.

[114] "All We Wanted Was a Decent Place to Rear the Children, Negro Mother Says," *St. Louis Star-Times.* 04 May 1948, p. 4.

[115] ibid. For an outstanding examination of the case, see Clara Germani's thesis *J. D. and Ethel Shelley: Celebrating the People behind the Landmark Shelley v. Kraemer Case.* Washington University in St. Louis, AMCS 502, 07 May 2019.

[116] "Shelley Et Ux v. Kraemer Et Ux," *Cases Adjudged in the Supreme Court of the United States at October Term 1947.* Esp. pp 1-4. Posted: n.d. Accessed: 21 Sep 2021) https://tile.loc.gov/storage-services/service/ll/usrep/usrep334/usrep334001/ usrep334001.pdf

[117] ibid.

[118] "Court's Ruling not a Simple Yes and No; What It Means," *St. Louis Star-Times.* 04 May 1948, p. 1.

[119] See p. 101, Theising, Andrew, ed. *In the Walnut Grove.* Florissant MO: Florissant Valley Historical Society, 2020.

[120] See "George L. Vaughn," *Findagrave.com.* Posted: n.d. Accessed: 02-02-2022. https://www.findagrave.com/memorial/11671934/george-l-vaughn

[121] "...Studied to Death...," *St. Louis Post-Dispatch.* 25 Jun 1955, p. 5.

[122] "Aldermen Under Fire for Delay...," *St. Louis Post-Dispatch.* 10 Feb 1956, p. 1A.

[123] ibid.

[124] Symington, James. "Letters from Readers: A Civil Rights Push in St. Louis in 1955," *St. Louis Post-Dispatch.* 11-16-05, p 8B.

[125] Jolly 27-28

[126] "Two Anti-Discrimination Bills Defeated...," *St. Louis Post-Dispatch.* 07 Dec 1956, p. 1A.

[127] "Approval Urged on Bill...," *St. Louis Post-Dispatch.* 13 Dec 1957, p. 3A.

[128] "Anti-Bias Bill Beaten...," *St. Louis Post-Dispatch.* 06 Feb 1959, p. 1A.

[129] "Tucker Urges...," *St. Louis Post-Dispatch.* 01 May 1959, p. 1A.

[130] "Aldermen Get Bill...," *St. Louis Post-Dispatch.* 19 Apr 1960.

[131] "Bill to Prevent Bias...," *St. Louis Post-Dispatch.* 28 Oct 1960.

[132] "Aldermen Pass Anti-Bias...," *St. Louis Post-Dispatch.* 19 May 1961, p. 1A.

[133] "Steamer Admiral Sues...," *St. Louis Globe-Democrat.* 30 Jun 1961, p. 6A.

[134] ibid.

[135] ibid.

[136] "'Integration' Threatens...," *Jet* 51

[137] ibid.

[138] "Woman a 'First' in St. Louis," *New York Times.* 05 July 1953, p 48.

[139] Corbett p. 294, and "First Woman in the Mayor's Cabinet," *St. Louis Post-Dispatch.* 07 July 1953, p. 1A.

[140] "Tucker Names Woman to Cabinet," *St. Louis Globe Democrat.* 05 Jul 1953, p. 1A.

[141] "Mayor Proclaims Friday as Human Rights Day," *St. Louis Post-Dispatch.* 07 Dec 1955, PDF p. 41.

[142] Valien 27

[143] . "4 with Ward Backing Win in School Races," *St. Louis Post-Dispatch.* 03 Apr 1957. p 1A. See also Lang, 2008, pp. 118-119; and "Win in St. Louis," *Baltimore Afro-American*, 12 Apr 1955.

[144] Lang 2008, 125

[145] "A New Day for Triple A," *St. Louis Post-Dispatch.* 11 Mar 1990, p. 8B.
[146] "Club's Fight to Stay in Forest Park Spanned Many Years," *St. Louis Post-Dispatch.* 11 Mar 1990, p. 12C)
[147] Gunther 211
[148] "Mayors to Take Stand on Rights," *New York Times.* 12 Jun 1963, p. 29. Emphasis added.
[149] "Awards for Tucker, Clayton Aldermen," *St. Louis Post-Dispatch.* 06 May 1962, p. 22A.
[150] Tucker 1963, p. 1.
[151] "Mayor Assails Disorder: Says It Harms Drive," *St. Louis Post-Dispatch.* 01 Sep 1963, p. 1A.
[152] This list (partial) is from a ten-page document signed by the leaders of the Human Relations Council (Father Paul Reinert SJ, president of St. Louis University, and Thomas Eliot, chancellor of Washington University), found in the Tucker Papers, Washington University Archives, Series 3, Box 13, Folder: "Civil Rights Record"

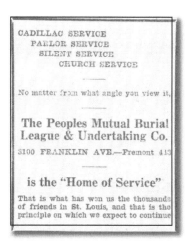

Above: Advertisement of "The Peoples Mutual Burial League and Undertaking Co.," which was owned by political boss Jordan Chambers. From "The Shout of a Rising Race," April 1926.

Below: A photo folder from the "ultra modern" Club Riviera, a popular night club owned by Chambers, 1950s. Theising photo; Author's collection.

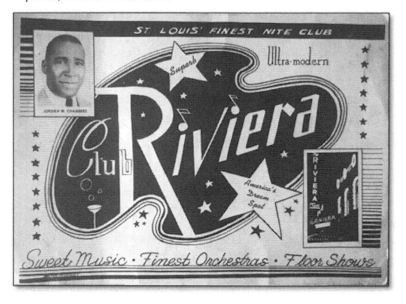

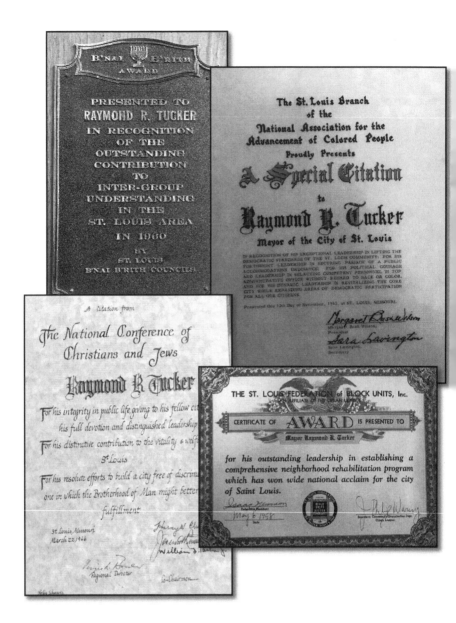

Some of Mayor Tucker's recognition for his achievements in civil rights, (clockwise from upper left) the B'nai B'rith Award for "outstanding contribution to inter-group understanding in St. Louis"; the STL NAACP citation for "exceptional," "forthright," and "dynamic" leadership on issues, as well as "political courage"; the STL Federation of Block Units (Urban League) award for "outstanding leadership" in establishing a nationally-recognized comprehensive neighborhood rehabilitation program; and a citation from the National Conference of Christians and Jews for "resolute efforts to build a city free of discrimination." Theising images, courtesy of the Tucker Family.

Chapter 4

Taking It to the Streets:

The Jefferson Bank Protest

Jefferson Bank Timeline

STL CORE demands Jefferson Bank respond to discriminatory hiring by 8/29

8/14: ESTL NAACP Protests Discrimination at East St. Louis Union Bank on Collinsville Ave.

AUG 1963

Jefferson Bank refuses to respond to CORE

8/29: Tucker develops 10-point plan to resolve discrimination; ALL banks sign it

8/30: Judge Scott orders protestors not to disrupt Jeff Bank business

8/30: CORE protest begins; nineteen are arrested late at night

SEP

~9/16: City prosecutor refuses to try these as criminal cases; Judge Scott names Wayne Millsap (the bank's lawyer) special prosecutor

9/23: Trials commence. Judge Scott rules defendants cannot submit certain evidence, nor examine certain witnesses

10/11: Tucker meets with CORE; all agree to 2 weeks cooling off period

OCT

10/12: Tucker meets with Jeff Bank, wants them to settle; reply: "go to hell"

10/24-25: Judge Scott finds all 19 guilty of court order violation; each is fined and sentenced to jail

10/25: All other banks start minority hiring; not Jeff Bank

10/29: Tucker demands Jeff Bank follow the 10 Point Plan it signed in August

10/31: Tucker brokers meeting of protestors and Human Relations Council

March: Jeff Bank changes hiring practices

MAR 1964

THE JEFFERSON BANK PROTEST
AUGUST 29-30, 1963

THE GREATEST CIVIL RIGHTS EVENT in the history of St. Louis was the Jefferson Bank Protest. Volumes have been written on it, and perhaps the most poignant is former Congressman William L. Clay's *The Jefferson Bank Confrontation*. This chapter is not designed to recast the entire chain of events, but rather to pull out those key portions that involved Mayor Tucker and how that action (or inaction, as the case may be) helps us understand the man. The Jefferson Bank Protest is a critical part of St. Louis' civil rights experience, and the full story is a worthy study in and of itself.

The Jefferson Bank Protest was significant in at least three different ways for understanding Mayor Tucker. First, it put to the test all the legal elements that had happened in the previous 10 years while Tucker was mayor: the *Brown v. Board* decision, the subsequent actions of desegregation in city (and social) institutions, the passage of a public accommodation law, the passage of an Equal Employment Opportunity law, and the establishment of an executive authority at both city and state levels to enforce EEO. Was it all just window dressing, or was it for real? This was the test!

Second, its timing was as the civil rights movement was approaching an apex. Martin Luther King Jr. had just given his *I Have a Dream* speech and President Kennedy had advanced the most significant piece of civil rights legislation in the 20th century (tragically, both of those men would be murdered before the movement had achieved all its legislative goals). There were forces at work at mid-century and timing mattered.

Third, the protest brought together all the elements of Mayor Tucker's personality. He responded in ways that were predictable and unpredictable, in ways that calmed and infuriated at the same time, and in ways that showed what St. Louis had been and could be.

The Setting: Leading Up to August 29

St. Louis CORE sent letters to leading banks and department stores demanding that the firms hire more African

167

Americans in the summer of 1963. The local NAACP had been working this issue since 1958, but CORE was ready to push for its demands—as had already taken place earlier that month with disruptive demonstrations by civil rights counterparts in East St. Louis.[1] In some cases, specific numbers of new hires were requested. Both banks and department stores called the request "quotas" and stated that it would be illegal for them to place employment limitations by race, as St. Louis had an Equal Employment Opportunity law since 1962. [2] To black demonstrators, the number was not a "quota" at all, but rather a "fair share of jobs."[3]

In East St. Louis on August 14, 1963, protesters lined up along the wall of Union Bank at the major intersection of Missouri and Collinsville Avenues, where three of the four corners were banks. They dropped to their knees to pray for change, and the newspapers photographed them and carried their cause on the front page far beyond the Illinois suburbs of St. Louis.[4] Then, people sat down on the floors inside. Arrests followed.

Jefferson Bank was chosen as the site of the St. Louis protest. According to a published interview with Norman Seay, a CORE leader, the bank dismissed its two black tellers when it moved from its location on the near North Side of the city to a location in the central business district.[5]

William L. Clay, another CORE leader, said "the bank chose itself," after providing an insensitive response to a letter to bank management from CORE. CORE's letter demanded that at least four African Americans be hired in white-collar positions. The bank's attorney, Wayne Millsap, said no, and added insult to injury by stating that "there were not 'four blacks in the city' qualified for white-collar jobs."[6] The insulting and insensitive response by Jefferson Bank steeled the willpower of CORE to plan a major protest.

CORE threatened to engage in "walk-ins, sit-ins, and lie-ins" at Jefferson Bank on Friday, August 30, if demands were not addressed by August 29.[7] In a last-minute effort to avert a crisis, a proposal came from Mayor Tucker on August 29. He worked with the St. Louis Council on Human Relations to develop a ten-point plan for progress on the issue. Meanwhile, thirty members of CORE met for two hours deciding how to proceed the next day.[8]

Tucker, the Professional, Gets Involved

Mayor Tucker saw what was happening and understood why it was happening. The bank (functionally) was violating the equal employment opportunity legislation that Tucker himself had advocated, signed, and implemented. CORE was calling out the bank's bad behavior. Tucker saw the Human Relations Council as the best vehicle to settle the dispute between the two parties. The council worked diligently to produce a document intended to mediate the dispute—necessarily taking a neutral position. The ten points prepared by the Human Relations Council and advanced by Mayor Tucker were:

1. to communicate a written statement of policy on equal employment opportunity to all levels of management within each bank;

2. to publicize their non-discriminatory policy so that all persons, regardless of race, color, or religion, will know that they will receive consideration for employment at the banks;

3. to review the employment records of present employees to

WHO WAS WAYNE MILLSAP? He was an attorney and represented Jefferson Bank. In his law practice, he was briefly associated with Lon O. Hocker, a leading Republican attorney. He was the Republican candidate for Board of Aldermen President in 1963 against Donald Gunn, and he was the son-in-law of Dillon Ross. Because of this relationship, Ross stepped down from Gunn's campaign when Millsap became the Republican nominee (he was unopposed). His campaign hinged on electing a Republican to the office as a "watchdog" against Tucker and his allies. (See "Wayne L. Millsap," St. Louis Post-Dispatch. 31 Mar 1963, PDF p. 127)

determine if anyone is working below his level or is being denied a promotion or transfer because of race;

4. to inform all recruitment sources, both public and private, of the banks' employment policy;
5. to inform schools where Negroes are enrolled of the desire of the banks to employ on the basis of merit and qualification;
6. to request the assistance of the St. Louis Urban League in recruiting qualified Negro workers;
7. to inform the Council on Human Relations and referral sources in the event that adequate numbers of qualified Negroes are not referred to the banks;
8. to encourage qualified employees to enroll in the American Institute of Banking for additional training which will help prepare them for promotion;
9. to discuss with the Missouri State Employment Division the possibility of establishing training programs for skilled jobs in the banks;
10. to periodically inform the Council on Human Relations of the results of these measures.[9]

This was a holistic approach to the problem. The first three points were related to the bank specifically: to make an internal commitment to honor the equal employment opportunity law, to publicize that policy commitment as an assurance to potential applicants, and to conduct an internal assessment to find existing employees who may have been affected by unfair practices. These were all actions that the banks could do quickly and easily. There were five points requiring outreach to recruiters and sources of training andalent. The remaining two points required reporting progress back to the Human Relations Council.

Note how the ten points are consistent with Tucker's professional ideals of neutral competence and working within the authority of various institutions. The points covered employers, sources of applicants, and over-sight. Seven banks involved in the dispute, **including Jefferson Bank**, signed on to the 10-point plan on August 29. For CORE, it was too little, too late. The demonstration was gaining un-stoppable momentum. Tucker tried to prevent the situation from escalating in the short-term, which didn't work, but he was still confident in the plan and that it would work in the long-term.

Violating the Court Order: August 30

The next day, August 30, Jefferson Bank attorney Wayne Millsap petitioned circuit court Judge Michael J. Scott for an injunction barring St. Louis CORE leaders from blocking access to the bank. Ray Howard, St. Louis CORE's attorney, was present. When Judge Scott asked him what assurance he could give that the demonstrations would be peaceful, Howard replied that he was uncertain what type of demonstration would take place, but that "it would be in the truest American sense."[10] Scott issued the temporary injunction and called for a hearing for a permanent injunction on September 26. St. Louis CORE generally, and eleven CORE leaders specifically, were named.[11] They were prohibited from *blocking the doors, sitting on the bank's floor, or otherwise disrupting the bank's normal business.*[12]

Judge Scott's injunction prohibited only behavior that disrupted the bank's operation. *Peaceful picketing outside was allowed.* About 4 p.m., two hours after Judge Scott issued the order on

WHO WAS MICHAEL SCOTT?
Judge of the Circuit Court in the City of St. Louis. He was from a large Irish family of 15 in the city's Kerry Patch neighborhood (approximately the site of Pruitt-Igoe). At age four, he was in a tragic streetcar accident that cost him both legs. It did not hold him back, though. With artificial legs, he played soccer and baseball. He finished his law degree at Saint Louis University, was an alderman at age 26 (Democrat, April 1933) and a circuit judge at 30 (Democrat, November 1936). He was especially prominent in the juvenile justice area. By the time of the Jefferson Bank trials, he had been on the bench for over 25 years. ("Judge Scott Is Man of Rare Ability," St. Louis Globe-Democrat, 26 Oct 1963, p. 1A).

171

August 30, picketers showed up and began walking outside the bank peacefully. Sheriff Martin Tozer served copies of the court order to several of them. The orderly demonstration did not last long. The crowd grew to over 100 people (both Blacks and whites). Protesters began to lock arms in order to block the path of Jefferson Bank customers. About fifty demonstrators entered the bank and began to sit on the floor. Sheriff's deputies jostled with some demonstrators at the door, but no arrests were made—*the court order did not have that provision.*[13]

William Clay said that most of the people in the protest were not CORE members.[14] In a pre-protest meeting in a parking lot, there was a vote approving picketing and blocking the doors. Clay and other leaders said they voted against blocking the doors, warned others not to violate the court order, and they themselves did not participate in that prohibited activity.[15]

The demonstrators left peacefully at 6:00 p.m., the bank's closing time. Bank attorney Millsap had already left the bank for Judge Scott's home to request that the Judge cite 23 demonstrators for contempt. Recollections of the events differ on when the request was granted. The *Post-Dispatch* reported that Millsap withdrew his request at the Judge's home when he learned that the demonstrators had left peacefully at 6 p.m., promising to secure the citation on Tuesday, September 3 (Monday was the Labor Day holiday). William Clay's 2008 chronicle suggests that the Judge granted the order three hours after the request on August 30, that Sheriff Tozer was serving the warrants at 10:30 p.m. that night, and that some demonstrators spent Labor Day weekend in jail awaiting arraignment—Clay himself stated that he surrendered that Sunday, September 1.[16]

It became apparent very quickly that Millsap's list of arrestees had improprieties. It contained 23 names, some of which were not even in town the previous 24 hours to participate in the CORE activity and others who were not connected to the case at all. Judge Scott winnowed the list down to nine and the Sheriff started executing the arrest warrants late into the night.[17] Clay noted the impropriety of issuing arrest orders after hours, in private, without presentation of evidence in public court. Even Millsap admitted that *he had no evidence that any of the nine played a role in disruptive tactics for which they were arrested.* [18] Hundreds of people held nightly demonstrations outside the jail where the arrested demonstrators were held.

Going Around and Beyond the NAACP

The St. Louis NAACP never took an official position on the Jefferson Bank protest—the protest was managed entirely by CORE. In fact, the St. Louis branch asked the NAACP national office to step in and curtail the activities of the East St. Louis branch at Jefferson Bank. James Milton Peake Jr., a 24-year-old white paraplegic, was the NAACP youth field secretary in East St. Louis and led militant protests for racial equality. He dropped out of college at Southern Illinois University Carbondale, where he had been arrested several times for demonstrations in Southern Illinois. He was a representative of the Student Nonviolent Coordinating Committee (SNCC) as well. The NAACP national office noted that Peake could do what he

WHO WAS MARTIN TOZER? Longtime politician associated with Jordan Chambers' 19th Ward (even though he didn't live there). He ran for Sheriff in 1952 with the intent of defeating machine-boss Thomas Callanan, whose organization had threatened Tozer's power. Once Tozer defeated Callanan in 1952, he held on to the Sheriff position and rose to political power in the late 1950s and 1960s. The Sheriff's position was highly partisan and based on patronage. Callanan died in 1959 and had never regained the power Tozer took from him. (See "The People Choose: Victory without a Machine," St. Louis Post-Dispatch. 05 Nov 1952, p. 2C)

wished as an individual, but his representation of the NAACP was limited to the Illinois side of the river.[19]

In East St. Louis, civil rights advocates met at Lincoln High School to create the "Civil Rights Coordinating Council of East St. Louis" to better align the work of East St. Louis and St. Louis civil rights activities. James Peake was put in charge of the implementation.[20] William Clay said that he welcomed the help from anyone allied with CORE's goals.[21]

Peake, like members of CORE, favored an aggressive approach to demonstrations. He participated in the CORE protest at Jefferson Bank. When the NAACP national office representative arrived in East St. Louis, the branch was in turmoil. The branch president, Rev. W. E. Wharton, tendered his resignation over the controversy of "irresponsible" and "extralegal" demonstrations that Peake and others encouraged.[22] Twenty of the 24 Executive Board members joined him. At issue was the lack of a clear statement from headquarters about these extralegal activities. Wharton was opposed to them, but the HQ man wanted him to settle his differences with the militant members like Peake. No for-mal statement was issued and never would be.

When Peake was arrested at Jefferson Bank and subsequently put on trial for violating a separate restraining order, Wyvetter H. Younge was his defense attorney. She argued that the initial court order was unnecessary and extraordinary, and that the protest was managed well by the police.[23] Younge was named temporary guardian of two minors who were arrested, one age 19 and one age 17.[24]

The *St. Louis Globe-Democrat* (again, the city's conservative paper) focused on James Peake's arrest. Under a headline "Bank Demonstration Leader Is Convicted Morals Offender," the paper said it believed "that the following [story of an individual] identified with the dispute over alleged discrimi-nation by the bank [is] in the public interest."[25] The paper conducted deep research on Peake and concluded he was "a lonesome, unhappy, inconsistent person with a high IQ and a tremendous drive to lead others," and that this was influenced "undoubtedly" by his confinement to a wheelchair since 1950 due to polio.[26]

The article went on for multiple columns about him, his

arrest record, his behavior in college, his grades, and his health conditions. The "morals charge" that so piqued the *Globe's* interest was an arrest at a tavern in Cairo IL, [a Kentucky-border city with its own history of racism] where he was "in the company of a 45-year-old Negro woman." She was charged with drunk and disorderly conduct, to which she pleaded guilty and was fined $14. He was tried for "indecent" behavior before a jury of only seven people—because the attorneys for both sides found so much partiality among the jury pool of 50, only seven were acceptable.[27] He was found guilty unanimously and fined $14.

**Taken into Custody:
The Nineteen**

Aldermanic President Donald Gunn, an ally of Mayor Tucker, criticized both protesters and law enforcement. He said court orders must be obeyed, and challenges to court orders are to be made through the appeals process. He was more critical of Tozer's late-night arrests of CORE members. He pointed out to the media that demonstrators were arrested before it had been determined **if there even was a**

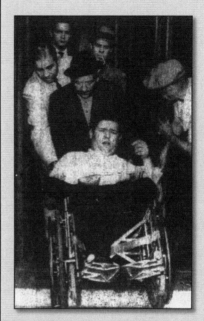

*WHO WAS JAMES PEAKE JR.?
Young civil rights activist in St. Louis and East St. Louis from Indiana. He had been a student at Southern Illinois University Carbondale when he became engaged in activism. He used a wheelchair for mobility, and it made for attention-grabbing media photos as he was removed from protests. He was deemed too militant by organizational leaders and removed from his posts in St. Louis and East St. Louis. He started his own group in St. Louis, but soon married and moved to New York. He died there at age 30. ("James Peake Jr.," Journal and Courier. (Lafayette IN) 03 Jan 1969, p. 5)*

violation of a court order or **if any of them were guilty** of the violation.[28]

Defense attorneys challenged Judge Scott's decisions on several fronts. They said this was a labor issue under federal jurisdiction, not a local issue. They questioned the propriety of how the court orders were disseminated. They questioned if the alleged violation rose to the level of *criminal* contempt instead of merely *civil* contempt.[29] There was indeed a special reason for that. Higher courts, state and federal, saw nothing wrong on appeal.

Nineteen protesters were prosecuted in three groups by Millsap and tried by Scott. The arrests happened earlier and many were freed on bond until the trial.

Tucker, the Institutionalist, Responds

Violating a court order raised the tension around the Jefferson Bank demonstration severely. Mayor Tucker "scolded" the demonstrators, to use Clay's term.[30] The Mayor validated the aims of Martin Luther King and the March on Washington, and said that the destruction of property and illegal or violent protests were intolerable to the city, as well as for the entire civil rights movement.[31]

Clay felt that there was no cause to call the protests violent and that Tucker was using code words to misrepresent the movement and its goals.[32] In Tucker's view, the bank demonstrators crossed a line. He respected anyone's right to challenge the validity of law and the need for law to change. In fact, he recognized repeatedly the need for law to change over time and the failure of old rules in serving a modern city. In William Clay's view, it was a "cynical conspiracy" against the civil rights movement by the media, the courts, the police, corporate leaders, and elected officials like Mayor Tucker.[33] In Tucker's institutionalist view, there was a process for protests and there was a process for changing laws, and they both needed respect.

The arrested demonstrators had a hearing on September 19th. Judge Scott had ordered the nine to submit depositions. All proclaimed their innocence, stating that they participated in demonstrations but did not block doors or otherwise violate the temporary injunction. The week before the nine were to go on trial for contempt of court, Judge Scott made a shocking decision (yet a legal one, according to the appellate courts): he would name a special prosecutor to handle the case for the State, and that prosecutor was Wayne Millsap— Jefferson Bank's attorney who had instigated the court order and the arrests.

If this were a civil case (private institution vs. private individual) Millsap could have been the attorney of record against the protesters. However, this was a criminal case (the people vs. private individual), and a government prosecutor had to represent "the people." Normally, Circuit Attorney Daniel P. Reardon, Jr. would have been the prosecutor. Reardon said at the outset that he considered this a civil matter and would only get involved if there were criminal actions. [34] Judge Scott used his discretionary power to select a special prosecutor to step in for

WHO WAS WYVETTER YOUNGE?
She was born Wyvetter Margaret Hoover in East St. Louis and obtained her law degree in St. Louis. She moved to St. Louis during her education and returned to East St. Louis when she married attorney Richard Younge. She was elected to the Illinois House of Representatives in 1975 and served until her death in 2008. She was one of the longest serving members of that body. (See "Longtime lawmaker...," Belleville News-Democrat, 28 Dec 2008, p. A1.)

WHO WAS NORMAN SEAY?
A founding member of CORE. He was active in the Urban League and the Pine Street YMCA from a young age, and was quite active in youth programs. He was the president of the Urban League's Federation of Block Units for many years. He was elected the committeeman of his 26th Ward, and was a political opponent of Sheriff Martin Tozer. (See "3 Democratic Ward Chiefs Challenged," St. Louis Post-Dispatch. 22 Jan 1960, p. 1) He became a teacher at Vashon High School but had to surrender his position after his arrest at the Jefferson Bank protest. (Kohler, Jeremy. "Norman R. Seay: Civil Rights Pioneer...," St. Louis Post-Dispatch. 19 Sep 2019, p. 10A)

the regular elected prosecutor. The choice of Millsap is difficult to understand from an impartial justice perspective.

Millsap, as special prosecutor, reviewed the depositions and Millsap determined that the nine should be charged with criminal contempt, as opposed to the less-serious civil contempt. CORE leaders saw this matter simply as the judiciary's "abuse of its awesome power to punish."[35] The trial commenced on September 23, 1963, with bank witnesses placing the defendants in the bank (itself not a violation of the order), but admitting under cross-examination that business was not disrupted.[36]

After that admission, Judge Scott refused to allow any further cross-examination of the prosecution witnesses—including Dillon Ross, who was both prosecutor Millsap's client and father-in-law. Further, Judge Scott allowed the prosecution to submit photos and news footage as evidence, but disallowed St. Louis CORE's request to submit refuting evidence.[37]

It makes no sense that Judge Scott had so much leeway, and that others with authority in the matter (like Circuit Attorney Reardon) did not step in.

Prosecuting the Violators: September 23

The prosecution presented its case with 30 witnesses over eight days. Judge Scott ordered a continuance until October 24, when he said he would decide. When that day came, Judge Scott pronounced all the defendants guilty, sentencing them to jail for periods of two to seven months, and levying fines between $500 and $1,000 each.[38] This was only the first group of demonstrators to be punished for contempt; as the protest continued, so did the arrests and the trials. In the end, 19 demonstrators were punished, some receiving jail sentences of one year and fines totaling $11,000, which were paid by the late great Johnetta Haley and the Alpha Kappa Alpha Sorority. She said in 1993, "It demonstrated to the community that we were willing to make sacrifices so our children would be able to have a better life."[39]

Judge Scott lectured the defendants before handing down sentences. "Our Negro citizens are entitled to fair and equal opportunities. To this end, in our Community many things have been done and numerous laws have been passed which are helping to provide those opportunities." He continued, "This Court did enjoin and prohibit unlawful interference with the business of the bank, because this is not in the American tradition." That last line harkens back to St. Louis CORE attorney Ray Howard's earlier statement that the demonstrations would be American in the truest sense. Scott concluded, "The Court looks with great sorrow and sadness upon this kind of contempt, because it is not in the best interest of the very persons who are involved."[40] Judge Scott's words were the end of a farcical trial that was filled with improprieties.

The sentences handed down to demonstrators for their civil disobedience were harsh. Jules Gerard, a law school professor at Washington University, writing for *Focus Midwest* magazine years later, called the sentences "outrageous" and the cases cited for such harshness was a "telling revelation" of the court's shortcomings.[41] Clay points to this as evidence that "the scales of justice are not balanced" and that judicial discretionary authority is "invariably use[d]…to mete out stronger penalties to minorities and the poor."[42]

William Clay recalls the three groups and the punishments they ultimately received. ($500=~$4,300 today)

Group One (October 24th):

Person	Jail Time	Fine
Marian Oldham	60 days	$500
William L. Clay	270 days	$1000
Robert Curtis	270 days	$1000
Charles Perkins	180 days	$500
Norman Seay	90 days	$500
Charles Oldham	90 days	$1000
Raymond Howard	60 days	$500
Herman Thompson	60 days	$500
Lucien Richard	90 days	$500

Group Two (October 25th):

Taylor Jones	1 year	$500
Louis Ford	1 year	$500
Ian Grand	180 days	$500
Benjamin Goins	90 days	$500
Roberta Tournour	120 days	$500
Kenneth Lee	60 days	$500
Ronald Glenn	60 days	$500

Group Three (also October 25th):

James Peake	1 year	$500
Michaela Grand	120 days	$500
Danny Pollock	60 days	$500

Source: Clay 2008 [43]

Tucker Meets with CORE: Friday, October 11

Tucker did meet privately behind the scenes with demonstrators, and attempted to broker a solution between the demonstrators, law enforcement, and the bank. The meeting with CORE leaders was lengthy. Handwritten notes in the Tucker Papers, presumably from this meeting, offer a slight glimpse behind the scenes. The notes probably were in the hand of Human Relations Council executive secretary Frank Campbell (formerly an executive with the Urban League), but there is a responding note page probably from Tucker himself. Both men were present.[44]

In true Tucker fashion, the meeting notes had "purpose" scribbled at the top, and that purpose was to decide what could be done about the Jefferson Bank situation. The meeting had three representatives from CORE: Norman Seay, Robert Curtis, and William Clay. The notes start out (though it is unclear who is saying this—perhaps Mr. Seay): "CORE no longer has full control" over the protest; there are not "one or two

WHO WAS ROBERT CURTIS? *Curtis was a longtime leader and activist of the Civil Rights movement in St. Louis. He received his law degree from Washington University. He was chairman of St. Louis CORE, and a founding member of ACTION in 1965. He was the attorney for the St. Louis Equal Employment Opportunity Commission and ran as a protest candidate for Missouri Governor in 1968. (See "Robert Curtis...," St. Louis Post-Dispatch, 19 Apr 1986, p. 4B.)*

[parties] controlling" the activity. The group felt that the "Mayor could use [his] office to bring some type of solution [double-underlined]."[45]

Curtis noted that the city kept money in the bank, and that the taxpayers' money should be deposited in a bank that doesn't practice race discrimination. Clay said he would not support stopping the protest unless there were assurances of even just an "honest discussion." He suggested, though, that the mayor could call for a "cooling-off period under certain conditions" that would include meeting with the local Fair Employment Practice Committee that Tucker had created.[46]

The last page of notes, perhaps from Mayor Tucker himself, capture the meeting's outcome: "Do not object to this setup: 2 weeks cooling off, then bank [will] work with [the state's Human Rights] Commission or [the city's Human Relations] Council to implement."[47]

Tucker Meets with Bank Officials: Saturday, October 12

Meanwhile, the demonstrations continued at both Jefferson Bank and the jail that housed the demonstrators throughout September and October. Tucker stayed away from the protests, though he had sympathy. He believed that his presence would only ignite an already-tense situation.[48] He had spent more than 2 hours listening to CORE leaders the day before.[49] His meeting with Jefferson Bank lasted only 30 minutes. The media reported that the bank meeting was congenial, but the meeting was undoubtedly tense. Clay's interpretation was that the bank executives told Mayor Tucker to "go to hell."[50] Tucker confided to his family what the exchange actually looked like—and Clay, basically, was correct.

Ross wanted protection for his bank and asked for the city to respond accordingly. Tucker pushed back. CORE leaders had told Tucker that this issue went beyond just Jefferson Bank, and that they were not going to stop until their hiring demands were met.

Tucker believed them and understood. He told Ross that he personally had been in discussion with specific leaders. Tucker stayed on message—he did not approve of illegal behavior, but he wanted the matter of human rights resolved and Ross had the power to end it. Tucker gave Ross an ultimatum: either make changes or "the police are going to get busy somewhere else" and not be able to respond to Jefferson Bank's needs.[51] Ross was furious: "You're condoning this!" The meeting ended abruptly.

This was exactly the same approach Tucker used in 1960, when the Missouri Restaurant Association's St. Louis Chapter pushed him for an opinion on the desegregation of lunch counters—a long tradition being challenged actively by the NAACP. Tucker responded that the city would not prosecute those engaging in peaceful sit-ins. "It certainly would appear that the best possible approach to the specific problem before you," said the professor, "would be the voluntary cessation of discriminatory practices by all restaurant operators in St. Louis."[52] Tucker's backing of the demonstrators in this case was the final push needed to secure their victory. The restaurant owners capitulated and adopted a resolution ending segregation. Margaret Bush Wilson, local NAACP president, savored her victory and agreed to work with the restaurants to implement the new agreement.

The Jefferson Bank executives (attorney Wayne Millsap, Executive Vice President Joseph McConnell, and President Dillon Ross) were angry, if not vengeful, over the protests. CORE attorneys, Millsap said, violated their professional ethics and he would pursue that with the Bar Association. He demanded that Father Joseph Nicholson, a priest who publicly supported the demonstrators, leave the bank's parking lot. When Alderman Joseph Clark approached Millsap, he was questioned whether or not he had an account at Jefferson Bank. The Alderman indicated he did and wished to speak to Dillon Ross (standing nearby) about the bank's hiring practices. Ross refused; he told the Alderman to go ahead and close his account.[53]

Ross called a press conference the morning after his session with the mayor. Bank executives lashed out at everyone involved. Executive Vice President Joseph McConnell likened the protesters to "animals," declaring the bank would never negotiate with CORE. He said he was "disgusted" with the various presentations and "angered" at the support the demonstration was getting from aldermen, ministers, and

WHO WAS DILLON ROSS?
He was the president of the Jefferson Bank, and a Democrat who was closely allied with Board of Aldermen President Donald Gunn. In fact, Ross was the treasurer of Gunn's 1963 campaign for a time. A decade earlier, Ross was the president of Southwest Bank when it was the scene of <u>The Great St. Louis Bank Robbery</u>. (See "Banker Resigns Post...," <u>Tucson Daily Citizen</u> (Tucson AZ), 21 Mar 1963, PDF p. 53. and "Scenes of Daring Bank Holdup...," <u>St. Louis Globe-Democrat</u>. 25 Apr 1953, p. 6A.)

physicians [54] (not to mention Mayor Tucker). Ross acknowledged that business at the bank was down and noted "several qualified Negroes had applied for jobs at the bank since the demonstrations started" but that no action will be taken under "a state of siege."

Ross' voice "showed emotion" as he read a prepared statement. "The issue is whether or not any ...institution in a free society should submit to threat.... If threats such as we have witnessed [here] become a way of life, no individual...will ever be safe again." [55] The bank had received bomb threats, he said. His words played on the fears that fueled racism, and the message was received if the letters sent to Mayor Tucker during these weeks were any indication. For example, consider the letter from Vivian C. Billen, 6900 block of Garner Ave., dated October 15, 1963, now echoed Ross' points of not giving in to threats. She called the protesters "animals," spoke of the old days when people carried "a gun for protection," and threatened to move out of the city. She quoted her suburban friends as saying, "Just keep the [Negroes] in the city and we'll gladly pay the earnings tax" and concluded with "how soon I leave depends on how soon they start moving into my neighborhood."[56] He ignored her, and the dozens like her.

Cooling Off: October 14-28

The result of Tucker's meeting with both sides of the Jefferson Bank protest was Tucker's call for a two-week "cooling off" period. He asked for a commitment from both sides by Monday, October 14. CORE leaders said they saw it as a distraction, though they agreed to it in the meeting. Clay personally called the idea a "devious maneuver" to "delay direct action" while "splintering opposition forces" (seemingly acknowledging the differences between NAACP and CORE, and later ACTION).[57] This was an acknowledgement of the divisions that existed between the various groups advocating for blacks in the Jefferson Bank Protest. CORE struggled to decide what to do and called a special meeting to discuss Tucker's proposal. Hundreds of people showed up, with reports ranging from 250 to 400.

To the chagrin of its leaders, the group voted to halt the demonstrations temporarily as Tucker requested. CORE leaders "accepted it, with guarded optimism...."[58] This vote was important. The CORE leadership did not get what it wanted, but admirably it consented to the will of the masses. The group, which had about 25 members planning the demonstrations in August, now drew a ten-fold crowd. Historian Clarence Lang suggested that CORE leadership may not have had functional control over its burgeoning membership, and, in fact, may have struggled just to keep pace with the growing activist base.[59] Being in such a position was advantageous from a resource perspective, but a disadvantage from a bargaining perspective— in the sense that the fight, rather than the peace mobilized many.

The cooling-off period may have stopped the public demonstrations, but quite a bit of activity happened behind the scenes. Black-interest organizations that received charitable contributions from white-led businesses were being "pressured" to issue statements against civil disobedience, as were individual leaders employed by local and state governments.[60]

The *Post-Dispatch* published an editorial calling on Jefferson Bank to do more. "It is regrettable that the Jefferson Bank management evidently chooses to make only a minimal response" to Mayor Tucker's ten-point plan from August 29.[61] The editorial noted that since August, other banks had hired 18 blacks into new positions. By the end of the month, that number was upward of 45, according to the Human Relations Council tracking.[62] None of this progress was at Jefferson Bank.

Protests Resume with Tucker: October 29

On October 29, Tucker demanded that the signatory parties, especially Jefferson Bank, implement his 10-point plan.[63] Lang described Tucker's pronouncement as being futile.[64] Jefferson Bank had signed the agreement but ignored it. The bank said it had no openings and made no hires, but Clay lists the hires made by Jefferson Bank: September 9, head teller; September 10, temporary clerk; September 13, permanent clerk; October 14, assistant collection manager. None were Black.[65] Jefferson Bank remained obstinate.

Demonstrations resumed throughout downtown. Leaflets were distributed around department stores calling for a Christmas-shopping boycott. People blocked buses by lying on the pavement ahead and behind them. Demonstrators stopped traffic in all directions at 6th and Washington. When the protesters were arraigned in court for their infraction, they started lying down on the courtroom floor and had to be removed on stretchers to awaiting police vehicles.[66]

When silent protesters filled the mayor's outer office on October 29, believing Tucker's public statement "seemed to criticize the demonstrators more than the bank," they peacefully sat down. When it was time for Mayor Tucker to leave at 5:30 p.m., he made a point to exit through the outer office (rather than the usual side door) to visually acknowledge them and see their signs. People made a path for the mayor and then followed him to his waiting car.[67]

The next day, October 30, demonstrators again showed up in Tucker's office wanting the mayor to utilize the full legal authority at the Human Relations Council's disposal and to do more to force the issue with Jefferson Bank. Tucker convened a meeting between protesters and the Human Relations Council in his office on the 31st. Demands were made to remove city funds from the bank. Though everyone knew it was not in the mayor's power to do this, his support of the measure was requested. Tucker stayed firm on his plan for the Council as a neutral mediator. The ten-point plan was working, albeit not to everyone's satisfaction, and Tucker was not about to change course in mid-stream.

Tucker and the Disagreement over Tools

The pressure on Jefferson Bank President Dillon Ross was growing. On November 5, the Missouri Commission on Human Rights made an inquiry. Ross sent a telegram to Commission Chairman J. Ben Searcy that the bank always had a nondiscriminatory employment policy and assured him of the bank's cooperation in the investigation. CORE considered Ross' statement absurd and produced evidence that qualified blacks were turned away from bank jobs, while less-qualified whites were hired.[68]

Tucker did have legal action at his discretion. The Fair Employment Practices Law was signed on November 30, 1962. It was created by Democrat William Clay and Republican Harold Elbert, and gave significant power to the city's Human Relations Council to launch investigations and levy fines up to $500 per day against violators.[69] The Council never used this power. Rather, according to Clay, the Council acted as a buffer between business interests and the activists.

On this point, Tucker's record is open to criticism. He helped initiate this power but pushed the council to remain a neutral arbiter—even after a formal complaint clearly had been levied against Jefferson Bank. It would have been unprecedented to use the council to its full power, but it certainly was possible and may well have pushed St. Louis to the forefront of progressive race relations had Tucker done so. It was a missed opportunity. His choices had a limiting effect on the council. However, Tucker was consistent in his action. Tucker the institutionalist avoided using the council's biggest weapon, undoubtedly in the hopes that his existing agreement (the ten points) could still carry the day, with the daily fines kept in reserve as back up.

Lang notes that the dominant model for interracial activity at the time was to "manage" the process bureaucratically.[70] Tucker certainly valued civil rights, but his approach here was through formal governance as Lang suggests. He saw integration as a (positive) process that was inevitable and needed to be managed. Tucker was enough of a realist to understand the pressures felt on both sides. He saw the role of formal governance being in the middle between the two groups, working to optimize solutions in the ever-changing landscape. This was not enough for William Clay. Anything short of wholesale reform of the system was inadequate and merely a "gimmick" for public relations benefit.[71] Clay's time for patience had passed.

The council's belief that it was a buffer was not a new position. In 1956, Tucker re-appointed the council's chairperson, Harry Pope, to a second two-year term.[72] Pope was the owner of a local cafeteria chain that refused to serve Blacks. The NAACP was opposed to the re-appointment.[73] William Clay was distraught. He outlined his complaints in a letter to Mayor Tucker, who provided a weak justification of his re-appointment of Pope. "This office is not familiar with any action of Mr. Pope as a member of the Council on Human Relations which has been injurious to any segment of the community. …It was thought that since he was familiar with the problem [of public accommodation], he would be of assistance to the council in arriving at a solution."[74] Clay considered the response a sign of Tucker's "contempt" for Blacks.[75]

While Tucker in 1956 probably saw Pope's as a routine reappointment, it was a mistake in practicality and sensitivity. Pope was on record that the council's next leader should not be anyone who was active with the Urban League, NAACP, or CORE, "as these people might have trouble adopting a patient attitude" toward the types of problems brought before the council.[76] When reminded that there were qualified Blacks for the position, Pope dug in. "We might as well just face it," he said. "[T]he places and problems that have to be attacked deal with white people" and he wondered if whites would speak freely to Blacks or "be embarrassed and hold back and not express themselves." [77] Pope's shallow and insensitive comments touched on a key truth that could not be denied—many whites were uncomfortable talking about race. The council under Pope's leadership was indeed only a buffer. Pope resigned under pressure in April and did not serve the new term.[78]

Pope, as chairman of the local unit of the Missouri Restaurant Association, voted to desegregate St. Louis area restaurants on November 15, 1960. The letter to members was drafted at their meeting with the assistance of attorney Margaret Bush Wilson, local NAACP president, and attorney Charles Oldham, national CORE chairman.[79] It was facilitated in the offices of the Human Relations Council. Mayor Tucker had pressed the issue with the Missouri Restaurant Association, noting that their practice violated the 14th Amendment rights of African Americans—and did this *before* there was a public accommodation law in the city (or nationally, for that matter).

In July 1963, a month prior to the Jefferson Bank protests, Tucker appointed Frank Campbell as Executive Secretary of the Council on Human Relations (replacing Chester E. Stovall, who was appointed to the mayor's cabinet). Pope's career in the field continued. He moved to the suburbs and in July 1964, Republican County Supervisor Lawrence K. Roos appointed Pope to serve on the County's version of the Human Relations Council.[80]

It Worked: Perspectives on Success

In the end, the protests were a success. The demonstrations stopped after about six months, when Jefferson Bank capitulated and hired six African Americans into white-collar jobs.[81] The Jefferson Bank Protest pushed St. Louis through a portal that it had been entering only very slowly. Over the next 42 months, Clay noted that 1,300 blacks were hired at department stores, hospitals, and insurance companies into positions previously blocked.[82] Another 800 blacks held white-collar jobs and managerial positions in the local banking industry.[83] It was a hard-fought victory.

Tucker's 10-point plan defined the council's neutral path. He wanted a direct solution between the bank and the demonstrators, and openly placed the Human Relations Council in a resource-only position for either side to engage should direct solutions falter. The council was to be notified if there were not an adequate number of qualified African Americans being referred directly to the banks, and periodically to be informed of progress around training and employment programs. Tucker stuck with his plan, and that worked too.

The Jefferson Bank Protest was a time when two perspectives were moving past each other. The banks had hired, in Margaret Bush Wilson's words, "more Negroes...in the last 60 days than had been hired in the last 60 years," but was that progress?[84] She acknowledged yes. Clay thought not.

From the banking industry perspective, it was a radical departure from the past and action that was taken reluctantly (and only after the protest forced it). In that sense, the demonstrators won a major victory. However, some—including future-Congressman William Clay—wanted much, much more. He wanted the city "to abolish the traditional pattern of discrimination" ("institutional racism" in today's terms) and to "censure the business community" for its long silence on the issue and its failure to "exert the moral force" that was at its command.[85] This comment was aimed directly at Mayor Tucker and the circles of Civic Progress, and was well-founded.

Clay also said that before the real problems of African Americans could be addressed, activists "must battle with white liberals and conservative Negroes about the methods to be used."[86] This position was consistent entirely with Martin Luther King's *Letter from a Birmingham Jail* that had been written just six months before. In that powerful letter, King called out white moderates for their self-justified inaction, based on some agreement with the movement's goals but disagreement with its methods.

Mayor Tucker, when he "scolded" the CORE demonstrators, was doing the very thing that King and Clay pointed out. Tucker genuinely saw violating the law as discrediting the movement's good work, and it put him in an untenable position as a neutral negotiator. There should be no surprise at this from Mayor Tucker. He was a party to the dispute—he was not being tone-deaf. He spent his career getting people to obey the law (smoke, merit, charter, accommodation); his discomfort in endorsing breaking a law is understandable (especially when he saw other avenues for change—albeit longer and slower). As Lang noted, the goal was to "manage" the situation.

Tucker did not place himself in the same vein as those elected officials in more southern cities who openly opposed civil rights—and whose vitriolic conduct had played out on news stories throughout the civil rights movement. "Civil rights leaders should adapt their tactics to the specific local situation," Tucker said. "Methods which are necessary in some localities where community leadership is opposed to their goals are surely not appropriate for St. Louis."[87] Tucker truly felt he was a friend of civil rights (Clay would disagree). Tucker said that rogue actions "debase the serious principles involved" with civil rights and he did take them seriously.[88]

At the same time, other politicians were reluctant to support budding civil rights in St. Louis. A. J. Cervantes, who would succeed Tucker as mayor in 1965, wrote in his autobiography that his aldermanic constituents in the 15th Ward "didn't think much of the lofty liberalism of the downtown civic leaders or the professional educators" regarding civil rights, and that he voted accordingly.[89] This was a direct criticism of Tucker and Tucker's circle, though Cervantes came around to the idea later.

Lang noted the several divisions within the Black community, with all having interest in the events at hand but with divergent approaches. The first division was between older established people and young people. Older persons, who had been involved in the local civil rights efforts for years, had risen to power in long-respected organizations such as the local Urban League and NAACP. Younger persons, who did not feel bound by the norms of activism embraced by the previous generation, gravitated toward newer channels and leaders, such as those offered by St. Louis CORE.[90]

The second division was between those valued civil disobedience and those who sought outright confrontation. Peaceful demonstrations, pickets, and boycotts were standard tactics of many civil rights activists. Others had no patience for "polite noncooperation," and sought to put white citizens in uneasy positions to force issues of racial injustice.[91]

The third division was between working-class demonstrators and professionals. The working class was the initial source of much of St. Louis CORE's strength in launching the Jefferson Bank protest. Professionals, of the sort led by physician Jerome Williams, sought to counter the "unruly conduct" of the working-class demonstrators.[92] All of these factions were present in front of Jefferson Bank at one time or another. As the protest evolved, schisms developed that motivated some to break away and others to join in.

The Rise of William L. Clay

Political scientist Lana Stein called Clay a "young rebel," who was willing to challenge both the mayoral alliances as well as the old guard of St. Louis's black community in pushing his political agenda.[93] Clay's lone term on the Board of Aldermen was a successful one. He helped push civil rights legislation on two key fronts—fair employment and public accommodations. He was a great fighter.

After the Jefferson Bank protest, Clay emerged as St. Louis's "civil rights hero," noted Stein.[94] He was shrewd and used his career path wisely. He first sought a formal government position on the Board of Aldermen in 1959 but shifted to ward committeeman after the Jefferson Bank protest. Clay saw the power of Jordan Chambers and Martin Tozer as ward committeemen and calculated that his agenda would succeed better from the wards than from the aldermanic chambers.

In 1965, Clay defeated his Jefferson Bank Protest colleague Norman Seay as committeeman of the 26th Ward and took over the empire once ruled by Jordan Chambers. Later, he took on the business manager position with the Steamfitters Union and helped that institution integrate. He had a position of great political strength, combining the power of a growing black electorate and the institutional power of one of the region's most prominent unions.[95] Clay used this power to seek patronage for loyal operatives and endorse political candidates— including Alfonso Cervantes in his bid to unseat Mayor Tucker.

The effect of Clay's shift had a significant impact on the civil rights movement locally. Lana Stein notes that other leaders of the civil rights movement followed Clay into the ward organizations, and civil rights became forever enmeshed with machine-style politics, characterized by "individualized rewards, factional loyalty, and other quid pro quo transactions." [96] This transition pushed civil rights further away from the institutional realm of Mayor Tucker and into the circles of ward politics.

William L. Clay, 1968.
Newspapers.com

Martin Luther King in St. Louis

Dr. King made at least six visits to St. Louis, all of them during Tucker's terms as mayor. Dr. Gwendolyn Moore of the Missouri History Museum suggested the number may be more like nine.[97]

His first publicized visit was on April 10, 1957, just a week after Mayor Tucker was re-elected by a landslide. He spoke at the St. Louis Freedom Rally, at the invitation of his dear friend John E. Nance. Dr. King was complimentary of what St. Louis had done. He said he was happy to be in St. Louis and was happy for the city's progress "in the area of human relations." He was pleased by how well integration (after *Brown v. Board*) had moved along and said, "this city is to be commended." He said St. Louis could be an example for cities in the Deep South. He said integration can be accomplished "smoothly and peacefully" and that this was laudable.[98]

A month later in Washington DC, he gave his *Give Us the Ballot* speech, where he spoke of liberals being so analytical and objective that they fail to take a side in the debate. He called them "lukewarm" liberals.[99]

When he came to St. Louis on June 21, 1961, he made a statement to the *Globe-Democrat:* "I often use St. Louis as an example of what other cities could do," but he added that it happens through acting in good faith. Even though St. Louis had made strides toward equality, it must do more.[100]

He was in St. Louis that week to address the National Baptist Convention's education auxiliary. His message, among other things, was a warning: if segregation was not addressed soon, "the 'deeply bitter' feelings of American Negroes may erupt into violence."[101]

On his visit to address the General Convention of the Protestant Episcopal Church in St. Louis on October 13, 1964, his first visit after the Jefferson Bank Protest, he remarked, "Segregation is on its deathbed," but "we've still got a long way to go."[102] He called out churches as still being bastions of segregation and pushed them to do more, even though he praised the advances made in public accommodation. (If he mentioned the Jefferson Bank Protest specifically, it was not noted.) He learned that he won the Nobel Peace Prize just hours after leaving St. Louis.

So Dr. King had a consistent theme of his own. He was quick to praise good work, and then quick to press for doing more. He was a believer in institutions, and then he called them out to take a stand on the correct side of the issues.

Good Work, and More to Do

To be certain, the record shows Dr. King approved of the good civil rights work done in St. Louis. To be certain, he called on the city to do more. Mayor Tucker was part of the good, and Mayor Tucker could have done more. The same could be said for others in St. Louis.

The city's history of racism is inexcusable. Racism has tainted everything about the city. We can praise people like Mayor John Darby in the 1840s for having the foresight to establish public space like Lafayette Park, and at the same time shame him for being insensitive to the complaints of the people he enslaved.[103] Yet there were individual acts of goodness amid the fog: Judge Bryan Mullanphy and the Lucy Delaney freedom suit come to mind.[104]

The Jefferson Bank Protest showed Mayor Tucker's behavior among many pressing circumstances, and it reasonably can be concluded that he was more a force for good than bad. He had a moral compass, and it showed up in his work. His institutionalist leanings were limiting on how far he would go. His consistent perspective of civil rights was ahead of his peers in the 1950s, but behind the times by the 1960s. Did he truly understand how quickly the world around him was changing? He may not have changed the world, but he changed part of it for the better.

Lenten Speaker

The Rev. Dr. Martin Luther King Jr., noonday Lenten
service speaker at Christ Church Cathedral today.

Hear One of World's Great Leaders
DR. MARTIN LUTHER KING
Montgomery, Alabama, Minister
IN FREEDOM RALLY AT KIEL
AUD. WED., APRIL 10 AT 8 P.M.
TO AVOID DISAPPOINTMENT GET AD-
MISSION SLIPS AT KIEL AUDITORIUM
BOX OFFICE, 3546 PAGE, JOE'S MUSIC
SHOPS, 2711 FRANKLIN, 4123 EASTON,
1500 BROADWAY IN EAST ST. LOUIS.
SEAT DONATION $1.00.
SPONSORED BY CITIZENS' COMMITTEE OF GREATER ST. LOUIS,
BENEFIT DR. KING'S CIVIL RIGHTS PROGRAM.

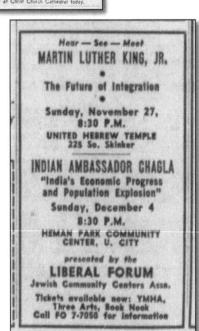

Hear — See — Meet
MARTIN LUTHER KING, JR.
*
The Future of Integration
*
Sunday, November 27,
8:30 P.M.
UNITED HEBREW TEMPLE
225 So. Skinker

INDIAN AMBASSADOR CHAGLA
"India's Economic Progress
and Population Explosion"
Sunday, December 4
8:30 P.M.
HEMAN PARK COMMUNITY
CENTER, U. CITY

presented by the

LIBERAL FORUM
Jewish Community Centers Assn.

Tickets available now: YMHA,
Three Arts, Book Nook
Call FO 7-7050 for information

REV. DR. MARTIN LUTHER KING JR., nationally known civil rights leader, addresses
the General Assembly Wednesday on "Christian Faith in Human Relations."

Advertisements from some of Dr. King's visits to St. Louis. Clockwise from upper left: at Christ Church Cathedral, March 1964; at Kiel Auditorium, April 1957; again at Kiel Auditorium, December 1957; and at United Hebrew Temple, November 1960. (Please note that Dr. King made visits to multiple sites/events/institutions while in the city.) Newspapers.com

ENDNOTES

---

[1] Lang 2009, 161

[2] "4th Firm Here Rejects Negro Job Demands," *St. Louis Post-Dispatch.* 28 Aug 1963, pp. 1A, 6.

[3] Lonesome, Buddy. "The Quota System," *St. Louis Argus.* 11 Oct 63 p. 10B, quoted in Clay 2008, 39.

[4] "70 Negroes Sing, Pray at Banks...," *St. Louis Post-Dispatch.* 14 Aug 1963, p. 1A.

[5] Lockhart, Linda. "Norman Seay Looks Back on Jefferson Bank and Local Struggle for Civil Rights," *St. Louis Beacon.* Posted 8-24-10. Accessed: 11-13-15. https://www.stlbeacon.org/#!/content/18213/norman_seay_looks_ba ck_on_ jefferson_bank_and_local_struggle_for_civil_rights)

[6] Clay 2008, 34. Clay does not give a primary citation for this quote; presumably it was Millsap's letter. A similar quote attributed to Millsap's letter to Robert Curtis was noted in "Negro Jobs (cont.)," *St. Louis Post-Dispatch.* 28 Aug 1963, p. 6A, col. 4.

[7] "CORE Barred from Causing Disorders at Jefferson Bank," *St. Louis Post-Dispatch.* 30 Aug 1963, p. 1A, 6A.

[8] ibid.

[9] ibid.

[10] "CORE Barred from Causing Disorders at Jefferson Bank," *St. Louis Post-Dispatch.* 30 Aug 1963, pp. 1A, 6.

[11] Clay 2008, 34, says 10 were named; the *Post-Dispatch* says 11; this research is using the account from the day.)

[12] Clay 2008, 34-35; and "CORE Barred from Causing Disorders at Jefferson Bank," *St. Louis Post-Dispatch.* 30 Aug 1963, pp. 1A, 6. Emphasis added.

[13] "Pickets Lock Arms at Bank, Block Path for Customers" and "Governor, Police Board to Confer on Bank Sit-In Held Despite Injunction," *St. Louis Post-Dispatch.* 31 Aug 1963, pp. 1A, 3A.

[14] "CORE Leaders Deny Demonstrating Inside of Jefferson Bank," *St. Louis Globe-Democrat.* 10 Dec 1963, p. 3A.

[15] ibid.

[16] See "Governor, Police Board to Confer on Bank Sit-In Held Despite Injunction," *St. Louis Post-Dispatch.* 31 Aug 1963, pp. 1A, 3A; and Clay 2008, 45-46.

[17] Clay 2008, 46

[18] "East St. Louisans Participate in Jefferson Bank Protests," *St. Louis Post-Dispatch.* 05 Oct 1963, p. 3A. Emphasis added.

[19] "Bank Protest (cont.)," *St. Louis Post-Dispatch.* 09 Oct 1963, p. 6A.

[20] "CORE Approves Two-Week Halt in Protests at Jefferson Bank," *St. Louis Post-Dispatch.* 14 Oct 1963, p. 1A.

[21] ibid.

[22] "20 of 24 Quit East Side NAACP Executive Panel," *St. Louis Post-Dispatch.* 17 Oct 1963, p. 1A

[23] ibid.

[24] "CORE Approves Two-Week Halt in Protests at Jefferson Bank," *St. Louis Post-Dispatch.* 14 Oct 1963, p. 1A. Wyvetter Margarite (*nee* Hoover) Younge (no direct relation to Walter), was the attorney for St. Louis CORE defendants during the Jefferson Bank Protest (sometimes spelled "Wyvetta" in Clay's account; see Clay 2008, 64). She went on to a long career in the Illinois House of Representatives representing East St. Louis, which had been her home before moving to St. Louis and to which she returned after marrying Richard Younge of East St. Louis.

[25] Herron, James and Timothy Hogan, "Bank Demonstration Leader Is Convicted Morals Offender," *St. Louis Globe-Democrat.* 15 Oct 1963, p. 1A.

[26] ibid.

[27] ibid.

[28] "Gunn Criticizes CORE, Quota Hiring Demands, Illegal Bias Protests," *St. Louis Globe-Democrat.* 09 Sep 1963, p. 3A. Emphasis added.

[29] "Judge Rejects CORE Motion...," *St. Louis Post-Dispatch.* 23 Sep 1963, p. 3A

[30] ibid. 80

[31] "Police Make Elaborate Efforts...,' *St. Louis Post-Dispatch.* 13 Oct 1963, cited in Clay 2008 38.

[32] Clay 2008, 80

[33] ibid. 36

[34] Swayzee II, Cleon. "Pickets Lock Arms at Bank...," *St. Louis Post-Dispatch.* 31 Aug 1963, p. 1A.

[35] Clay 2008, 61

[36] ibid.

[37] ibid. 63-64

[38] ibid. 127

[39] Clay 2008, 128; and Eardley, Linda. "Marchers Recall Civil Rights...," *St. Louis Post-Dispatch.* 28 Aug 1993, p. 4A. Ms. Haley was the author's colleague at SIUE in East St. Louis.

[40] "Text of Judge Scott's Pre-Sentence Statement," *St. Louis Globe-Democrat.* 25 Oct 63, p. 1.; cited in Clay 2008, 126.
[41] Gerard, Jules B. "Jefferson Bank dispute Rocks St Louis," *Focus/Midwest*, 5:36, 1967. p. 14; in Clay 2008, 132.
[42] Clay 2008, 134
[43] Clay 2008, pp. 127-128
[44] These dates of Oct 11 and 12 are confirmed by "Tucker Urges 2-Week Truce...," *St. Louis Post-Dispatch.* 13 Oct 1963, p. 1A.
[45] *Untitled handwritten notes.* WUSTL Archives, Tucker Papers, Series 3, Box 13, Folder: "Equal Employment Opportunity 10/1/63-12/31/63."
[46] ibid.
[47] ibid.
[48] Tucker, John interview, 2013
[49] Clay 2008, 70-71
[50] ibid. 71
[51] Tucker, John interview, 2013
[52] "Integration Gain Made in St. Louis," *New York Times.* 13 Nov. 1960, p. 70.
[53] Clay 2008, 136
[54] "Bank Officers and Mayor Meet on Dispute over Negro Jobs," *St. Louis Post. Dispatch.* 12 Oct 1963, pp. 1A, 3A.
[55] ibid.
[56] Billen letter. WUSTL Archives, Tucker Papers, Series 3, Box 13, Folder: "Equal Employment Opportunity 10/1/63-12/31/63."
[57] Clay 2008, 71
[58] ibid.
[59] Lang 2009, 173
[60] Clay 2008, 77-78
[61] "Inescapable Obligations," *St. Louis Post-Dispatch.* 25 Oct 1963, p. 8C.
[62] "Forward as One Community," *St. Louis Post-Dispatch.* 29 Oct 1963, p. 8C; cited in Clay 2008, 80.
[63] Clay 2008, 80
[64] Lang 2009, 167
[65] Clay 2008, 80
[66] ibid. 82
[67] "Ministers Urge...," *St. Louis Post-Dispatch.* 30 Oct 1963, pp. 1A, 3A.
[68] Clay 2008, 81
[69] ibid. 76

[70] Lang 2009, 82

[71] Clay 2008, 75

[72] There may be some confusion over when the Council started. The Council on Human Relations was created by Mayor Darst and held its first meeting on June 28, 1949. See "Human Relations Council...," *St. Louis Star-Times*. 24 Jun 1949 p. 11.

[73] Raymond Tucker Papers, Series 1, Box 10, cited in Stein, 127.

[74] *NAACP Youth Council Journal*, 12 Jan 56, Vol 1, No 2, p. 4; cited in Clay 2008, 75.

[75] Clay 2008, 75

[76] Raymond Tucker Papers, Series 1, Box 10, cited in Stein, 128.

[77] ibid.

[78] "Pope Resigns," *St. Louis Argus,* 4-13-56, cited in Lang 2009, 98.

[79] "Café Group Will Ask Members...," *St. Louis Post-Dispatch*. 15 Nov 1960, p. 14A.

[80] "Roos Appoints Seven Members...," *St. Louis Post-Dispatch*. 01 Jul 1964, p. 3A.

[81] Schneider 22

[82] Clay 2008, 177

[83] ibid.

[84] ibid. 49

[85] ibid. 81

[86] "CORE Approves Two-Week Halt in Protests at Jefferson Bank," *St. Louis Post-Dispatch*. 14 Oct 1963, p. 1A.

[87] "Mayor Assails Disorder: Says It Harms Drive," *St. Louis Post-Dispatch*. 01 Sep 1963, p. 1A.

[88] ibid.

[89] Cervantes 9-10

[90] Lang 2009, 170

[91] ibid.

[92] ibid.

[93] Stein 132

[94] ibid.

[95] See Stein 132-133, and Clay 2004, 26-27.

[96] Stein 133

[97] Edgel, Holly. "A Monumental Figure: 4 Times Martin Luther King Jr. Spoke in St. Louis," *St. Louis Public Radio*. Posted: 14 Jan 2018. Accessed: 02 Feb 2022. https://news.stlpublicradio.org/arts/2018-01-14/a-monumental-figure-4-times-martin-luther-king-jr-spoke-in-st-louis

[98] King, "Address Delivered at St. Louis Freedom Rally," 1957

[99] King, "Give Us the Ballot," 1957

[100] "Equal Housing, Work Urged by Rev. King," *St. Louis Globe Democrat.* 21 Jun 1961, p. 10A.

[101] "King Warns Negro Feelings Could Erupt Into Violence," *St. Louis Globe-Democrat.* 24 Jun 1961, p. 3A.

[102] "Dr. King Urges Church Attack on Inequality," *St. Louis Post-Dispatch.* 13 Oct 1964, p. 5A.

[103] See Theising, ed., *In the Walnut Grove*, p. 39.

[104] ibid. 133

1957 Mayoral General Campaign Ad, St. Louis
Globe-Democrat.

Snapshots of Mayor Tucker, June 1964. This is probably the West End Community Conference "Interracial Housing Tour," in the 5500-5600 blocks of Delmar Boulevard. Courtesy of the Tucker Family

Groundbreaking at the Gateway Arch, June 23, 1959. Mayor Tucker (center) tosses the symbolic spade of dirt, while R. E. MacDonald (president of MacDonald Construction—the builder) beams with joy at left. Alderman Archie Blaine stands behind MacDonald with hands folded. In the light suit applauding at right is former mayor Aloys Kaufmann, and next to him, leaning for a better view, is civic icon Morton D. May. Moore Photo, 1959. Courtesy of the Tucker Family. (edited out of this photo at right, ironically, is former Mayor Bernard Dickmann)

Chapter 5

Tying Up Loose Ends:

The Charter, the Suburbs, and
Building the Gateway Arch

Gateway Arch Timeline

1935

STL voters approve bonds, FDR matches funds; demolition of the riverfront site underway, 1935-1937

Nat'l Park Service calls for train track removal, sparking hot debate, 1940

1940

Eero Saarinen (Finland) wins national competition with his arch design, 1948; his famous father, Eliel Saarinen, also submitted a design

Site (temporarily) becomes a municipal parking lot, 1946

1945

President Truman dedicates the site, 1950

1950

1955

STL voters approve another bond issue, 1955

Tucker resolves the volatile train track issue, 1957

Tucker hosts official ground-breaking, 1959

Tucker makes city's final payment, awards contract to the lowest bidder, MacDonald Construction Co., 1962

1960

1965

Construction, 1962-1968

Gateway Arch opens to the public, 1968 (after Tucker left office)

1970

THE 1950S WERE DYNAMIC TIMES. It was a period of unprecedented federal investment in cities and locales—for highways, land clearance, public housing, airports, education and more. It was the decade of heavy suburbanization and a population baby boom. Technology was dazzling! It was a time of war, both hot (Korean Conflict) and cold (Soviet Union). The institutions of government were functioning at high levels and with renewed vigor and efficiency.

The great scholar Max Weber (he was German, so pronounce it *Mahx VAY-bayr*) defined institutions for us back in the early 1900s. Institutions were power arrangements that delivered *work* to customers or constituents. They were organizations that went beyond the individuals who occupied them. The presidency was bigger than Dwight Eisenhower. The governorship of Missouri was bigger than Phil Donnelly. The mayoralty was bigger than Raymond Tucker. Tucker knew this and valued it. He valued the *process* of government work, knowing that changing a *process* would last long after he was out of office.

Society was changing too. Family sizes were large back then and a lot of housing was not. Kids were encouraged to play outside and there were plenty of neighborhood attractions for them—clubs, movie theaters, skating rinks, baseball diamonds, amusement parks.

People valued togetherness (despite racial divisions in that concept) and there were plenty of organizations to facilitate that. In St. Louis' African American community, there was the Pine Street YMCA, a variety of Black professional organizations, at least two newspapers, and strong African American churches. White communities had those organizations also, as well as large Masonic and Scottish Rite organizations, and the Missouri Athletic Club for those who could afford it.

Robert Putnam's brilliant volume called *Bowling Alone* discussed the disappearance of these social connections in the decades after Tucker. No more bowling leagues, no more taverns at the factory gates, the decline of social groups.

Nightclubs were everywhere back then and just didn't hold their allure in future generations.

Disposable income had made it all possible. Scholar Rosemary Feurer makes this point in her work.[1] The G.I. Bill sent millions of (mostly white) veterans to college for the first time in their families' history. The bill was passed in 1944. Cities and towns received about eight million veterans returning from combat and occupation duties by 1947 (Operation Magic Carpet). This meant that by the early 1950s, a wave of highly educated people was unleashed to transform businesses, establish new households in suburbia, and build the new middle class. Society has lost this concept of social investment.

St. Louis embraced a LOT of institutional change in the Tucker years. The city-suburb region was being transformed, more or less with his leadership: Civic Progress (in its long-term form) in 1954, the Metropolitan St. Louis Sewer District in 1954, one of the very first public television stations in the country (KETC) in 1954, the expansion of Lambert Field (the Yamasaki terminal that stands today) in 1956, Downtown St. Louis Inc. in 1958, the construction of the (later-named) Abram Federal Building on Market Street in 1961, the Junior College District (St. Louis Community College) in 1962, the consolidation of mass transit under the Bi-State Development Agency in 1963, the creation of the McDonnell Planetarium in Forest Park (then the world's largest, designed by Gyo Obata), the University of Missouri-St. Louis in 1963, and the East-West Gateway Council of Governments in 1965 (technically six months after Tucker left office, but the groundwork was laid), and progress on the flood wall protection system by the Army Corps of Engineers that began under Darst and wasn't projected to be finished until 1967, but most of which happened during the Tucker Era. St. Louis was a wildly different place after Tucker than before.

Tourist sites were changing too: There was Gaslight Square in the late 1950s, the St. Louis Playboy Club in 1962, and even an attempt to move the Museum of Transport (at the museum's request) from Kirkwood to downtown in 1962. It was to have been located on Laclede's Landing between the Eads and Veterans (now MLK) Bridges, and happened over the same period as the push for preservation of Laclede's Landing in 1965 (as well as the mirror image of Chouteau's Landing and visions for East St. Louis) by creative minds like preservation architect Ted Wofford, AIA, and artist Saunders Schultz.[2]

The Tucker Era was certainly one of institutional change. So much of it was embraced, but quite a bit of it was rejected. Tucker led St. Louis through some difficult discussions. City voters—for whatever their reasons—were just not receptive. Unknowingly, they may have been squandering St. Louis' last chance for greatness.

Paradigm-Shifting Plans

St. Louis was facing some gigantic decisions, though the average citizen may not have known it. There were big decisions being made in Washington DC after World War Two. St. Louis, if it wanted part of it, had to be aggressive. There were political, military, industrial, and technological decisions being made at the same time. The city would need a conscious and coordinated effort to stay on top of it all. The various chambers of commerce played an especially important role, largely without success, though new institutions emerged. St. Louis had thrown its hat into the ring for major projects, such as hosting the United Nations Headquarters and the Air Force Academy.

For the institutions that existed already, there were some loose ends. The city's charter remained a stumbling block for the efficient operation of a modern government. Then there was the growing imbalance between city and suburb. Finally, there was the Arch project—long ago designed, approved, site-ready and perpetually stalled over some train tracks. Mayor Tucker was not content to let these projects just founder.

ONE LAST SWING AT CHARTER CHANGE

Mayor Tucker saw a need for charter change during his first term, even more so than in 1950. He conceived of a new Board of Freeholders in 1956 that would have one year to come up with a document and present it to the people.

Some changes in the 1957 charter were consistent with the 1950 charter—such as increased fiscal controls in the mayor's office, changes to city department structures, and special regulation of traffic problems. However, this version called for the mayor's salary to be raised to $25,000 (over $225,000 in today's dollars) (Donald Gunn would step back from the Board President position in 1959 due to a low salary).[3] Further, it seemed to have a back-door statement for Civil Rights, where it could "define and prohibit...all acts [and] conduct [including businesses]...detrimental to the [welfare of inhabitants]."[4]

The biggest change would be to the Board of Aldermen. Instead of 28 wards electing one member and a board president elected city-wide, it would be cut in half. There would be 14 aldermen, half elected directly from their seven newly created wards and half elected at large. The board president would still be elected city-wide.[5] The plan came to be known as the "7-7-1 Plan" and that was the new charter's nickname in the media and meetings.

The 7-7-1 plan had an operational advantage that Tucker liked. It would necessarily diminish—if not eliminate—what he saw as the evils of politicians on the board: spot zoning and aldermanic courtesy (not challenging aldermen on items specific to their wards). These provisions wreaked havoc on the city plan by messing with land use and gave unfair advantage to well-connected individuals.

Taking Sides

The city's upper-management crowd extolled the virtues of the new charter. Mayor Tucker gave a speech embracing the change as necessary and urgent. It was backed by the League of Women Voters, the Chamber of Commerce, the CEOs of Civic Progress, both newspapers, former Mayor Aloys Kaufmann, Board President Donald Gunn, and Comptroller John Poelker. Everyone else hated it.

Once again, Mayor Tucker had upset key constituencies. First were those who relied on partisanship and dealmaking. Only *one* of the city's Democratic ward organizations endorsed the plan—the other 27 organizations *of the mayor's own party* did not. Second, the Mayor alienated the African American voter base. Cutting back on the number of aldermen would mean cutting back on the number of seats held by African Americans. Further, many African Americans saw at-large voting as a way to keep African Americans out of office by diluting the Black vote. The NAACP would not support it, and NAACP attorney David M. Grant, one of the elected Freeholders, did not sign the final released document.

There was another rallying cry against the new charter—taxes, taxes, taxes! Recall that *Dillon's Rule* means the city only has the power given to it in its charter, so the forward-thinking freeholders listed out all the things the city would have the power to tax if it wanted to. Article Ten of the proposed charter listed them out, alphabetically, and there was a paragraph of potential taxes for nearly each letter of the alphabet.

A: abstractors of land titles, acetylene gas, accounting machines, acids, acoustical supplies...

B: baby sitter agencies, badminton or tennis courts, bail bondsmen, bakers...

C: cables, calculating machines, cameras, carnivals, carpentry, carpets...

D: dairies, dance halls and studios, dealers or distributors of goods, decorating, delivery goods...

E: electricity, electric appliances, electric or compressed hammers, electrical transcription, electrical work...

F: fans, farmers markets, feather renovating, feed brokers, ferries and boats, fertilizers, filling stations...

G: galvanizing, garages, garbage removers, gas and gas appliances, gasoline...

H: halls, hardware, hauling, hawkers, hucksters, heating, hoisting...

I: ice, incinerators, income or other tax returns or services, industrial instruments, information or inspection bureaus...

J: janitor service, jewelry, job wagons, jobbers...

K: kalsomining, kitchen equipment

L: labor or public relations counselors, laboratories, laboratory equipment, lamps, landscaping...

M: machine shops, machinery of all kinds, machinery designing, magazines, mail order houses...

N: natural gas companies, navigation companies or steamboat lines, news agents...

O: office buildings, office uniforms, office equipment, oil companies...
P: packing or slaughter houses, paint sprayers, painting, paper, paper hanging...
Q: quarries
R: race tracks, radios, radio equipment, radio or television broadcasting stations, railroads...
S: safes, safe depositories, salary brokers or buyers, sales counseling, sand blasting, sash material...
T: tailors, tanks, tanners, tape machines, tariff bureaus, tattooing, taxicabs...
U: umbrellas, underwriters, upholsterers, upholstering, ushering
V: vacuum cleaners, vaults, vehicles, vending machines...
W: wall paper cleaning, washing machines, watches, watchmen...[6]

There was nothing for the letters X, Y, and Z. It was as if they took a Labor Department survey of American jobs and just copied the list (and could justify stopping with W).

All citizens of St. Louis, if they wanted to, could find something on that list that was then untaxed and would soon have the potential for being taxed. Every occupation, every major object in the average home, the tools (and clothes) one would see at work were all on the list. This was the charter's fatal error. People thought these taxes would all be implemented at once (rather than just giving the city permission to tax them someday if the city chose to). The charter was defeated handily.

Tucker's friend Donald Gunn, President of the Board of Aldermen, was censured by a majority his members for his support of the 1957 charter, as was Jack Dwyer, City Treasurer and chair of the only Democratic committee to endorse it.[7]

Tucker, the pragmatist, looked at the next available option. In his first talk with reporters after the defeat, he said, "I have supported the method by which an entirely new charter is proposed," and acknowledged "this has been defeated." The next method was amendment of the existing charter. "There now appears to be agreement among both [sides] that modernization is needed."[8] He added, "We who supported the

212

adoption of the new charter should not be discouraged.... I have the utmost confidence in the judgment of the people of St. Louis. ...We can revise the charter for the benefit of all."[9]

In the year 2021, through the amendment process, the Board of Aldermen of the City of St. Louis voted to cut its size in half, the total number Tucker proposed in 1957. The individual aldermen would represent 14 different wards, though.

Re-election by a Big Margin

Between the time when the freeholders first convened and the new charter was put on the ballot, St. Louis had another mayoral election. Tucker had won acclaim for his management of the city. *National Geographic*, *Harpers*, and the *Saturday Evening Post* all did profiles of the old city with bold ideas that was being dragged into midcentury kicking and screaming by a professor who knew what was good for all of them. [10] Despite Tucker's landslide re-election (a 41,000-vote margin!), his endorsement for the charter didn't resonate. People seemed to like him and his methods, but not his ideas. They seemed to have enjoyed being asked, though.

Turnout was respectable by voters. The newspapers and universities gave attention and effort to the big ideas. Tucker was getting tired, though, of the voters' conservative ways. Leave it to a new politician to come up with the next big idea.

AUTHENTICATION OF THE CHARTER

On this 7th day of May, 1957, we the undersigned Chairman, Vice Chairman, Secretary, and the other members of the Board of Freeholders elected pursuant to Ordinance No. 47690 of The City of St. Louis, State of Missouri, hereby certify that the above and foregoing is a true and complete copy of the new or revised Charter of The City of St. Louis prepared by us for submission to the qualified voters of the City for ratification, as provided in Section 32 of Article VI of the Constitution of the State of Missouri.

IN WITNESS WHEREOF we have hereunto subscribed our names.

ATTEST:

GEORGE L. STEMMLER, *Chairman*

DR. RALPH A. KINSELLA

MRS. CONRAD SOMMER, *Vice Chairman*

MELVIN H. KRAH

C. B. BROUSSARD, *Secretary*

JOHN J. NALLY

FREDERICK E. BUSSE

HENRY B. PFLAGER

JOHN F. X. CALLANAN

WILLIAM A. WEBB

MAJOR B. EINSTEIN

FRANK L. G. WEISS

DAVID M. GRANT

David M. Grant's signature clearly is missing from this official copy of the 1957 proposed charter. As the NAACP's attorney, he refused to sign the final product when the organization refused to endorse it. Theising image; Author's collection.

214

MERGING CITY AND SUBURB

Change was in the air in 1957. The city was examining its charter, the county was looking at consolidation of suburbs, and there was a formal study of merging the two.[11] Alfonso J. Cervantes, that "young, energetic, and politically ambitious St. Louis alderman," started the whole discussion.[12] He was 34 years old and the chairman of the aldermanic committee on traffic. He was looking at ways to alleviate the traffic jams that many leaders felt pushed frustrated folks to suburbia.

While trying to devise a plan to better work with suburbia, someone pointed out that the Missouri Constitution offered the possibility of formally linking St. Louis the city and St. Louis the county. Cervantes pushed for the idea and set up the Citizens' Committee for City-County Co-Ordination in 1955. Cervantes was a candidate for President of the Board of Aldermen (a city-wide office) and incorporated the idea into his platform.[13]

There were four possible choices laid out by the "new" Missouri Constitution of 1945. These were: 1.) merger of all governments in St. Louis city and county into one giant municipal government called the "City of St. Louis"; 2.) re-entry of the City of St. Louis as another city in the County of St. Louis; 3.) enlargement of the city's boundary by annexing parts of the county; or 4.) creating one or more metropolitan districts for administering services common to the areas (e.g., a police district that served across city and county lines; a fire district that consolidated the urban and suburban departments; or perhaps a public works district that maintained local roads without regard for municipal boundaries.[14] The only thing leaders could agree on was to convene a Board of Freeholders to start the discussion. Signatures were being gathered to launch the idea. In a speech before the Missouri Municipal League, Mayor Tucker said that rapid suburbanization could only be addressed "after exhaustive studies," warning that Cervantes' committee was being "hasty" in addressing far-reaching and permanent solutions.[15]

Their First Clash

This was one of the first major policy clashes the two had,

and Cervantes saw the dismissal of his idea as a threat to his path to higher office.[16] When Cervantes saw that top civic and business leaders were taking their cues from Tucker and not financing his committee, he paused the petition drive on the matter. Meanwhile, political scientists from Washington University and Saint Louis University had proposed doing a major study of St. Louis structure and service delivery. They approached the Ford Foundation for funding. When Tucker learned of this, he saw it as the solution to the hasty planning of the Cervantes committee, which was still seeking funding for its work.

Tucker publicly supported the university study, called *The Metropolitan St. Louis Survey.* He worked with James S. McDonnell (and the McDonnell Aircraft Charitable Trust) to secure the matching funding ($50,000) for the Ford Foundation grant ($250,000). The mayor endorsed the study, the county supervisor endorsed it, corporate leaders lent their support, and the money was in hand. It was the Ford Foundation's first grant in the subject area and it started in the summer of 1956.[17] Tucker won this battle, and Cervantes had to sit on his hands for the next year.

The survey team dug deeply into data, documents, and interviews with over 2,000 residents of the region. The committee debated the findings and produced a series of reports, culminating with a book-length report called *Path of Progress for Metropolitan St. Louis.* One of the consultants was Louis Brownlow, the man who helped Franklin Roosevelt restructure the national executive branch some 25 years earlier.

An outside scholar participating in the discussion noted the "obeisance to political reality" that dominated the survey. Shouldn't "they be creating some sort of model…which does not give primary consideration to whether Democrats or Republicans control the County?"[18] The outsider was right. The survey team was paying great attention to the ability to implement the plan—and it indeed mattered which party controlled the County.

One of the reasons for this partisan concern was uncovered in the survey data. The Republican City Committee endorsed "federation" of city and county.[19] However, key Republican leaders in the county were vehemently opposed to merger because the metropolitan-wide jurisdiction would contain a majority of Democrat voters.[20] "The partisans, especially the Republicans, were unwilling or unable to separate political considerations from metropolitan solutions." [21] In the conservative small suburban towns, mayors already shot down the county's trial balloon on suburban consolidation. They didn't want to merge with their neighbors and they had no desire to merge with the central city either.

Just Pick One

Coming out of the study phase, the scholarly panel made its recommendation: establish an expansive metropolitan service government (choice #4). Nevertheless, it was not the panel's decision to make. They could make recommendations, and lay out arguments for and against, but only an actual Board of Freeholders could have the power to submit something specific to the voters—and county voters were not keen on choice #4.

Cervantes' petition drive in the city, along with a parallel effort in the county, led to the creation of a Board of Freeholders to consider some kind of merger from the four constitutional choices. The freeholders debated (sometimes hotly) the various choices in front of them. A total of five proposals was submitted by various factions of the board, using different structural elements and various combinations of the constitutional choices. However, it came down to a battle between choice #1 (merger) and choice #4 (service district). When the two were put to a head-to-head vote, choice #4 won by a single vote.[22] It became known as the *St. Louis District Plan.*

Cervantes led the district campaign in the city; no one really wanted to lead the campaign in the county. After losing three months of the campaign calendar (from May to August), a civic-minded car dealer, unfamiliar to most people, stepped into the role.[23]

Mayor Tucker was not happy; many noted his silence and lack of enthusiasm. The ideal choice for him was a complete merger of all jurisdictions (choice #1), but he understood that this was impractical, so having the city re-enter the county was the next best option (choice #2). It would at least put city and suburb in the same sandbox. When the board advanced choice #4, Tucker withdrew his support of the effort.

The post-mortem case study declared his withdrawal to be "the most crippling blow" to the effort.[24] He argued in a "carefully reasoned" statement a month before the election: The district plan was "unsound" and "inefficient," and it "failed to reflect the economic, social, and cultural interdependence of the area." Further, it didn't eliminate any units of government, so this new district was actually *in addition to* the plethora of wards and governments that functionally created the problem purporting to be fixed.[25] The measure failed miserably in city and suburb.

One More Try

Almost immediately, though, the merger concept was resurrected. Those freeholders who supported choice #1: merger (like Mayor Tucker wanted), came up with a plan and a method to get it before the voters that didn't require another freeholder board. This time it was called the *St. Louis Borough Plan*. They took the idea to Mayor Tucker in advance and asked him to champion the effort. Tucker abstained. He thought it lacked order and clarity, and that it would encourage premature decisions that would have negative long-term consequences. The group designed it all without Mayor Tucker, who probably was the strongest voice on the subject to be found locally.

Instead of using the freeholder route, the supporters used a petition drive to make it an amendment to the state constitution. Charles Vatterott, a major contractor who built suburban subdivisions, was the effort's chairman. It would be easy to get enough signatures to put it on the ballot statewide, but the ballot wording was necessarily brief. The new merged government would have been structured into 22 boroughs, with seven wholly in the county, eight wholly in the city, and seven that straddled the old city-county line.[26] The expectation that volunteers and donations would appear automatically to support the effort proved to be a tragic mistake.[27]

One editorial opposing the plan quoted a line purported to be from Mayor Tucker: he believes in marriage, but he does not believe in marrying the first woman who comes along.[28] Even civic leaders who had initially endorsed the Borough Plan changed their minds and announced their opposition, including Mrs. George Gellhorn—a longtime civic powerhouse in St. Louis, a founder of the League of Women Voters (which did not endorse), and mother of famed journalist Martha Gellhorn.[29]

The voters across Missouri defeated it in November 1962. The Republican National Committeeman for Missouri had called the plan a "governmental monstrosity."[30] To help calm the electorate, Mayor Tucker and the new Republican County Supervisor, Lawrence K. Roos, made a joint presentation on the importance of coordinating services and strengthening the city-county relationship.[31]

See, I Told You So

The city had been declining on many fronts in the 1960s, and especially so after Mayor Tucker left office in 1965. The Rand Report from 1973 noted how severe the decline was in those years after Mayor Tucker. "If industrial location trends during the last half of the 1960s (that is, after the Tucker Administration) continue for another five years, St. Louis County will contain that share of metropolitan business activity usually characteristic of a central city."[32] It did.

"Large in-migrations of groups that vary from the existing population—such as rural low-income families—appear to hasten the departure of more affluent families to the suburbs."[33] This applied to both whites and Blacks.

Decentralization has made revenue "progressively more difficult to generate locally."[34] Downtown was no longer the shopping hub. Union Station carried only a fraction of the rail passenger traffic it used to. Jobs were moving out of the city just like residents were. It was the movement of wealth to the suburbs that was behind all of this, more related to class than race. Tucker's pursuit of choice #1 during the reform era would have addressed that.

The Rand Report also suggested St. Louis, with all its struggles, could have treated itself as a large "suburb" to the County (suggesting it could be one that catered to African Americans) rather than try to revive the traditional central city functions and leverage various fiscal mechanisms to tap the County's wealth.[35] Ironically, Tucker's pursuit of choice #2 back in 1959 would have enabled that as well.

FINISHING THE ARCH

One of the nagging projects that had been on the shelf for a long time was the Gateway Arch. It was a fantastic plan that offered opportunity to give downtown St. Louis a distinct asset of international prominence. So much energy and effort had gone into it. It was a shame that progress stalled. If Tucker did not put renewed energy into it, this big opportunity could pass by St. Louis. This was not a new concern, though.

One Man's Vision

Luther Ely Smith was on an inbound train coming from Indiana in the autumn of 1933. He had been appointed by President Calvin Coolidge six years earlier to spearhead the development of the George Rogers Clark Memorial on the Wabash River in Vincennes. As Smith crossed the Eads Bridge into St. Louis, he could not help but envision something great on this riverfront, something more impressive to visitors than just rows of warehouses, something that would far surpass when he had accomplished in Indiana.[36] He called a meeting to discuss the idea with the city's new mayor, Bernard F. Dickmann. Dickmann loved it and presented it to his cabinet a few weeks later in December.

Dickmann himself went to the White House to seek Franklin Roosevelt's support of the $30 million memorial.[37] Roosevelt approved the idea, but did not commit to the entire budget. Voters had approved a $2.25 million bond issue to start the work on September 10, 1935 with nearly 71% of the vote in favor.[38] All elements of the city looked forward to the creation of jobs, higher property values, and the financial investment in the city. Roosevelt was prepared to finance the federal government's $6.75 million match of the project through the Emergency Relief Appropriations Act of 1935. The Attorney General ruled that the president could not make such an authorization. [39] Dickmann was furious and threatened to withhold support of FDR in the fall elections. Thankfully, the Assistant Attorney General found a loophole that the president could exploit—but only if the land could be declared of historical importance. Interior Secretary Harold Ickes determined that it was historically important and said "I think we ought to go through with it under whatever guise." [40] Roosevelt signed the appropriation just before Christmas 1935.

Mayor Bernard Dickmann presided over the greatest federal demolition project the city had known to that point—the clearing of 37 blocks of riverfront property to build a national memorial to the Louisiana Purchase. Dickmann ceremoniously started the demolition himself, autographing bricks for those who wanted them.

Progress was quick and visible—exactly what politicians want their constituents to see. There must have been some sloppy accounting, though. In 1940, though, it was discovered that $417,657 of the federal appropriation had lapsed and reverted back to the U.S. Treasury the previous year. [41] On top of this loss, the city's matching funds ($139,213, or one-third of the appropriation) were held by the National Park Service (NPS) and would not be returned unless the idea of a memorial disappeared.

Dickmann was in a tough spot but was able to reach an understanding with federal officials. The federal authorities would provide WPA funds that could be used creatively to keep the project alive, and the city would need to sell more bonds at the local level to continue funding its portion of the $6.75 million memorial. The financial problem with the feds was resolved for the time being, but another barrier loomed with the railroads.

Fighting the Railroad

The riverfront tracks, so unsightly in the mind of Luther Ely Smith that he conceived of the grand memorial, had to be moved or replaced. The feds could not be part of the negotiation—only a final approver of the plan from an "ultimate project" perspective. [42] In fact, an early NPS official, Daniel Cox Fahey, had stated before and restated in 1940 that ideally there would be no tracks separating the memorial from the Mississippi. It was suggested that passenger lines be removed first, and freight lines be removed later. Fahey had hoped that this would become the accepted goal of all parties involved and resolve the disputes over location. Instead, he heightened the cantankerous debate to a new level.[43]

A high-level Park Service advisor, Frank Wright, became involved in the debate. He favored the federal government putting some money into the problem, but did not suggest an amount. He also would not endorse *any* of the ideas put forward about the tracks. Wright's conversations only emboldened the National Park Service's point man on the issue, Superintendent John Nagle, to step back from negotiations and let the local interests settle the matter. Dickmann was furious at Wright's involvement. He did not want Washington DC upsetting the negotiations around St. Louis' tracks and the Terminal Railroad didn't want it either.[44]

Dickmann called Wright to St. Louis for a "showdown" on the matter. The mayor continued to push the Terminal Railroad Association (TRRA) for removal of its tracks, which had been the position of NPS before it stepped back. TRRA proposed a dual-use line (passenger and freight) in front of the memorial that would be, roughly, at grade.[45]

Wright's meeting with Dickmann went nowhere. Subsequent meetings with the railroads also did not go well. It was decided that each of the interests (St. Louis, TRRA, and the Park Service) appoint an engineer to a study committee. The Park Service declined to participate in the committee, but did reject the TRRA plan for dual-use tracks in front of the memorial. Basically, all the work done to this point was thrown out.[46]

The TRRA's president, Philip Watson Jr., already had strained his credibility with the Park Service. Nagle felt that Watson wasted time with useless arguments and red herrings.[47] Watson had also strained his relationship with Mayor Dickmann by opposing the smoke elimination ordinance that Tucker had help fashion. It was then that Watson started using national defense as an argument against moving any rail tracks. With World War II looming, Watson said it was "unthinkable" to remove the riverfront tracks because of the requirements "to meet the emergency growing out of the national defense program."[48]

Frustrations were high. The city's Board of Estimate and Apportionment decided to play hardball. Just a few weeks after the engineering committee met, the Board took action to revoke TRRA's permit to use the riverfront tracks. This action required *another* team of engineers to work on re-routing the city's railroad traffic around the riverfront. Amid all this turmoil, a new solution emerged—a tunnel through the memorial site. It would allow the memorial to have uninterrupted access to the river, it would allow the railroads to keep some version of a riverfront line, and it would allow the project to move forward. It was also the most expensive solution that could have been devised: at least $3 million ($56 million in today's dollars).[49]

Secretary of the Interior Harold Ickes noted that the tunnel plan did address the NPS concern about river access, but that the feds did not have the money to pay for it. TRRA already was on the record that it would not pay for the government's project. The City of St. Louis was mortgaged to the hilt from several Depression-era bond issues generally, as well as specifically for this project. At least now it was just a money problem.[50]

The year was 1940. The studies continued. The land clearance continued. Luther Ely Smith, leading citizen on the matter and president of the nonprofit board working with the NPS, believed that since everyone wanted to see progress overall, the individual matters would work themselves out.[51]

After Dickmann lost elected office in 1941, Republican Mayor William Dee Becker picked up the negotiations with TRRA. Becker had been born across the river in East St. Louis, graduated from Harvard and then St. Louis University for law, and had served as a judge in St. Louis for 24 years before running for mayor. He was a talented and seasoned leader. Under Becker there were more meetings, more officials, more plans and a higher price tag. What had been a $3 million tunnel had ballooned in a new TRRA study to new approaches, temporary tracks (leaving the permanent track question undecided), and a price tag of at least $5 million. TRRA justified its position based on the war emergency.[52]

Becker was furious. He formally charged the TRRA with "obstructionist" tactics and was using the war emergency as a convenient excuse to delay the matter. This led to more study, more negotiations, and little progress. Becker's untimely death in 1943 meant that yet another mayor would be involved in the project, Republican Aloys Kaufmann, who had been President of the Board of Aldermen.[53]

Kaufmann inherited the office just as the federal WPA program was ending—and it was WPA money that had been used to keep the memorial work going. It had been a beneficial program for the project and for St. Louis (and the country). All told, the WPA had contributed $959,504 to the memorial project—more than double the funds that had lapsed in 1939-40.[54] Now, Mayor Kaufmann had an unfinished memorial, an ongoing disagreement with TRRA on the riverfront tracks, and no congressional appropriation to move it any further.[55]

Congress became focused on funding the war effort and was in no position to allocate money for the memorial. It would be years before there could be any kind of serious funding discussion. By that time the early champions were gone or moved on—Roosevelt was dead, Dickmann was out of office, Interior Secretary Harold Ickes stepped down. Only Luther Ely Smith was the constant, bringing on new officials, keeping the plan front-of-mind, and pushing the project ever forward. The war effort left St. Louis with a naked riverfront. In 1946, the National Park Service, which now owned the land, signed an agreement to allow the city to operate the space as a parking lot.[56] It would be unfortunate if that were deemed the land's best use after all the promises.

While there was no money for further site development under the Kaufmann Administration, the memorial association called for a $225,000 international design competition ($3 million in today's dollars). Luther Ely Smith worked with the American Institute of Architects to manage the process, with Smith himself underwriting the last $40,000 of the cost from his personal wealth until other funders could step in (a half-million today).[57]

Ideas for the memorial poured in from all directions. Finnish architect Eero Saarinen's arch was a hit, in St. Louis and around the country. The *New York Times* declared it to be "a modern monument—fitting, beautiful, and impressive."[58] Of course there were detractors who called it a giant hairpin, a grand hitching post, and even a Mussolini-like monument to fascism.[59] These criticisms were all dismissed (though the last one did warrant a written response from the selection committee, since the defeat of fascism was fresh in everyone's minds). Now that a design was chosen, Saarinen's voice weighed in on the negotiations. He proclaimed that if the railroad tracks were allowed to block access to the river, he would withdraw his participation.[60]

Luther Ely Smith was growing tired. He no longer had the stamina to be the cheerleader, fundraiser, introduction-maker, liaison, and all-around champion of the project. On the occasion of his 75th birthday, in 1948, he stepped down as president of the Jefferson National Expansion Memorial Association. (He was 58 when it all started.) One of his last acts was the selection of Eero Saarinen's design. He wrote a glowing letter to Saarinen: "it was your design, your marvelous conception, your brilliant forecast into the future, that has made the realization of the dream possible—a dream that you and the wonderful genius at your command and the able assistance of your associates are going to achieve far beyond the remotest possibility that we had dared visualize in the beginning."[61] He dropped dead of a heart attack in the street in 1951. The 76-year old attorney was walking from his home on Pershing toward his office at 7th and Locust, when he was stricken in front of the Park Plaza Hotel at Maryland Ave. and Kingshighway. The man who envisioned a new riverfront had shepherded the project from conception to land clearance to design competition and selection, was gone. Finishing the dream would be left to another team and another mayor.

Getting It Done

In the year 1950, the project from the 1930s now touched its third decade and construction was still a long way off. Mayor Joseph Darst was in his first year of office and former Mayor Kaufmann took over the powerful St. Louis Chamber of Commerce. Darst had been a good friend of former Missouri Senator and now President Harry S. Truman, and called on his old friend for help. Fearing that interest in the project was lagging, Darst asked Truman to "dedicate" the site. On June 10, 1950, Truman obliged.

This renewed national interest seemed to mean the stars were aligning for the aging endeavor. However, two weeks after Truman lifted local spirits on the project, North Korea invaded South Korea and Congress was once again focused on a war effort rather than funding memorials. It would be another four years before Congress would appropriate any money to the St. Louis project.

However, the bickering continued. Darst was growing furious. He threatened that if city officials and the TRRA didn't get together on a plan for the tracks, he would "go to Washington and seek to have the riverfront deeded back to the city for public housing."[62]

St. Louis Congressman John B. Sullivan, who had served in Dickmann's inner-circle in the 1930s, like Joseph Darst and Raymond Tucker, introduced a bill to fund the Arch in 1950. A subcommittee authorized $5 million of funding, but it went nowhere as the Korean War heated up. In the meantime, the city built baseball diamonds and a flower garden on the riverfront.

Federal officials were growing tired of the project. In 1953, at the end of Darst's single term, there was a threat from the feds to "throw the whole thing back in the lap of the city." By this time, millions had been spent and millions more needed.[63]

To battle the federal fatigue for the project, new Missouri Senator Stuart Symington (a former executive with Emerson Electric) pushed through a resolution of support, without funding, favoring memorial completion. His goal was to keep the federal government on-record in support of the project.

Congressman John Sullivan died suddenly in 1951, and the following year his widow, Leonor Kretzer Sullivan, was elected to fill the vacancy. She proved to be a formidable politician and won reelection eleven times. Congresswoman Leonor K. Sullivan introduced a funding measure in the fall of 1953 for $5 million for the project. The *authorization* was approved in May 1954, but Congress did not have the money for the *appropriation* in the budget that started on October 1.[64] In those days, the federal budget had to be balanced as a matter of principle. The riverfront parking lot remained unchanged five years after Truman dedicated it as the memorial site. Even though the *appropriation* didn't happen, the *authorization* remained.

Building the Arch (at last)

It was not until 1956, though, that President Eisenhower managed to balance the federal budget enough to allow memorial funding, $3 million was allocated solely to relocate the riverfront railroad tracks—which had been a sticking point for so many years.[65] The award was later reduced to $2.64 million, but at least a federal appropriation showed up![66] This action had the power to break the long-stalled negotiations loose.

By this time, Raymond Tucker had been in office for three years. He was in the middle of executing grand plans across the city and the naked riverfront was an underutilized asset. He worked closely with Congresswoman Sullivan. With federal money starting to flow, as well as approval of local bond money in 1955, it was time to settle the track issue once and for all.

Philip Watson, president of the TRRA, had died suddenly after surgery in 1946. (His son-in-law was Lawrence K. Roos, Republican leader of St. Louis County.) He was replaced by Armstrong Chinn.[67] Chinn was of the same mindset of Watson —delay, delay, delay. Chinn hired yet another engineering firm to study the issue, telling the press there was no "thought control" placed on them. The report suggested keeping the tracks as-is—bringing back the same old TRRA position of status-quo.[68] The TRRA announced in February of 1958 that it had yet another plan that would keep the tracks at surface level—basically throwing all of the previous work out the window. "We couldn't do anything until they were removed," Tucker recalled in later years. "There had been endless discussion and nothing accomplished."

Tucker called representatives of the Terminal Railroad Association, the National Park Service, and the Memorial Association to his office.[69] The meeting took place on November 15, 1957, in classic Tucker fashion—facts, debate, consensus, compromise. The mayor broke the work into three key decisions. "First, without talking about the cost or who would pay what, we would come up with a design which would be acceptable to everybody, including Mr. Saarinen," Tucker said. Second, Tucker pushed the group to agree on the estimated cost, without regard to who would pay. The final piece was to discuss the division of payment.[70] It worked.

Tucker, the engineer, devised a technical solution that was previously not considered and saved the project. The TRRA had wanted tracks to stay at their existing ground level. The Park Service wanted the tracks below grade in a tunnel. Tucker suggested cutting a channel instead, riprapping the sides with stone, and placing a concrete slab over the top.[71] It was the easy construction style the TRRA wanted; it functionally put the tracks below grade, which the Park Service wanted, by building the memorial site up higher. It was considerably cheaper than tunnel construction, which made everyone happy. Though the TRRA tried to wriggle out of the deal briefly in 1958, in the end, the TRRA committed $500,000 to the project.[72] It was a small sum, but previously it had said it would pay nothing. After more than a decade of debate, the matter finally was settled. Chinn turned over the half-million dollars to Mayor Tucker to satisfy the TRRA's portion of the project on June 16, 1958.[73] Eight weeks later, Chinn died suddenly after surgery—just like his predecessor. Russell Dearmont, President of the Missouri Pacific Railroad and a longtime director of the TRRA, replaced him.

That December, Russell Dearmont received the prestigious St. Louis Award for, as the *Post-Dispatch* described, changing the TRRA's "obstructionist attitude."[74] One has to wonder if it was Dearmont's success that caused the change, or the sudden funerals of TRRA executives!

Mayor Tucker arrived at what was then called the municipal parking lot on June 23, 1959 for the groundbreaking ceremonies. The project had languished for nearly 25 years and had been the frustration of five mayoral administrations.

Money continued to be a problem. The city requested $8.19 million from the federal government to help move the project forward. President Eisenhower cut it to $1.65 million. The city scaled back its request to $4.6 million—which the city said was the minimum needed to keep the project on track for completion in 1964, the city's bicentennial. Congress allocated $2.9 million in the 1960 budget—bicentennial be damned.[75] It was enough to begin excavation of the site and construction of the museum. MacDonald Construction Company received the initial contract for the base work.

After years of wrangling, the money to build the Arch finally was authorized. In one of his last budget actions in office, President Eisenhower proposed $9.5 million to finish the project. John F. Kennedy signed the appropriations bill on August 3, 1961.[76] Unfortunately, the delay in decision-making meant that costs were rising while the budget remained flat.

When the bids were opened, the lowest bid was from

This CharmCraft postcard of the proposed Arch and stadium from the early 1960s had the following message from 1964: "Dear Mother, This description [of planned downtown development] sounds as though St. Louis is like me—more things planned than will ever get done, but I have been surprised before…. I can't see that the arch pictured will be much of an addition to the landscape, but it will be an improvement to have something done to the riverfront. Love, Martha" Theising image; Author's collection.

This image shows the Arch in its original 1947 design, which was shorter and more rounded. Saarinen modified the design from the proposed 590 feet high to 630 feet—so that its height and width would be the same. Robert Osserman (interviewing Saarinen colleague Bruce Detmers) suggests it was in part due to the construction of taller buildings in St. Louis (Saarinen wanted the Arch to dominate it surroundings) and due to the designer's "predilection for perfect geometric shapes," adjusting the Arch so that it could be "exactly inscribed in a square." (Osserman, Robert. "How the Gateway Arch Got its Shape," Nexus Network Journal, 12:2, 2010, pp. 167-189. Quotes from pp. 179-180.)

MacDonald Construction for $12,139,918—about 50% higher than anticipated.[77] It did not deter Tucker. Cost-cutting measures were identified and some creative revenue streams were tapped.

On March 14, 1962, Mayor Tucker went to the Old Courthouse to formally award the contract to MacDonald. He handed a check to Conrad Wirth, National Park Service director, for $2.5 million as the city's final payment of its $7.5 million construction contribution. In total, from the beginning, the federal government spent $24 million, the city $7.5 million, and TRRA $500,000, for a total investment of $32 million.[78] Tucker had done his part and stepped aside. The project ultimately spanned the administrations of six mayors and five presidents before it was completed and opened in 1968.

Tucker had been an institutionalist all along. He had confidence in the institutions involved to make the best decision. He saw value in pursuing the Arch, not only for its historical significance, but as a tool to kick-start downtown revitalization. The new downtown was already bubbling with proposals to complement Arch construction. A downtown stadium was being built and the Civic Center Redevelopment Corporation was prepared to demolish the few remaining slums of the Mill Creek Valley. For a time starting in 1963, Walt Disney considered building an amusement venue near the Arch to be called "Riverfront Square."[79]

Tucker flew to Los Angeles to meet with Disney in March, 1963. The new theme park was to be entirely indoors and feature historic themes around Thomas Jefferson, Daniel Boone, and Mark Twain.[80] There remains wide speculation as to why the deal fell through. St. Louis may have been a ruse so that Disney could amass land holdings in Florida without suspicion, or if the Florida land purchase was to pressure St. Louis into cutting a deal.[81] Disney had a public tussle with August Busch surrounding a business deal in Houston, and that may have soured the relationship in St. Louis as well.[82] Busch had planned to build an Anheuser-Busch museum next to the Disney building, which would focus on Clydesdales, brewing beer, and the family's history. Disney did not want his name to be used to market beer (or the Playboy Club, which was also going up in St. Louis).[83] According to his family, the pragmatic

Tucker told Disney that it was futile of him to challenge Busch on any project in St. Louis and would be a waste of his money.[84]

Disney withdrew his money and his plans in the summer of 1965—weeks after Tucker was defeated for re-election—and announced his Florida plans that November.   August Busch was so impressed with Disney's plans that he developed his own theme park a few years later—not in St. Louis but in Los Angeles—while civic leaders in St. Louis later bought elements from the New York World's Fair in 1965 to create a new attraction to replace Disney's idea.

The Gateway Arch has served as an anchor for St. Louis' downtown for generations. It was an engineering marvel, and it took an engineer to break loose the details of the construction that had bedeviled the project for so long. Though Disney did not build there, the Arch spawned considerable construction along the St. Louis riverfront and forever changed the city's skyline. The experience showed that Tucker knew the power of corporate St. Louis in making economic development decisions.

Tucker changed the city of St. Louis at a time when change was coming from all directions: social, economic, and political. The city would have been different regardless of who was in the mayor's office, but would a lesser mayor have shirked responsibilities and missed opportunities? Would a partisan boss have engaged communities or expanded the decision-making table? Was the city better off for having tried ideas like charter reform or the earnings tax? In one sense, he was just another leader with his own priorities in a long line of them. In another sense, he changed the region forever by being the right man at the right time. Being mayor was his apotheosis.

Sauer photo, c. 1963. Courtesy of the Tucker Family.

ENDNOTES

[1] For example, see Feurer's appearance in *Made in USA: The East St. Louis Story* from KETC Public Television, available online.
[2] Ted Wofford is a brilliant man who rolled up his sleeves to preserve so many of Missouri's landmarks—including the Governor's Mansion in Jefferson City and the St. Vincent DePaul Church complex in St. Louis that was potentially destroyed by Interstate 55 (as well as designing many of our favorite buildings, like the old county library headquarters in Frontenac and the Rep in Webster Groves). His papers are in the process of being donated to Washington University, like Mayor Tucker. The late Saunders (Sandy) Schultz designed many things, but most notably the carved-brick and applied sculpture in the high-rise apartment buildings of Mill Creek Valley along I-64/US40 (search for the "Council Tower" building—you'll recognize it). Please see his legacy website: saundersschultz.com.
[3] Stein 105-106
[4] *Proposed Charter*, item #31, pp. 3-4
[5] Stein 106
[6] *Proposed Charter* 79-82
[7] See "Gunn Not Candidate...," *St. Louis Post-Dispatch*. 18 Jan 1959, p. 1A.
[8] "Tucker Says Charter Can Be Amended...," *St. Louis Post-Dispatch*. 08 Aug 1957, p. 1A, 4A.
[9] ibid.
[10] See: *National Geographic*, November 1965 (covering Tucker's achievements while in office); Avis Carlson's essay in *Harper's* March 1956; and Joe Alex Morris' essay "How to Rescue a City" in the *Saturday Evening Post,* 18 Aug 1956.
[11] Eliot 31
[12] Schmandt et al, 5
[13] ibid.
[14] ibid.
[15] "Mayor Urges Thorough Study...," *St. Louis Post-Dispatch*, 20 Oct 1955, p. 5D.
[16] Schmandt et al 6
[17] ibid. 7
[18] Eliot 33

[19] "G.O.P. Pledges Support…," *St. Louis Post-Dispatch.* 10 Mar 1957, p. 3A.

[20] Eliot 34

[21] ibid. 35

[22] Schmandt 23-25

[23] Greer with Long 62

[24] Schmandt 42

[25] ibid. 42-43

[26] Sengstock et al 12, 54

[27] Washington, S. 10

[28] "Borough Plan…It Is Not the Answer!!," *Neighborhood News*, 01 Nov 1962, p. 1.

[29] "3 Who Backed Borough Plan…," *St. Louis Globe-Democrat*, 02 Nov 1962, p. 4A.

[30] Corley, Francis C. "Going Places!," *Gerald Journal* (Gerald, MO), 02 Nov 1962, p. 3.

[31] "City and County Officials Will Work…," *St. Louis Post-Dispatch.* 08 Nov 1962, p. 3A.

[32] Williams, Barbara R. *St. Louis Final Report.* Santa Monica CA: Rand Corporation, August 1973. p. vi

[33] ibid.

[34] ibid. vii

[35] ibid.

[36] Tranel 6-7

[37] Campbell 31

[38] ibid. 37

[39] ibid. Interestingly, this same Attorney General, Homer Cummings, was a staunch fighter for FDR's New Deal programs and was the man who secretly drafted FDR's "packing the court" plan.

[40] ibid. 38

[41] Brown, Sharon chap. 3

[42] ibid., see esp. "Railroad Negotiations"

[43] ibid.

[44] ibid.

[45] ibid.

[46] ibid.

[47] ibid.

[48] ibid.

[49] ibid.

[50] ibid.

[51] ibid.

[52] ibid.
[53] ibid.
[54] ibid.
[55] ibid.
[56] Campbell 52
[57] Brown chap. 4
[58] See Louchheim, Aline B. "For a Modern Monument: An Audacious Design," *New York Times*. 29 Fed 1948; cited in Bellavia, Regina. *Cultural Landscape Report for the Jefferson National Expansion Memorial*. St. Louis: National Park Service, 1996, p. 37.
[59] Brown chap. 4
[60] ibid.
[61] Smith to Saarinen, cited in Máire Murphy, p. 131, f. 249
[62] Hagen 537
[63] ibid. 538
[64] Brown, Sharon A., vi.
[65] ibid. 539
[66] ibid. 541
[67] "Armstrong Chinn New President of Terminal Railroad," *St. Louis Globe Democrat*. 10 Dec 1946, p. 5.
[68] "Chinn Proposed Hiring Firm That Indorsed Tracks for Riverfront," *St. Louis Post-Dispatch*. 12 May 1957, p1A.
[69] Hagen 541
[70] ibid.
[71] ibid.
[72] ibid.
[73] "Terminal Pays in $500,000 to Shift Tracks," *St. Louis Post-Dispatch*. 16 Jun 1958 p. 3.
[74] "Thanks to Russell Dearmont," *St. Louis Post Dispatch*. 06 Dec 1958, p 4.
[75] Hagen 541
[76] ibid.
[77] ibid.
[78] ibid. 542
[79] Pierce, Todd James. *Walt Disney and Riverfront Square—Part 1*. Posted 25 Feb 2013. Accessed 31 Jan 2015. http://www.disneyhistoryinstitute.com/2013/03/walt-disney-and-riverfront-square-part-1.html
[80] Campbell 137
[81] ibid. 138

[82] Pierce, John Todd. *Walt Disney and Riverfront Square— Part 10.* Posted 06 May 2013. Accessed 31 Jan 2015. http://www.disneyhistoryinstitute.com/2013/05/walt-disney-and-riverfront-square-part.html
[83] ibid.
[84] Tucker, John interview 2013

Mayor Tucker presents a celebratory proclamation to the Federation of Block Units, May 2, 1958. From left: Leo Bohanon, J. Philip Waring, H. H. Webb, Tucker, Isaac Newman (Federation President), Fannie Torian, Norman Seay. Lane photo. Courtesy of the Tucker Family. This same photo appeared on the front page of the Argus on May 2, 1958.

The mayor and some presidents: (from top) with Harry Truman at City Hall; with JFK's inter-gov't committee (arrow pointing to RRT), and as part of LBJ's Education Task Force, receiving a presidential pen. All courtesy of the Tucker Family.

Chapter 6

The End of a Career
and a Life:
Tucker's Departure and Legacy

Finishing a Lifetime of Public Service

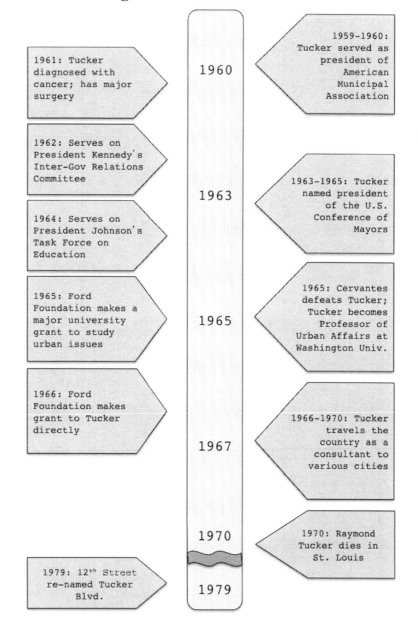

1961: Tucker diagnosed with cancer; has major surgery

1962: Serves on President Kennedy's Inter-Gov Relations Committee

1964: Serves on President Johnson's Task Force on Education

1965: Ford Foundation makes a major university grant to study urban issues

1966: Ford Foundation makes grant to Tucker directly

1979: 12th Street re-named Tucker Blvd.

1960

1963

1965

1967

1970

1979

1959-1960: Tucker served as president of American Municipal Association

1963-1965: Tucker named president of the U.S. Conference of Mayors

1965: Cervantes defeats Tucker; Tucker becomes Professor of Urban Affairs at Washington Univ.

1966-1970: Tucker travels the country as a consultant to various cities

1970: Raymond Tucker dies in St. Louis

THE RETURN OF POLITICS

A. J. CERVANTES THREW HIS HAT IN THE RING for the President of the Board of Aldermen in 1955. The incumbent was Donald Gunn, long a Tucker ally. The *Post-Dispatch* noted that Cervantes was a key opponent to Mayor Tucker's vetoes of neighborhood spot-zoning, voting 48 times to override. While complimenting Cervantes' energy and community recognition, the paper did not endorse him because of "his participation in the plague that is ruining St. Louis corner by corner, block by block."[1] The *Post* further said that Cervantes had "almost unbroken subservience to the vicious practice of 'aldermanic courtesy,' [meaning] that he has made it his business to favor petty, selfish demands of individuals over the welfare of entire neighborhoods."[2] This editorial was posted the day after Cervantes' father died of a sudden heart attack at 72.[3] Gunn beat Cervantes by a 2-to-1 margin.

Cervantes was putting Tucker on notice. He was challenging Tucker's political team. When Donald Gunn announced that he was not going to run for another term as Board President in 1959, two men filed to replace him. The first was the bombastic alderman from the 22nd ward, Alfred Harris, and the second was Cervantes. The outspoken Harris had been critical of Tucker in board debates and Cervantes clearly was a rising star among the politicians.[4]

Gunn laid out the pragmatic reasons for stepping down. "Neither my large and growing family nor my active law practice can afford the time which the last four years have required me to invest in the office. ...[The] salary it carries in no way compensates for the time it demands."[5] He was still loyal to Raymond Tucker. In fact, he had chaired Tucker's 1961 re-election committee.

Tucker endorsed Cervantes as Gunn's replacement, and spoke out against Harris. Harris, noted the *Post-Dispatch*, was "an irresponsible messenger boy for special interests and the darling of the ward bosses who once dreamed of putting Tom Callanan in the mayor's chair."[6] Politics made strange bedfellows in this case, or perhaps better: *the enemy of my enemy is my friend.* Cervantes won easily.

Back and Forth

Gunn could not stay away. He filed his candidacy against Cervantes in 1963 and the *Post-Dispatch* happily endorsed him. Basically calling Cervantes the lesser of evils in 1959, the paper endorsed Gunn for his return to office. "Mr. Cervantes's record [as board president] was not good enough to make him a truly strong candidate in the mold of Mayor Tucker. Nothing has happened in the last four years to persuade us to revise that judgment."[7] He beat the incumbent Cervantes in the primary by just 400 votes, and faced Republican attorney Wayne Millsap for the general municipal contest. He beat Millsap, too, but it was closer than expected. Republicans gained their largest city vote count since 1951.[8] The Tucker-endorsed candidate barely won the primary over the ward politician candidate, and the Republicans showed substantial gains. The electorate was changing. What should have caught more attention than it did was that African American voters in the 26th Ward (Committeeman Norman Seay and Alderman William L. Clay) went for Cervantes.

Skeptics thought Mayor Tucker and his old friend Donald Gunn had made an agreement. If Gunn won, Tucker would retire early and the charter would make Board President Gunn become mayor.[9] "It's a lie," said Tucker. "There is not a word of truth in it. I am going to serve out my term."[10] Asked if he would run for an unprecedented fourth term, Mayor Tucker said, "We'll talk about that some other time."[11] At the end of that year, the *Post* reported, "It is no secret that Mayor Tucker has not been too popular with a number of Democratic organization leaders, and some have been looking around for a candidate to oppose Tucker in the March 1965 primary," while many suspected that Tucker intended to go one more term.[12]

Reports were circulating in January 1964 that Cervantes was going to challenge Mayor Tucker for the Democratic nomination, more than a year early.[13] Cervantes was without elected office for the first time since 1949. He was too young and too ambitious to stay away for long. He spent his time planning his mayoral bid.

Aiming for the Mayor's Office

The first candidate to file for mayor in the 1965 municipal election was Alfonso Juan Cervantes. Since Tucker had not announced his intentions yet, Cervantes had the floor to himself and made his case to the newspapers. He promised a "dynamic and imaginative new program" for the city's progress, and said "thinking people" want a mayor "who is aware of their needs" and advances policies to make "their everyday lives safe, happy and prosperous."[14] His home address was #51 Westmoreland Place, one of the city's most exclusive streets. The 10th Ward endorsed him immediately, while he was the only name on the ballot.

Meanwhile, Tucker considered his options. He was not set on pursuing a fourth term. [15] After the Cervantes announcement, he received a letter asking him to pursue a fourth term. It was signed by brewery chief August A. Busch Jr. (who was the chairman of St. Louis' 1964 Bicentennial Celebration Committee), bank chairman James P. Hickok (who was the leader of the Civic Center Development Corporation, builder of the new downtown stadium), and insurance executive Sidney W. Souers (who was a commissioner of Bi-State Development Agency that implemented Tucker's long vision of a regional transit authority).[16] The men basically represented what would become Tucker's re-election theme: finish the job. It worked.

On Christmas Eve, it was announced that Circuit Attorney Daniel P. Reardon Jr. intended to file. This was seen as advantageous for Tucker, since Reardon would draw votes away from Cervantes.[17] It must have been reassuring to Mayor Tucker, but it didn't last. Reardon withdrew a month later.[18]

The "Progress Gap"

Cervantes went on the attack early. He opened his campaign assailing the "progress gap" that existed under Tucker. He blamed Tucker for the loss of residents and more than 45,000 jobs, and the taxes on the remaining residents had doubled per capita. The economic base had to be broadened, he said, with new ideas.[19] The two faced off in a debate at the Lindenwood Park Community Center. Tucker relied on his record. Cervantes kept hitting him with consistent messaging: "progress gap," "new ideas," declining statistics. It led to a lack of confidence by young people, said the 44-year-old candidate to the 69-year-old incumbent.[20]

Cervantes won ward endorsements more than Tucker did, but that was not new. Tucker never won them all. This time, though, Tucker felt the heat. He knew he had always had support from the city's conservatives—but they were moving to the suburbs and the Republican enclave being built by Lawrence K. Roos. Two Republican candidates filed for mayor, so that meant conservative voters would be more likely to vote in the Republican primary. Tucker reached out to them: "The blunt political facts of life in St. Louis today are that if you want to have any choice at all who will be your next mayor, you must vote in the Democratic primary." Continuing his appeal, he said, "I am proud of the fact that members of both parties have been active in the resurgence of our city" and "without the help of all our citizens" his programs would not have happened. "I know I have been the recipient of many Republican and independent votes in the past and humbly ask for them again."[21]

Tucker did not have the broad support of African Americans. He never did. Even though State Senator Theodore McNeal (the first African American state senator in Missouri) urged support for Tucker, there were opposing voices too. McNeal said, "I believe it would be ethically and morally wrong for the Negro community not to support [Tucker]. Nothing that is morally or ethically wrong can be politically right."[22]

Constable Leroy Tyus, committeeman of the 20th Ward, pointed to Homer G. Phillips Hospital. "It would be hard to find a place where the 'progress gap' is more clearly evident than in this hospital." He went on to say how the intern program was neglected, salaries were lower, and the place suffered from "a program of planned decay" that intentionally would set the hospital up for closure.[23] The closure of Homer G. Phillips remained an active rumor in the community.

The *Post-Dispatch* made an appeal to voters to show up. Everyone—not just the mainline Democrats—would be needed to help Tucker win. "St. Louis has come too far in the last 12 years to be turned over to the *fixers*."[24] The day's editorial cartoon was captioned "Bad Officials are Elected by Good People Who Don't Vote."

The "Triumph of Tradition"

Tucker was blunt in his campaign against Cervantes. "I do not believe a majority of the citizens want to take a chance by turning control of City Hall over to the politicians."[25] He remarked that Cervantes would have to pay back all the ward politicians he wooed during the campaign. Cervantes team was attracting "a motley crew" of political wannabes. He vowed to always put the broad interests of the city ahead of the narrow interests of the wards.[26] It didn't work.

Tucker lost the primary to Cervantes by a large margin— 81,000 to 67,000.[27] Both men said they were starting vacations immediately thereafter.[28] Cervantes said his win was "dictated by the independent voter," and noted "Mayor Tucker was [not] able to garner the...support in the Negro community." In the end, African American voters just didn't vote for Tucker. They had been split all along, and Jordan Chambers' long grudge against Tucker lasted longer than Chambers himself did. Ernest Calloway wrote, "Much of the anti-Tucker influence in the Negro community was institutional and politically habit forming. It developed under...Jordan W. Chambers...and the rank-and-file Negro voter had never been able to 'kick the habit.'"[29]

The ward politicians were back in control, for the first time in a long time. Almost immediately, Cervantes was making headlines. He announced a 10% budget cut for all major agencies, and city workers feared for their jobs.[30] He hired a "chauffeur-pilot" to potentially fly the mayor to his destinations, noting that the city might lease an airplane "occasionally."[31] He hired his brother as an "unpaid consultant."[32] He also said that there would be "stepped up efforts" to collect medical bills at

Homer G. Phillips Hospital and time clocks would be installed in all city departments.[33]

His name would make the front cover of *Life Magazine* in 1970 for his association with the old political boss and mob attorney Morris Shenker, whom Cervantes named, of all people, to lead a new anti-crime commission. There would be dogging criticism that he had mob affiliations, though he denied them and there was never any concrete proof. One of the questionable activities, recorded by Pulitzer Prize winning investigative reporter Denny Walsh, was his interest in the Consolidated Service Car Company from 1951, which was sold to Bi-State Development Agency seven months after he took office for $625,000 [34] (over $6 million today).

A Rare Leader

Raymond R. Tucker was an exceptional man. In a very real sense, he was "the right man" at "the right time." He brought a strong skill set and a good sense of right and wrong. He was a selfless public servant who was loyal to his convictions.

According to Mayor Tucker's son, the candidate would return excess campaign dollars proportionately to all his donors after each election.[35] Maybe the best example of mid-century's uncluttered perspective is Mayor Tucker himself. *Look Magazine*, in awarding St. Louis the All-America City Award, said Mayor Tucker started a renaissance. The editorial praised Tucker's reform efforts (even the unsuccessful ones) and the humility of the man himself. "Tucker and his wife live in an old brick house he inherited. His mayor's salary of $10,000 (about $93,000 today) is far less than he formerly earned in private life as a professor and a smoke-abatement expert. But he refuses to let such shortcomings dampen his energy with which he drives for a better St. Louis."[36]

His son said that Mayor Tucker only wanted enough money to buy a new suit every year and to take his wife out to dinner once a week—Medart's was a favorite place.[37] Tucker didn't work afternoons on Wednesdays, and one must wonder if that was date night for Edythe and him.

Issues of Health

Mayor Tucker suffered a significant health issue late in his second term. Around the holiday season in 1960, he developed an acute lung infection that required medical intervention. As a result of that, doctors diagnosed him with lung cancer (carcinoma) in the spring of 1961, amid his re-election to a third term. Many people attributed his surprisingly narrow primary win in March of that year (1,200 votes) to overconfidence of his supporters, but it may have been that the candidate had something heavy on his mind all along. His right lung was removed at Barnes Hospital on June 7.

Tucker did well during and after surgery. He had asked to be kept informed of city business during his recovery in the hospital and at home.[38] His staff obliged, and the mayor was conducting business from his hospital bed. He returned to city hall on July 31 on a reduced schedule and was not full-time again until September 5.

One of the pressing issues he faced from his sick bed was the potential budget shortfall. A new pay plan for city workers was being implemented and the administration was unsure how it would affect the budget, so the mayor ordered budgetary allotments to departments be made on a monthly basis. "The guillotine will fall monthly," said the mayor only half-jokingly. Any unspent money from the monthly allowance would have to be returned to the treasury.[39]

He took a vacation trip once he was mobile fully again. He went to the American Municipal Association meeting in Seattle, and then took the Labor Day weekend for a visit to Victoria, British Columbia.[40] There is no evidence that his health prevented him from doing any of his duties thereafter, though his surgery perhaps sparked the occasional rumor of his retirement before completing his new term.

Return to Academia

Professor Tucker resumed his academic career at Washington University, this time as a professor of urban affairs.

He still did some clean-air consulting and had time to serve on environmental task forces.[41]

He gave many lectures about urban affairs. He lamented that the American people had "accepted, virtually without debate, the challenge of [outer] space and have committed tens of billions of dollars to it," but "we struggle to organize and finance efforts to cope with earthbound problems."[42] He focused his attention to resource allocation, which he felt was holding back quality of life for many in St. Louis and other cities.

The Ford Foundation, which had funded the survey of the St. Louis region in the late 1950s during the second term, took a liking to Tucker and St. Louis. In 1965, only days before Tucker's departure from city hall, the foundation made a gigantic matching grant to Washington University ($15 million) and St. Louis University ($5 million) (combined, that's over $175 million in today's dollars). It was an investment in urban universities and the third largest grant ever made by the foundation to that time.[43] In 1966, Tucker received his own grant from the Ford Foundation to explore targeted resource allocation and municipal cooperation with representatives from 25 cities, this at the time President Johnson was still unleashing his Great Society programs.[44] This basically made Tucker a consultant for cities everywhere. He was able to travel across the country as part of his work and, according to his son, he loved every minute of it.[45]

Quietly Fading Away

Those were Tucker's parting words on his last day in office. "…It's his show [now]. That's the way it should be. I'll just quietly fade away."[46] He joked that he spoke about the rebirth of the city so many times that he felt like an obstetrician![47] As he was getting into his official car for the last time, he said to a reporter: "You asked about my plans. Well, I'll tell you what I'm going to do first. I'm going home and have lunch with Mrs. Tucker, and then I'm going out this afternoon and buy an automobile of my own."[48]

The media extolled his service, and it was deserved. He had "brought new honor and respect to St. Louis and himself." He had served on President Kennedy's Intergovernmental Relations Committee and on President Johnson's Task Force on Education. He had been president of the American Municipal Association and, at the time of his departure, president of the United States Conference of Mayors.[49]

He changed the way the government worked. He established the first retirement and pension plan for city workers. He pushed for new city charters twice, but he also amended the old one that citizens seemed so attached to. He fought for the earnings tax with the Missouri Legislature and made it a permanent revenue stream that has been the lifeblood of the city ever since.[50]

He changed the way the city looked physically. He said that when he came to the Mayor's Office, the city was in dire need of capital investment. The people needed the facilities and structures that could "create the environment in which the city and the people could expand and grow."[51] He drastically changed the riverfront, settling the disputes that had held back Gateway Arch construction and making the decision to locate the new interstate bridge at Poplar Street downtown instead of further south at Chippewa.[52] The resulting bridge, commonly called the Poplar Street Bridge, was cutting-edge technology. It was designed by Sverdrup and Parcel to be flat, so that the view of the Arch would be unobstructed for drivers. It was constructed by and of Bethlehem Steel. It was the longest steel girder bridge in the world, according to souvenir postcards of the day.[53]

On January 12, 1964, the city adopted a new flag for its bicentennial, a wonderful piece of modern art described as having "movement and dynamic quality." It was designed by Theodore Sizer of Yale University's Art Department, and, in a 2020 Twitter contest, the city's flag was declared the best flag in the world.

Resting in Peace

Raymond Tucker died on November 23, 1970, exactly fifty years after his father passed (within 24 hours). His father had been a smoke inspector for the city and was removed from the job when a new administration came to power, forever influencing young Raymond's view of smoke and politics. A modest funeral was held at the old family parish, SS. Mary and Joseph, in the Carondelet neighborhood. The parish priest celebrated the Mass. There was music but no choir. Mayor Tucker requested that he not be eulogized.[54] About 300 mourners were present, including Mayor Cervantes and Tucker's old friend Donald Gunn. His parish priest, Father Edward Feuerbacher, said that if Tucker were there to speak to the assembled, he would say, "Remember what I have done. Forgive any offense, any hurts. I tried to do what I thought was right."[55]

The interment was private. His parents had been buried from that church as well. He was not laid to rest with his parents at the Mount Olive Cemetery. Instead, his family arranged to have him interred next to the dear old friend who helped launch his career, Joseph Darst. The two rest eternally in neighboring crypts in the beautifully mid-century designed mausoleum by the lake at Calvary Cemetery.

On November 16, 1979, the Board of Aldermen voted to rename the street on which city hall stands in memory of Mayor Tucker. The Raymond R. Tucker Memorial Boulevard (formerly 12th Street) runs from Geyer Avenue in the south to O'Fallon Street in the north.[56] In 2013, the Missouri Legislature renamed the "Poplar Street" Bridge after retired Congressman William L. Clay—the man who helped deprive Tucker of an unprecedented fourth term. Coincidentally, there's not an exit to Tucker Boulevard for bridge traffic.

Mayor Tucker's crypt in the beautiful Calvary Cemetery mausoleum, adjacent to his dear friend, Mayor Darst. Theising photo.

ENDNOTES

[1] "Gunn or Cervantes," *St. Louis Post-Dispatch.* 09 Mar 1955, p. 2C.

[2] ibid.

[3] "A. A. Cervantes, 72...," *St. Louis Globe Democrat.* 09 Mar 1955, p. 7A.

[4] "Cervantes Will Oppose Harris," *St. Louis Globe-Democrat.* 18 Jan 1959, p. 1A.

[5] "Donald Gunn Cites Low Salary...," *St. Louis Globe-Democrat.* 20 Jan 1959, p. 3.

[6] "Everybody Sweats," *St. Louis Post-Dispatch,* 06 Mar 1959, p. 2C.

[7] "For Donald Gunn," *St. Louis Post-Dispatch,* 21 Feb 1963, p. 2C.

[8] "Gunn Wins...," *St. Louis Post-Dispatch.* 03 Apr 1963, p. 1A.

[9] This happened in 1943, when Mayor Becker died in office and Board President Aloys P. Kaufmann filled out the term, winning election to a following full term in 1945.

[10] "Cervantes-Gunn Race...," *St. Louis Globe-Democrat,* 19-20 Jan 1963, p. 3A.

[11] ibid.

[12] "Reardon (cont.)...," *St. Louis Post-Dispatch,* 15 Dec 1963, p. 4A.

[13] "Alderman Clay...," *St. Louis Post-Dispatch.* 15 Jan 1964, p. 3A.

[14] "A.J. Cervantes First to File...," *St. Louis Post-Dispatch.* 03 Dec 1964, p. 3A.

[15] Tucker, John interview 2013

[16] "Mayor Tucker Will Run...," *St. Louis Post-Dispatch.* 21 Dec 1964, p. 1A.

[17] "Reardon Entry...," *St. Louis Post-Dispatch.* 24 Dec 1964, p. 1A.

[18] "Out of Mayor Race," *Kansas City Times.* 23 Jan 1965, p. 47.

[19] "Mayor Tucker Faces Battle," *Kansas City Star.* 31 Jan 1965, p. 16A.

[20] "Tucker Appears with Cervantes...," *St. Louis Post-Dispatch.* 02 Feb 1965, p. 3A.

[21] "Tucker Appeals for GOP Support," *St. Louis Post-Dispatch.* 06 Feb 1965, p. 5A.

[22] "Tucker Appears with Cervantes...," *St. Louis Post-Dispatch.* 02 Feb 1965, p. 3A.

[23] ibid.

[24] "For Tucker and Poelker," *St. Louis Post-Dispatch.* 08 Mar 1965, p. 12A. emphasis added.

[25] Stein 115

[26] ibid.

[27] Numbers are rounded. See any of the numerous articles on the outcome, such as "Tucker Upset by Cervantes," *St. Joseph Gazette.* 10 Mar 1965, p. 1.

[28] "Cervantes Says Aim Is Better...," *St. Louis Post-Dispatch.* 11 Mar 1965, p. 1A, 8A.

[29] "Where Was the 'Delivery' Vote," *St. Louis Post-Dispatch.* 24 Mar 1965, p. 2C.

[30] "Cervantes Said to Plan...," *St. Louis Post-Dispatch.* 13 Apr 1965, p. 1A.

[31] "Mayor Hires...," *St. Louis Post-Dispatch.* 22 Apr 1965, p. 3A.

[32] "Catholic Paper Opposes Job for Fr. Cervantes," *St. Louis Post-Dispatch.* 29 May 1965, p. 1A.

[33] "Mayor Orders...," *St. Louis Post-Dispatch.* 30 Apr 1965, p. 1A, 3A.

[34] "Life Accuses St. Louis Mayor...," *New York Times.* 25 May 1970, p. 67.

[35] Tucker, John interview, 2013

[36] "Mayor Tucker Started It," *Look Magazine,* excerpted in *St. Louis Post-Dispatch.* 30 Nov 1957, p. 4A.

[37] Tucker, John interview, 2013

[38] See "Mayor Tucker Returns Home from Hospital," *St. Louis Post-Dispatch.* 23 Jun 1961, p. 1A; and "Back at City Hall," *St. Louis Post-Dispatch.* 31 Jul 1961, p. 1A.

[39] "Mayor Orders Allotment...," *St. Louis Post-Dispatch.* 23 Jun 1961, p. 1A.

[40] "Tucker to Combine Parley, Vacation," *St. Louis Globe-Democrat.* 25 Aug 1961, p. 13A.

[41] "Tucker to be Consultant...," *St. Louis Post-Dispatch.* 23 Mar 1967, p. 3A.

[42] "Public is Slow to Cope...," *St. Louis Post-Dispatch.* 15 May 1965, p. 3A.

[43] "Investment in St. Louis," *St. Louis Post-Dispatch.* 22 Jun 1965, p. 2B.

[44] "Experiment in St. Louis," *St. Louis Post-Dispatch.* 14 May 1966, p. 4A.

[45] Tucker, John interview, 2013

[46] Dickson, Terry. "Tucker Looks Toward...," *St. Louis Post-Dispatch.* 25 Apr 1965, p. 3K.

[47] ibid.

[48] ibid.

[49] ibid. This article says he was president of the "National League of Cities," which was the then-current name of the old American Municipal Association.

[50] ibid.

[51] ibid.

[52] For downtown location story, see "The Interstate Bridge Between St. Louis and East St. Louis," *NEXTSTL (Policy and Commentary, Transportation)* posted: 06 Apr 2012, accessed: 16 Jul 2017. www.nextstl.com; and for the Chippewa Bridge, see "Cahokia Bridge Approved...," *St. Louis Post-Dispatch.* 31 May 1955, p. 3A.

[53] See the postcard *New Poplar Street Bridge*, St. Louis: Charm Craft Publishers, c. 1965.

[54] "Simple Service at Parish Church...," *St. Louis Post-Dispatch.* 27 Nov 1970, p. 3E.

[55] ibid.

[56] Sutin, Phil. "Tax Break for Stix on Renovations," *St. Louis Post-Dispatch.* 16 Nov 1979, p. 1A, 10A. The author personally is disappointed that editors at the time did not make this name change the title lead for the story, but instead kept it more of an afterthought. It was a much bigger and lasting deal than Mr. Stix's project (the headline), which has been vacant for many years at the time of this writing.

Epilogue

The More We Know...

Revelations by authors, documentarians, and scholars since 2000 cast a pall over this entire mid-century era, and with cause. Dr. Linda Morice (2022) and Dr. Denise DeGarmo (2006) both produced shocking work on the toxic waste contamination that stemmed from Mallinckrodt's Manhattan Project work in North St. Louis. *The Pruitt-Igoe Myth* (2011) is an outstanding look at how government at all levels failed to provide support for the people who were supposed to be in its care. Vivian Gibson's memoir of growing up in Mill Creek (2020), as well as the documentary *The Color of Medicine* about Homer G. Phillips Hospital, show with first-hand accounts of what African American culture was lost in Mill Creek and the Ville. Finally, the film *Target: St. Louis* (2018) reveals details of the U.S. Army's exploitation of poor African Americans in St. Louis for Cold War radiation experiments.

A lot of these things happened on Mayor Tucker's watch. Yes, some began long before he held office. Yes, some happened after he left. Yes, a lot of it may have been beyond his control. Yet, all of it overlapped with his terms as mayor, with his vision for the city, and with his pursuit of the city's quality of life. It cannot be ignored because, as mid-century President Harry Truman said of chief executives, *the buck stops here*. It is worth studying what influence he had or didn't have or refused to use in these cases.

Historic Moments During the Tucker Years

05/06/1953: St. Louis playwright William Inge wins the Pulitzer Prize for *Picnic*

04/24/1953: The Great St. Louis Bank Robbery took place; became a 1959 feature film starring Steve McQueen

1ST TERM

07/14/1954: Hottest day ever recorded in STL—115 degrees

06/19/1957: Heaviest rainfall ever recorded in downtown STL—8.5" in 14 hours

04/17/1957: The National Personnel Records Center opens at 9700 Page Ave.; was one of the 20 largest buildings in the world! Bldg burned in spectacular fire, 07/12/1973.

2ND TERM

08/30/1958: First metro STL McDonald's opens, 9915 Watson Rd.

02/10/1959: An F4 tornado ripped through STL near Oakland and Hampton, hitting Gaslight Square and killing 21 people.

02/28/1961: The feature film *Hoodlum Priest* premiered in STL; about a local Jesuit. Entered at Cannes Film Fest.

07/01/1963: Post Office begins using ZIP codes

02/14/1964: President Johnson visits STL to celebrate its bicentennial.

10/15/1964: Cardinals win the World Series in STL over Yankees

3RD TERM

01/10/1962: Busiest day in STL Fire Dept. A grain elevator explosion took 120 fire-fighters 20 hours to control. At the same time, a 5-alarm fire began at Gaslight Square, and then another 5-alarm fire happened at the Ambassador Hotel. The temp was five below zero that night.

Tucker's may be the best-documented mayoral administration in St. Louis history. Multiple thousands of pages were
reviewed for this work—memos, reports, interviews, news
accounts, and published information. There are hundreds of
boxes each containing thousands of pages in various archives.
To search it all would mean delaying this book another five
years. So many of the living memories are gone. Television
archives offer even more perspectives (all largely unexplored for
this work). I have great trust in the community's capacity for
this kind of research, and I encourage future scholars and artists
to continue these investigative tracks. Science comes from
comparison. May this book be one step toward understanding
the context and be a solid block on which future work is
compared or constructed.

*Right: Mayor Tucker
admires the new city flag
on a 1964 bicentennial
license plate. (Uncredited
staff photo.)
Above: the old city flag.
(City of St. Louis photo,
1964.) Both courtesy of
the Tucker Family.*

Raymond R. Tucker press photo. Weitman photo, about 1961. Courtesy of the Tucker Family

Honoring STL Artists: Keys to the city are presented to opera singer Grace Bumbry in 1962 (courtesy of the Tucker Family) and composer W. C. Handy in 1953 (Globe-Democrat).

Acknowledgements

THIS WORK BEGAN ABOUT 2006 as a study/history of the **Metropolitan St. Louis Sewer District.** I began by interviewing several hard-working leaders behind the scenes—such as Chuck Etwert, Karl Tyminski, and John Siscel—who gave me great insight to the operations of the district. It is an interesting agency worthy of scholarly study.

As I examined the history of the district in 1954, I noticed the larger forces of the era—suburbanization, federal investment, city-county merger, etc.—and began to focus on the elected officials at the time. **Mayor Raymond Tucker** stood out and became the focus of my research for the next 15+ years.

…And so, here we are in 2024. After considerable input, review, revisions, and modifications, this work finally is in a position for public presentation, review, and feedback. It has been the work of a career for me; not quite as long as my efforts in East St. Louis, but clearly the second place.

It is a challenge for me to compile a comprehensive list of those who worked with me on this project in various ways, but I have kept a list over the years knowing that this day was coming and that these individuals helped me in substantial ways.

One cannot do this kind of work without **the support of family**. I am grateful for the support of my son, Evan Theising, and my partner, Alexis Elward. They were always willing minds to consider my thoughts, perspectives, and to help settle my questions. I am further grateful to my extended family, especially Susan Andrews and the late Colonel Stanley Brown. I am saddened that Stan did not live to see the fruition of this project. All gave feedback of various sorts to the project and manuscript.

At Southern Illinois University Edwardsville, I am grateful to the staff of the **Institute (later Initiative) for Urban Research**, especially Hugh Pavitt, Rhonda Penelton, Jim Hanlon, and the administrative support from Heather Birdsell, Julie Tucker Eudy, and Carrie Smolar. I am also grateful to the student researchers who helped me as research assistants or under directed studies. Top among them is Sara Washington, someone who truly came to appreciate the contributions of a mayor like Raymond Tucker and whose work informed this research directly. Other research assistance came from Anthony Dietz, Patience Ferry, Alexandra Hurley, Lindsey Luehrsen, Delia Major, Carlos Scurloc, and Peter Witte.

At Washington University in St. Louis, particularly at **the Brown School of Social Work** where I have taught urban-based coursework since 2010, I am grateful to the graduate students who helped me as summer research interns. Hassan Arab, Yiyi Tao, Yiye (Yoko) Wu, and Jason Yuan. The Special Collections Librarian Miranda Rectenwald was most supportive of the hundreds of hours spent in the Olin Library archives back in 2019.

Finally, I am grateful to my colleagues in the **Department of Political Science** at SIUE, who gave me support and encouragement during my years of research, including sabbatical. All of them were very helpful in different ways, including Dr. Ken Moffett, my supportive chair; Dr. Nicholas Guehlstorf, who chaired my sabbatical research review committee; and my other dear colleagues in the department that provided guidance and review. Thank you! Dr. Jessica Harris (Historical Studies) provided meaningful support for my studies of civil rights and providing her interpretations of the writings of MLK.

Further, colleagues from other institutions helped out in so many ways: Dr. Todd Swanstrom and Dr. Lana Stein from the **University of Missouri-St. Louis**; Dr. Dennis Judd, my life-long mentor, most recently from the **University of Illinois-Chicago**; Dr. Andrew Hurley and Dr. Mark Tranel, both of the **University of Missouri-St. Louis**; and especially Dr. Mark Abbott, planning historian extraordinaire, of **Harris-Stowe State University**. I acknowledge the many groups convened by Dr. Abbott, including **the St. Louis Writers Group** that gave me feedback on early drafts and included several of the aforementioned folks, plus others such as Emily Jaycox of the **Missouri History Museum Library and Research Center** and Jasmin Aber of the **Creative Exchange Lab** (CEL). It was a great honor to meet Percy Green through CEL and its support of my work. Dr. Kris Smith of **Lindenwood University** gave especially good feedback. Thank you for sharing your brilliance.

I am grateful to **the Raymond Tucker Family** for their support. The Mayor's grandson, Timothy Tucker, is a personal friend with an impressive presence in the St. Louis economic development field. He shared his family's trove of archival material. Most significantly, though, he arranged an interview with his father, John Tucker—the son of Mayor Raymond Tucker who had first-hand accounts of several stories shared herein. I am sorry that John did not live to see the publication of this work. I am grateful to Lucy Tucker and Tucker Doxsee for their manuscript review and discussion.

I could go on for pages acknowledging the many kindnesses shown me by supporters of this work. The special collections folks at **St. Louis Public Library** were very kind, especially Kirwin Roach and Amanda Bahr-Evola. Cathy Smentkowski at the **St. Louis Mayor's Office** was a kind connection to city resources.

If I have omitted anyone, please forgive my error. It is not because I did not value your input; it was only because of my poor memory. Thank you especially.

Mayor Tucker valued the city of St. Louis with his whole heart. I do too. It is an imperfect but wonderful place. It has rough spots that are balanced by deep pools of kindness—even in places where casual observers cannot see it. There is a genuine love that I have seen, and to those people who have shared that love and make it city a better place for all, this work is dedicated.

Mayor Tucker visits with James S. McDonnell at the McDonnell Aircraft facility at Lambert Field, c. 1960. Uncredited photo. Courtesy of the Tucker Family.

Raymond Tucker is inaugurated as the 38th mayor of St. Louis in the city hall rotunda, April 21, 1953. He was sworn-in by Judge Edward M. Ruddy of the St. Louis Court of Appeals. Uncredited photo. Courtesy of the Tucker Family.

Bibliography

Newspaper articles, minor documents, and web-only features are given full citation in the endnotes to each chapter. The bibliography is reserved for published pieces or major research held in print form by area libraries.

Abbott, Mark. "The Seeds of Regionalism: Harland Bartholomew and the Origins of St. Louis Regionalism," *The Confluence.* Jeffrey Smith, ed. St. Charles MO: Lindenwood University. Fall 2009. Pp. 6-19.

Abbott, Mark. "A Document That Changed America," *St. Louis Plans.* Mark Tranel, ed. St. Louis: Missouri Historical Society Press. Pp. 17-55, 2007.

Allison, Oscar Hugh. *Raymond R. Tucker: The Smoke Elimination Years, 1934-1950.* Ph.D. Dissertation, Department of Philosophy, Washington University in St. Louis. St. Louis: 1978.

Bartholomew, Harland and the City Plan Commission. *Annual Report of the City Plan Commission of St. Louis, 1916-17.* St. Louis: Wilson Printing Co. 1917.

Bartholomew, Harland and the City Plan Commission. *Problems of St. Louis: Being a Description, from the City Planning Perspective....* St. Louis: Nixon-Jones Printing Co. 1917.

Bartholomew, Harland and the City Plan Commission. *St. Louis After World War II.* St. Louis: City Plan Commission, December 1942.

Beckmann, Vernal. *A Historical Analysis of the Public Speaking of Mayor Raymond R. Tucker with Specific Emphasis on Two Selected Speeches.* MS Thesis, Department of

Communications, Southern Illinois University. Carbondale IL: 1959.

Bellavia, Regina. *Cultural Landscape Report for the Jefferson National Expansion Memorial.* St. Louis: National Park Service, 1996

Benton, Mark. " 'Saving' the City: Harland Bartholomew and Administrative Evil in St. Louis," *Public Integrity* 20:2 (2018) pp. 194-206.

Brown, Sharon. "Administrative History: Jefferson National Expansion Memorial, 1935-1980," *Jefferson National Expansion Memorial National Historic Site.* 1984. Posted: Jan 2004; Accessed: 01 Oct 2024 and earlier. https://npshistory.com/publications/jeff/adhi.pdf

Campbell, Tracy. *The Gateway Arch: A Biography.* New Haven: Yale University Press, 2014.

Cervantes, Alphonso J. *Mr Mayor.* Los Angeles: Nash Publishing, 1974.

City Plan Commission. "A Study for a Comprehensive Plan for Redevelopment of the Central City Area of St. Louis." St. Louis City Plan Commission, January 21, 1954.

Clay, William L. (2004) *Bill Clay: A Political Voice at the Grassroots.* St. Louis: Missouri Historical Society Press, 2004.

Clay, William L. (2008) *The Jefferson Bank Confrontation: The Struggle for Civil Rights in St. Louis.* St. Louis: W. L. Clay Scholarship and Research Foundation, 2008.

Coibion, William H. *Descriptive Statement of Land Use and Circulation Pattern—Scheme C-3 Dated June 18, 1956, for Mill Creek Valley, prepared by St. Louis Plan Commission.* Raymond R. Tucker Records, Office of the Mayor, Series 1, Box 13, Folder "Land Clearance and Housing Authorities, June 1955 to August 31, 1956." St. Louis: Washington University Archives.

Comptroller General of the US, "St. Louis, Missouri," *Inadequate Relocation Assistance to Families Displaced from Certain Urban Renewal Projects in Kansas and Missouri.* Washington DC: Government Printing Office, June 1964. Online copy is available here: https://www.gao.gov/assets/b-118754-d09686.pdf

Cook, Fannie. *Mrs. Palmer's Honey.* Garden City NY: Doubleday, 1946.

Corbett, Katharine T. *In Her Place: A Guide to St. Louis Women's History.* St. Louis: Missouri History Museum, 1999.

Eliot, Thomas H. "Dilemmas in Metropolitan Research," *Midwest Journal of Political Science.* Chicago: Midwest Political Science Association, 2:1, Feb 1958, pp. 26-39.

Fagerstrom, Ron. *Mill Creek Valley: A Soul of St. Louis.* St. Louis: Privately published, 2000.

Farris, Charles L. *St. Louis Story, or the Blues Have a Silver Lining.* Manuscript. Tucker Papers, Series 2, Box 16, Folder: "Land Clearance and Housing Authorities, Jan. 1, 1961 to _____". St. Louis: Washington University Archives.

Flint, Barbara. *Zoning and Residential Segregation: A Social and Physical History, 1910-1940.* Dissertation. Department of History, University of Chicago. Chicago: Dec 1977.

GAO Report, see Comptroller General.

Gibson, Vivian. *The Last Children of Mill Creek,* Cleveland: Belt Publishing, 2020.

Grant, Gail Milissa. *At the Elbows of My Elders: One Family's Journey toward Civil Rights.* St. Louis: Missouri History Museum, 2007.

Greenberg, Cara. *Mid-Century Modern: Furniture of the 1950s.* New York: Harmony Books, 1984.

Greer, Scott, with Norton E. Long. *Metropolitics: A Study of Political Culture.* New York: John Wiley and Sons, 1963

Griffenhagen, E. O. and the Mayor's Survey Committee. *General Organization Structure of the Government of the City of St. Louis.* St. Louis: Griffenhagen and Associates, 1940.

Hagen, Harry M. *This Is Our St. Louis.* St. Louis: Knight Publishing, 1970.

Heathcott, Joseph. "The Whole City Is Our Laboratory: Harland Bartholomew and the Production of Urban Knowledge," *Journal of Planning History.* 2005-11, Vol.4 (4), p.322-355.

Henry, Virginia Anne. *The Sequent Occupance of Mill Creek Valley.* Dissertation, Department of Geography, Washington University in St. Louis, June 1947. [Not directly cited, but very helpful in this research.]

Horne, Ph.D., Malaika B. *Mother Wit: Exalting Motherhood while Honoring a Great Mother.* Pittsburgh: Dorrance Publishing, 2017.

" 'Integration' Threatens to Close St. Louis Hospital," *Jet.* Chicago: Johnson Publishing, 21:1, 26 Oct 1961.

Jolly, Kenneth. *Black Liberation in the Midwest.* New York: Routledge, 2006.

Kemper, Donald J. "Catholic Integration in St. Louis, 1935-1947," *Missouri Historical Review* LXXIII:1, October 1978, Columbia MO: State Historical Society of Missouri, pp. 1-22. 3 endnote 29

King Jr., Martin Luther. (1957) *A Realistic Look at the Question of Progress in the Area of Race Relation.* Address Delivered at St. Louis Freedom Rally. St. Louis: 10 Apr 1957. In *The Papers of Martin Luther King Jr., Volume IV: Symbol of the Movement, January 1957- December 1958.* Clayborne

Carson et al, eds. Los Angeles: University of California Press, 2000.

King Jr., Martin Luther. (1957) *Give Us the Ballot.* In *The Papers of Martin Luther King Jr., Volume IV: Symbol of the Movement, January 1957- December 1958.* Clayborne Carson et al, eds. Los Angeles: University of California Press, 2000.

Kirschten, Ernest. *Catfish and Crystal.* Garden City NY: Doubleday and Company, 1960.

Lang, Clarence. *Grassroots at the Gateway: Class Politics and Black Freedom Struggle in St. Louis.* Ann Arbor: University of Michigan Press, 2009.

Lee, Mordecai. *Bureaus of Efficiency: Reforming Local Government in the Progressive Era.* Milwaukee: Marquette University Press, 2008.

Matherne, Max. *Jacksonian Reformation: Political Patronage and Republican Identity.* Doctoral Dissertation, University of Tennessee Knoxville, August 2019. Posted Aug 2019, Accessed 21 Sep 2021. https://trace.tennessee.edu/cgi/viewcontent. cgi?article=7321&context=utk_graddiss

Mayors Survey/Advisory Committee (see Griffenhagen)

Meehan, Eugene. *The Quality of Federal Policymaking.* Columbia: University of Missouri Press, 1979.

March, David D. *The History of Missouri*, Vol. II. New York: Lewis Historical Publishing Co., 1967.

Murphy, Máire Agnes. *The Metropolitan Project: Leadership, Policy, and Development in St. Louis, Missouri, 1945-1980.* Dissertation, Department of History, University of Virginia, May 2004.

Myers, John Samuel. *The Principles and Organizaiton of the Merit System in St. Louis.* Doctoral dissertation, political science. St. Louis: Washington University, June 1936.

Peirce, Neal. *The Great Plains States of America*. New York:
W. W. Norton Co., 1973.

Perald, Libby. "Mill Creek Valley: A Symptom of Void
St. Louis," *Issues Magazinse: The Vacancy Issue*.
Spring 2013. St. Louis: Washington University in
St. Louis. http://issuu.com/issuesmagazinewashu/
docs/issues_sp2013

Primm, James Neal. *Lion of the Valley: St. Louis, Missouri*.
Boulder CO: Pruett Publishing, 1981.

Proposed Charter of the City of St. Louis. St. Louis: Board of
Freeholders, 07 May 1957.

Roosevelt, Theodore. (1913) *An Autobiography*. New York:
Charles Scribner's Sons, 1920. A copy can be found
here: https://www.gutenberg.org/ebooks/3335

Rumbold, Charlotte. *Housing Conditions in St. Louis: Report of the
Housing Committee of the Civic League of St. Louis*.
St. Louis: Civic League of St. Louis, 1908.

St. Louis Civil Defense Commission. January 1953. *The
St. Louis Civil Defense Plan*. St. Louis: Office of Civil
Defense (Referenced but not used as a direct citation;
provided for convenience. Located in the St. Louis
research section of the St. Louis Public Central Library.)

St. Louis Housing Authority and Land Clearance for
Redevelopment Authority, *untitled brochure*, August 1960.
Tucker Papers, Series 2, Box 16, Folder "Land
Clearance and Housing Authorities, June 1, 1960 to
Dec. 31, 1960." St. Louis: Washington University
Archives.

Schmandt, Henry J., Paul G. Steinbicker, and George D.
Wendel. *Metropolitan Reform in St. Louis: A Case Study*.
New York: Holt, Reinhart, and Winston, 1961.

Schneider, Msgr. Nicholas. *Joseph Elmer Cardinal Ritter: His Life and Times.* Ligouri MO: Ligouri Publications, 2008.

Sculpture City. *St. Louis's Invisible Monument: Mill Creek Valley.* Posted: 22 Octboer 2013. Accessed: 05 March 2015. http://sculpturecitystl.com/journal/st-louis-invisible-monument-mill-creek-valley/

Sengstock, Frank S., Phillip A. Fellin, Lawrence E. Nicholson, and Charles I. Mundale. *Consolidation: Building a Bridge between City and Suburb.* St. Louis: Heffernan Press, 1964.

Sobel, Irwin, Werner Hirsch, and Harry Harris. *The Negro in the St. Louis Economy, 1954.* St. Louis: Urban League of St. Louis Inc., 1954.

Steffens, Lincoln. *The Shame of the Cities.* New York: McClure, Phillips, and Co., 1904

Stein, Lana. *St. Louis Politics: The Triumph of Tradition.* St. Louis: Missouri Historical Society Press, 2002.

Taylor, Anne Cleester. St. Louis: Washington University School of Law. Posted: n.d. 2013. Accessed: 05 December 2014. http://law.wustl.edu/staff/taylor/slpl/stacentc.htm

Taylor, Frederick Winslow. *The Principles of Scientific Management.* New York: Harper and Brothers, 1911.

Theising, Andrew. Ed. *In the Walnut Grove: A Consideration of the People Enslaved in and around Florissant, Missouri.* St. Louis: Florissant Valley Historical Society, 2020.

Toft, Carolyn Hewes. (Phillips) *National Register of Historic Places Inventory Nomination Form for Homer G. Phillips Hospital.* Posted: 3-31-1982. Accessed 16 Dec 2014. http://www.dnr.mo.gov/shpo/nps-nr/82004738.pdf

Toft, Carolyn Hewes. (Kessler) "George Edward Kessler (1862-1923)," *Landmarks Association of St. Louis.* https://

www.landmarksstl.org/architects/bio/george_edward_
kessler/ Posted n.d. Accessed: 21 Sep 2021.

Tranel, Mark. "Luther Ely Smith: Father of the Gateway Arch,"
The Confluence Spring/Summer 2012, pp. 6-15.

Tucker, John. Personal interview with. Town and Country,
MO. 13 December 2013.

Tucker, Raymond R. 1953. *Why St. Louis Must have the City
Earnings Tax.* St. Louis: Mayor's Office, 1953.

Tucker, Raymond R. 1957. *Introductory Remarks of Mayor Raymond
R. Tucker…before the Housing Subcommittee…November 5,
1957.* Tucker Papers, Series 2, Box 16, Folder "Land
Clearance and Housing Authorities, April 1957 to June
30, 1958." St. Louis: Washington University Archives.

Tucker, Raymond R. 1963. *Mayor's Remarks, First Meeting,
St. Louis Commission on Equal Employment Opportunity.* 02
Aug 1963. Tucker Papers, Series 3, Box 13, Folder:
"Equal Employment Opportunity, July 1, 1963 to
September 30, 1963. St. Louis: Washington University
Archives.

Valien, Bonita H. *The St. Louis Story: A Study of Desegregation.*
New York: Anti-Defamation League of
B'nai B'rith, 1956. HathiTrust document.

Vexler, Robert I. *St. Louis: A Chronological and Documentary
History, 1762-1970.* Dobbs Ferry NY: Oceana
Publications Inc., 1974.

Washington, Sara. *Tucker (Paper 3).* Edwardsville: SIUE
Department of Political Science. Undergraduate essay
for POLS310-009 (Instructor: Andrew Theising).
Spring 2010.

Watson, Clinton T. and Charles L. Farris. *Plan for Relocation of
Displaced Mill Creek Valley Occupants (condensed from Official
"Relocation Plan for Mill Creek Valley Project),* Tucker
Papers, Series 2, Box 17, Folder "Mill Creek Project,

Feb. 1958 to ___." St. Louis: Washington University Archives.

Weingroff, Richard F. "Three States Claim First Interstate Highway," *Public Roads*. 60:1, Summer 1996. Posted: n.d. Accessed: 02 Feb 2022. https://highways.dot. gov/public-roads/summer-1996/three-states-claim-first-interstate-highway

Welek, Mary. "Jordan Chambers: Black Politician and Boss," *Journal of Negro History*. 57:4, October 1972. Pp. 352-369.

Williams, Barbara R. *St. Louis: A City and Its Suburbs*. Washington DC: Rand Corporation, August 1973. Posted: August 2019. Accessed: 27 Jan 2022. https://metrostl.com/wp-content/uploads/2019/08/The-Rand-Report.pdf

Witt Ph.D., Msgr. Michael. *Saint Louis: The Story of Evangelization of America's Heartland, Volume Three: The Age of Cardinals*. St. Louis: The Miriam Press, 2018.

Mayor Tucker (below, second from left) receives an honorary doctorate (above) from Washington University in St. Louis 1955. Courtesy of the Tucker Family

Index

City Plan, Comprehensive (1947) viii, 73, 89
City Plan for St. Louis (1907) 73-74
Civic Progress (organization) 58, 190, 208, 210
Civil Defense Plan (1953) 40, 103
Clay, William (Activist, Congressman) 138, 139, 149, 167, 168,
   172, 174, 176, 179, 180, 181, 182, 185, 186, 187, 188, 189, 190,
   191, 192-193, 242, 250
Cochran, John (Congressman) 133
Coibion, William (City Planner) 89, 91
Compton, Arthur Holly 138
Cook, Fannie 81-82, 142, 143
CORE (Congress of/on Racial Equality) 138-139, 167-170, 171-
   174, 175, 178, 179, 181-183, 185, 187, 188-189, 190, 191, 192
Curtis, Robert 180, 181, 182

D

Daly, Richard (Arch activist) 139
Darst, Joseph (Mayor) 6, 13, 35, 36, 37, 38, 39, 40, 41, 42, 45, 57,
   58, 84, 92, 123, 144, 208, 225, 226, 250, 251
Darst, Katherine 13
Davis, J. Lionberger 75
Davison, Rosemary 122
Delaney, Lucy 192
Dickens, Charles (Dickensian) 2, 72
Dickmann, Bernard (Mayor) iv, 5, 6, 9, 10, 16, 18, 19, 23, 27, 29,
   31, 32, 33, 35, 45, 78, 84, 123, 133, 204, 220, 221, 222, 223,
   224
Dillon's Rule 145, 147, 211
Disney, Walt viii, 230, 231
Donnelly, Phil (Governor) 93, 207
DuBois, W.E.B. 136, 137
Duckett, Herbert 135

E

Eagleton, Mark 41-46
Eisenhower, Dwight (President) 77, 207, 227, 228, 229
Election of 1953, (Primary: Tucker/Eagleton; General:
   Tucker/Stifel) 41-46, 47
Election of 1957 (Primary: Tucker/Callanan) 213
Election of 1961 (Primary: Tucker/Holloran) 241, 247
Election of 1965 (Primary: Tucker/Cervantes) 242, 243, 244,
   245

Johnson, Lyndon B. (LBJ) (President) 248
Jones v. Mayer case (1968) 147

Vaughn, George L. 147, 150
Ville, The (neighborhood) 81, 82, 83, 92, 255 (see also Elleardsville)

W

Washington University 3, 4, 5, 33, 65, 70, 89, 137, 138, 151, 179, 181, 216; 233 n2; 247, 248, 261, 274, 282
Watson, Philip 222, 227
Weber, Max 207
Wilson, Margaret Bush 114, 137, 183, 189, 190
Wofford, Ted 209; 233 n2

X, Y, Z

X, Malcolm 136
Yamasaki, Minoru iv, ix, 61, 208
Younge M.D., Walter 99, 151, 198 n24
Younge, Wyvetter 174, 177, 198 n24
Zeckendorf, William 84
Zuercher S.J., Rev. Joseph P. 129

About the Author

DR. ANDREW THEISING is emeritus professor of Political Science at Southern Illinois University Edwardsville and, by special arrangement between institutions, has taught in the Brown School of Social Work at Tucker's alma mater, Washington University in St. Louis, since 2010. He continues to teach coursework at WashU.

He has produced multiple volumes on East St. Louis, Illinois, the focus of his scholarship. His award-winning research has been used by media nation-wide, including *The New York Times, Sports Illustrated,* and *the PBS NewsHour.*

His recent books include *Hemingway's Saint Louis* (2020), *In the Walnut Grove: A Consideration of the People Enslaved in and around Florissant MO* (2020), and *Main Street USA: The Life and Photography of H. H. Bregstone* (2018)—featured in that year's St. Louis Jewish Book Festival.

His research and artifact collections can be found at Southern Illinois University Edwardsville, the St. Clair County IL Historical Society, and the Newberry Library in Chicago.

His family came to the city of St. Louis in 1857. He is active in various community nonprofits, including the East St. Louis Historical Society and the Florissant Valley Historical Society.

Made in the USA
Columbia, SC
08 December 2024

48769554R00161